THE RELATIONAL LEADER

A REVOLUTIONARY FRAMEWORK TO ENGAGE YOUR TEAM

Frank McIntosh

Course Technology PTR

A part of Cengage Learning

COURSE TECHNOLOGY
CENGAGE Learning™

Australia, Brazil, Japan, Korea, Mexico, Singapore, Spain, United Kingdom, United States

COURSE TECHNOLOGY
CENGAGE Learning™

The Relational Leader: A Revolutionary Framework to Engage Your Team
Frank McIntosh

Publisher and General Manager, Course Technology PTR:
Stacy L. Hiquet

Associate Director of Marketing:
Sarah Panella

Manager of Editorial Services:
Heather Talbot

Marketing Manager:
Mark Hughes

Acquisitions Editor:
Mitzi Koontz

Development Editor:
Kim Benbow

Project Editor:
Kim Benbow

Interior Layout Tech:
William Hartman

Cover Designer:
Luke Fletcher

Indexer:
Larry Sweazy

Proofreader:
Melba Hopper

For product information and technology assistance, contact us at **Cengage Learning Customer & Sales Support, 1-800-354-9706.**

For permission to use material from this text or product, submit all requests online at **cengage.com/permissions**. Further permissions questions can be e-mailed to **permissionrequest@cengage.com**.

All images © Cengage Learning unless otherwise noted.

Library of Congress Control Number: 2009941743

ISBN-13: 978-1-4354-5558-0

ISBN-10: 1-4354-5558-4

Course Technology, a part of Cengage Learning
20 Channel Center Street
Boston, MA 02210
USA

Cengage Learning is a leading provider of customized learning solutions with office locations around the globe, including Singapore, the United Kingdom, Australia, Mexico, Brazil, and Japan. Locate your local office at: **international.cengage.com/region**

Cengage Learning products are represented in Canada by Nelson Education, Ltd.

For your lifelong learning solutions, visit **courseptr.com**.

Visit our corporate Web site at **cengage.com**.

Printed in the United States of America
1 2 3 4 5 6 7 12 11 10

To my wife and partner, Carolyn, and my three daughters Kelly, Meredith, and Caitlin for your love and support.

Acknowledgments

I have wanted to write a book since my college days some 40 years ago. My career got in the way, but since retirement came along, I renewed my zest for the idea. My thanks to Jim Duncan for pushing me past the dream to actually beginning to write and for not abandoning me afterward.

I am grateful to my wife and partner, Carolyn, for her support along the way and for the support of my children, Kelly, Meredith, and Caitlin, who were always encouraging. Special thanks to Caitlin who volunteered her artistic talents in creating the original illustrations for the book, as well as designing my website and other business materials.

My deepest appreciation to all the folks featured in the book who took the time to talk with me, encourage me, and share stories of their exceptional careers: Bob Adams, Bob Albin, Bob Brightfelt, Alan Burkhard, Chris Coons, Nathan Hill, Michelle Hollandsworth, Jim Kelly, Mike Kozikowski, Sue Linderman, Ed McKenna, Russ Owen, Pam Seaholm, Skip Schoenhals, and Mark Suwyn. They were an inspiration to me and proof that any mountain can be scaled with the right attitude.

My thanks to Charlie Cawley and Ed Woolard whose legend alone encouraged me to do my best.

My personal story was made possible because of the assistance of colleagues who believed in me and were willing to share their talents throughout the journey of my career. They include Jack Talcott, Dale Baxter, Bill Annino, Doug Andre, Tracy Birney, and Lucy O'Donnell. My appreciation goes out to all the wonderful staff and colleagues with whom I have worked—so many of you played a role in the content of this book.

My gratitude to all those who read the book as it was coming together and offered their advice to improve it, particularly my brother Howard and my friend Joe Brady (who also introduced me to Cengage Learning), to Rob Eppes and Marshall Howard for their insight, and to my sister Marie for her constant encouragement.

Thanks to the folks at Cengage Learning, specifically Mitzi Koontz for believing I had something worth saying and editors Kim Benbow and Sandy Doell for their talent, patience, and understanding.

About the Author

Frank McIntosh was inducted into the Delaware Business Leaders Hall of Fame in 2008 and is one of 40 members culled from the state's rich business history. Junior Achievement of Delaware, where he served as President and CEO for 25 years, was recognized frequently with significant national honors for its performance. Frank assisted in the launch and provided board, personnel, and fund development for Junior Achievement operations in Ireland, Cote d'Ivoire, Benin, Uzbekistan, Oman, United Arab Emirates, and Bahrain in addition to numerous individual JA franchises across the United States, including its national headquarters. He has served his community as president of the Delaware PTA and as a national PTA board member, chair of the Governor's Mentoring Commission, member of the Advisory Council for the College of Business at Delaware State University, chairman of the Financial Advisory Committee for the state's largest school district, Christina. Frank is known for his vision, passion, dedication, and performance.

Contents

Chapter 11
The Long and Winding Road. **209**

Appendix
The Company Barometer Questionnaire **227**

Index. **231**

Introduction

How we lead has everything to do with the behavior of those we lead. It is in the "how" that we produce results of a different measure. Virtually any leadership style will generate an effect on the followers. It is up to us as leaders to select one method that will create the most positive results for all our stakeholders, be they stockholders, equity partners, employees, customers, vendors, or the community. Knowing that there are many different styles and hybrids of those styles can be very confusing.

Because leadership is often ignored at the undergraduate and graduate levels, we are often left to ourselves to pick our own style. Sometimes, oftentimes, it just evolves according to the type of person you are without regard to what might be best for the group you lead. It would be best to have a framework to use as a compass point, in both good times and bad, so that you can project a consistent message and methodology to your people. That framework, I believe, is *relational leadership.*

Of course, relational leadership is the subject of this book. You will be exposed to the principles of this style. More importantly, you will see how the principles, when applied in tandem, can produce substantial results. The application of the relational leadership principles will enable you to look in the mirror before going to sleep and allow you to say, "I am doing the best I can to lead my team to the best possible results." When you can do that, you will definitely sleep better and wake up refreshed. As you read through this book, you will begin to see yourself in a different light. You will be able to apply the tenants of relational leadership to who you are and, at the same time, understand how to adapt to them. When these principles come together, it will be a very powerful moment for you.

When a person tries to mimic someone else, it usually doesn't play out too well. They are who they are, and you are who you are. So you have to be you. In knowing who you are, you know your strengths and where you need to improve or shift gears. Relational leadership begins and ends with people. How you approach people and the environment you provide for them to work in revolves around seven attributes: fairness, character, trust, fun, celebration, attentiveness, and purpose. Applying these attributes collectively through your own personality is what it takes to be successful.

I believe it is true that people frequently make life more complex than it needs to be. I have found that most situations can be handled straightforwardly if you have a system in place to guide you in your relationships. The answers to life's problems are often terribly obvious. These answers begin with taking personal responsibility for your actions, consistently doing the right thing, understanding what people respond to, and understanding that simple observation and listening will tell you almost all you need to know about a situation.

The dominant style of leadership in our nation's history is referred to as "command and control." For the most part, it has served us well. After all, our economic, political, government, social, and religious success is beyond all that preceded it. Shouldn't this be enough as we move forward? In my view, the answer is no.

Our world is changing. It is no longer Soviet Russia versus the USA with the rest of the world lined up as cheerleaders behind one or the other. Nations around the world, particularly in Asia, are waking up to market economies. The Middle East is demanding attention for its ideals. Europe is rethinking its own relationships. With all these cultures emerging on the world scene, it seems clear that a different way of dealing with people needs to rise to the forefront. At home, our institutions are challenged with an ethical abyss. Our scruples are becoming unglued. The attitude of "me first" is rampant wherever you look in our culture. It is time to rethink how we interact with people, be it on our home ground or around the globe.

Now is the time to get back on track. A leadership style is emerging that can be the portal to change. Relational leaders value people first and foremost, and their actions are dictated by this belief. This book will explore how institutional leaders can make claim once again to ethical, fair, and purposeful practices that underscore the value of human beings as the linchpins of our society.

To that end it is vital that today's leaders pay attention to the stakeholder most often ignored—the community. Enlightened leaders have always understood this idea. Today, though, we must move beyond enlightened leaders and reach out to others in the business world, asking them to extend their time and resources to the community in which they live.

The actions of a few have soiled the image of the entire business community. Americans have lost trust in business leadership, and more and more are thinking of business leaders as greedy and thoughtless. Rebuilding trust is not easy; it takes time. The only way I know how to do this is by acting ethically and becoming visible in the community. Allow your fellow citizens to see the real you—a person who is honest and cares. Relational leaders will be volunteers who help nurture and grow our communities.

Relational leaders fundamentally understand certain principles; they understand how people react to the stimulus that surrounds them. They know that people who are browbeaten will cower. People who are disrespected get angry. People who are treated unfairly, conspire. They know that where there is no trust, people steal. Where this is no fun, people wilt. Where there is no purpose, people lag. Where there is no celebration, people regret. Where there is no character, people cheat. Where no one listens, people shut up. Feel free to substitute your own words, but you get the picture. People are people; they react to the circumstances around them, and in the case of negative stimuli, it is enough to make an organization dysfunctional.

We understand the power of environment on people's output, yet our leaders engage in similar unconstructive behaviors every day. It is no wonder that our institutions seemingly are becoming more dishonest by the day. Our political, business, civic, and public leaders are involved in corruption, immorality, and unethical behavior with increasing regularity. It's starting to feel a little like the last days of ancient Rome around these proud United States.

But we can take back our institutions and create a style of leadership that is positive and energizing, where people feel purpose and respect and trust. I am not talking about being evangelical; I am talking about being decent human beings who recognize that our lasting independence is achieved through dependence on each other. This book speaks to the leaders who are prepared to make a difference in their world, to lead our country back to prominence, and to limit excess.

One of the essential concepts I put forth is that lasting independence can only be achieved through dependence upon each other. Relational leadership recognizes that each person has worth and that it is the challenge of the leader to bring out the best possible work product from each contributor. Investment in the human spirit is paramount to success.

The active practice of relational leadership is effective when the leader is competent in his field and understands how his business or organization operates. Great relational skills and no business skills will likely end up with a bankrupt organization! That's not the objective. So you have to put together a team that has the operational skill set and let them work in a relational environment. Now, you have the real deal!

In this book, I speak plainly through common sense, logic, and stories that illustrate the points I am making. The reading should be interesting and informative and provide a clear path that an individual reader can internalize and act upon. Through the examples contained on these pages, you will learn to become a leader who is respected and followed. In fact, isn't the aim of any leader to be respected for his abilities and followed for his view of the future?

As you read through these thoughts, precepts, axioms, and stories you will find comfort in the fact that it is all doable. It's not easy, mind you—it takes discipline and commitment. You should approach the task of becoming relational as if it were a marathon, not a sprint.

Observation, self-analysis, sensibility, and listening are the key skills to becoming relational. What makes it fun is that most everyone can lead at some level. Once you become purposeful about being a relational leader and you begin to see results from your efforts, you will want to get better and better at the task. Believe me—leaders are needed at every level of an organization. Organizations laden with relational leaders succeed because they fundamentally understand the value of people and extract the most out of every interaction. In an organization that is emerging as relational, those participating in the "heavy lifting" will be easy to spot. The top leadership of a relational organization will want to push these concepts and principles from the top down through the organization.

I started on this journey 40 years ago, and I am still learning. That is the nature of relationships and leadership. My career efforts were recognized in 2008 when I was inducted into the Delaware Business Leaders Hall of Fame. For me it was a humbling experience, one that I was unsure that I deserved. Many of the Laureates are internationally famous, have directed vast business organizations, and all have made a lasting mark on Delaware business as well as American business. At the time of my induction, there were just 38 Laureates culled from the rich business history of the state. I am proud to be one of them and to share with you the methods I employed to achieve success.

The reflections I give you represent what I strived to do throughout my career in Junior Achievement. I strove to build my organization's effectiveness so that we could impact hundreds of thousands of students as they planned their journeys through life. I did not do it alone; I had many advisors along the way. To embellish this subject matter, I invited some of these individuals to share their thinking with me. These are people I admire for their business sense, personal ethics, and because they are wonderful human beings. Some of them I adopted as mentors; others I learned from because they offered so much insight about the human condition. In the pages ahead, you will read about many of their life stories and benefit directly from their own words and experiences. They may use different approaches, but they share commonalities that are relational in nature. It is what makes them great. I have had the privilege of seeing them from a unique vantage point—I have worked with all of them but not necessarily for them. I will share their perspectives with you to help you become the great leader that is inside of you.

KEEP IN MIND:

- Relational leadership recognizes that each person has worth and that it is the challenge of the leader to bring out the best possible work product from each contributor.
- Lasting independence can only be achieved through dependence upon each other.
- Put together a team with the operational skill set and let them work in a relational environment.
- Observation, self-analysis, sensibility, and listening are all skills that we either have or can acquire. They are the key competencies to becoming relational.
- Volunteer in your community and let people see you as the honest and caring person you are.

Chapter 1

Illustrating the Case for Relational Leadership

"It is not the critic who counts: not the man who points out how the strong man stumbles or where the doer of deeds could have done better. The credit belongs to the man who is actually in the arena, whose face is marred by dust and sweat and blood, who strives valiantly, who errs and comes up short again and again, because there is no effort without error or shortcoming, but who knows the great enthusiasms, the great devotions, who spends himself for a worthy cause; who, at the best, knows, in the end, the triumph of high achievement, and who, at the worst, if he fails, at least he fails while daring greatly, so that his place shall never be with those cold and timid souls who knew neither victory nor defeat."

—*Theodore Roosevelt*
"Citizenship in a Republic"
Speech at the Sorbonne, Paris, April 23, 1910

■ A Little Background on the Author
■ An Overview of the Relational Model
■ A Tale of Two Organizations
■ Summary

Leadership is packaged in many different sizes and shapes. Where there is a leader, there are followers. It doesn't matter if the leader is good or bad at the task; there are still followers. It doesn't matter if the outcomes the leader is driving followers toward are good (think Nelson Mandela) or bad (think Jim Jones). In the pure nature of leadership, what *does* matter is if people understand what you are doing and follow you.

Promoting and developing effective leadership is critical to our success in this complicated, fast paced, and ever-changing world we live in. The concept of *relational leadership* is not as widely known as some other styles, and implementation models are relatively scarce. However, if we can embrace it and implement its principles in our organizations, we can begin to ameliorate our circumstances. It is time to put aside the greed, immorality, and unethical behavior that is so prevalent in our society today. Becoming a relational leader is a solution to these burgeoning problems.

What you will learn about relational leadership is that it is centered on people and how the leader relates to them. It provides a methodology for a group of attributes—like trust, celebration, attentiveness, and fairness—to be applied toward advancing and honoring the role people play in an organization. The pillars of the model, taken and implemented as a whole, give an organization a framework to develop a strong work ethic and excellent productive outcomes.

A Little Background on the Author

I started my career as a district manager for Junior Achievement of Eastern Massachusetts, a nonprofit organization whose mission is to teach kids about business, economics, and finance. I was accountable for managing the territory covering the North Shore of Boston. I was responsible for a company-owned building and three tenants. I had one full-time and five part-time employees working for me, and I didn't have the foggiest idea of how to lead this team. In the very early days, I can tell you that the word "leadership" probably never even entered my mind. I think it was more of a survival mentality.

None of my college courses dealt with the subject of leadership. There was a lot of "how-to" and technical stuff but nothing about motivating and energizing people. The organization provided very little in the way of training. There must have been an assumption that if you went to college, you knew these things, although I am not sure where this thinking might have originated.

I did have pertinent experience during my years as a student in Junior Achievement (JA) in high school and later as a volunteer in college. I was privileged to be a member of the National Speakers Corps; I had the opportunity to train with experts in the art of public speaking and travel around the country giving talks on behalf of the organization. Leading the student-run company (the organization's only program at the time) and attending regional and national conferences helped build my confidence. I had good instincts, and the JA experience began to kick in after about six months on the job. I had a sense about what might be right and some ideas about how people would like to be treated. I dove into my job with the attitude of "nothing ventured, nothing gained." My thinking was, if you don't do something, you won't succeed at anything.

Thus began my journey toward discovering the power of relational leadership. Over the next 35 or so years, I would build a practicing theory of leadership that was based on the following five activities:

- Observing
- Listening
- Analyzing
- Testing
- Enacting

I made it my business to carefully watch people who had more experience than me. I looked at their mannerisms and actions. I carefully listened to their expressions and words. I assessed the effectiveness of their methods and made a determination of what to incorporate into how I acted and spoke. As time wore on, I got better at this and had better subjects to study. One of the great benefits of working for Junior Achievement was the people you meet and associate with. From very early on in my career, I was around very successful business people and educators, so I had lots of opportunity to employ my observations and listening skills.

The key to my success was the ability to discern the attributes that I could incorporate into my *modus operandi*. There are just some things that are not going to work for you, while others fit very nicely. For instance, I am not very mechanical; I know that. People who are mechanical generally have effective analytical skills. Therefore, I knew that exhaustive analysis of a problem was probably not going to work too well for me. By nature, I am intuitive. I needed to square up with people who demonstrated similar traits.

Once I had determined that there was substance to a particular individual's style, I would try it out, a little bit at a time. If it worked effectively and I was getting the type of results I hoped for, then I would incorporate it into my ongoing style. Over time I could see myself developing into a leader. I had beliefs and systems that were working for me. I was gaining respect and receiving promotions. People began coming to me for advice. I think that is a true sign that what you are doing is working. All the while I kept looking, listening, analyzing, testing, and enacting.

An Overview of the Relational Model

What evolved from this activity was a method of operation that I call *relational leadership*. I don't claim to have coined this phraseology. It is descriptive of what happens in the model. It has stood the test of time, and it has produced excellent and consistent results.

The relational leader places people at the center of her thinking and actions. People are the core of the model; people define the model. People are thought of in broad terms, so in a business situation they include employees, customers, vendors, shareholders, and community. Whatever the leader does, people and their needs are always on her mind.

In the model, shown in Figure 1.1, the core is surrounded by three elements: fidelity, appreciation, and value. Within the three elements there are seven attributes representing fairness, character, trust, fun, celebration, attentiveness, and purpose. The core and its elements are in play at all times in *relationalism*. When the model is fully in place, all attributes work in unison at all times. Therefore, you do not sacrifice trust for fun in any activity in which your organization engages. This means you can't ridicule another person in the name of fun, regardless of how "funny" it might be, because that violates the concept of trust. Likewise, you would not celebrate the acquisition of software without a license because it violates the concept of character.

As you can see, the intertwining circles suggest that each piece of the model is vital to the other. For this to work at maximum effectiveness, every part works together somewhat like a complex gear box. And like gears, your relationalism must be greased from time to time. This means assessing where you are at vis-à-vis your relational goals. Before talking about goals and assessment, see Table 1.1 for the definitions of the relational terms I've introduced.

You may have noticed that value calls upon the leader to take accountability, whereas in fidelity and appreciation, the whole organization is accountable. In the case of value in organizational structure, attentiveness and purpose primarily fall into the blend of the leader/manager role. Of course it is desirable for all people within the team to contribute their skills and commitment, but that task is secondary to the leader/manager position.

NOTE

A common definition of *leader* is a person who does the right things versus a *manager* as a person who does things right. The leader thinks about what the organization is about and why, while the manager is largely concerned about the how. Also, it is certainly possible to be both at the same time. In the case of value, these individuals are responsible for maintaining the focus on relationalism within the organization.

Relationship Diagram

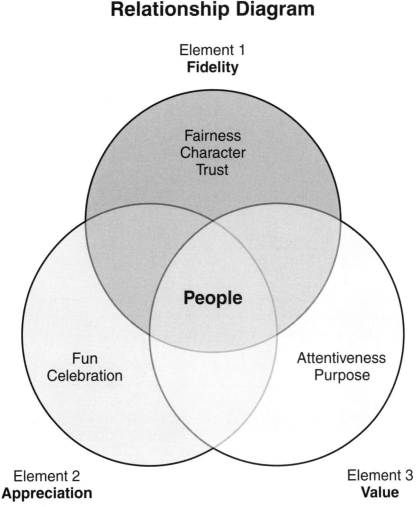

Element 1
Fidelity

Fairness
Character
Trust

People

Fun
Celebration

Attentiveness
Purpose

Element 2
Appreciation

Element 3
Value

Figure 1.1 *The relationship of the core to the elements in the relational leadership model.*

TABLE 1.1 Terms Used in the Relational Leadership Model

Core	Definition
People	The employees, customers, vendors, shareholders, and community involved with your team.

Elements	Definition
Fidelity	Encapsulates the attributes of fairness, character, and trust.
Appreciation	Encapsulates the attributes of fun and celebration.
Value	Encapsulates the attributes of attentiveness and purpose.

Attributes	Definition
Fairness	Organization displays no self-interest, favoritism, or prejudice to achieve balance between conflicting interests. There is openness to appropriate action and words.
Character	Organization holds to high standards of ethics and morality.
Trust	Organization consistently adheres to its precepts, particularly relating to people.
Fun	Organization promotes activities that support enjoyment, laughter, and relaxation.
Celebrate	Organization regularly honors both small and large accomplishments.
Attentiveness	Leaders observe and listen to their people. Leaders self-observe for alignment to precepts of the organization.
Purpose	Leaders promote an honorable and fulfilling intention to the organization.

It is up to these stewards of the organization to be attentive, to listen and observe, to gauge the temperature, and to adjust wherever appropriate so that the people remain enthused and dedicated. Likewise, the leader/manager is responsible for promoting and maintaining the purpose of the organization. He reinforces the mission in the sense of its integrity and contribution to the betterment of society. He also keeps the people on task, on goal.

Regarding fidelity and appreciation, these elements tend to be shared activities. Obviously, leadership is vital, but the employees, vendors, and customers must support and actively engage in the processes for them to be effective. The "buy in" extends equally to all parts of the organization.

I have mentioned assessment as an important part of the role of the relational leader. This is because it is critical for the leader to know where she stands with her people regarding the style she has chosen to move the organization forward. Relational leadership as defined here is not common.

It is also true that many people fall prey to the excesses that can be found in *Command and Control* organizations. People are a bit jaded about their work situation. There is a lack of trust in senior management. There is an attitude in many businesses that suggests, you have a job, I pay you, and at the end of the day we're even. I will deal with this subject in more detail later and provide you with a tool you can use in the assessment.

A Tale of Two Organizations

Now that you have a working idea of what the relational leadership model looks like, I would like to tell you two real stories about very different organizations—one that demonstrates the model and another that doesn't. As you read through the stories, try to match up what is going on with the components of relational leadership, either for or against.

One anecdote is about a school and its principal. I selected this one because I want to underscore that the model can be applied to any type of group. It does not have to be a business entity. The other is a start-up bank. Again, the model applies, even though this company has only been in existence for about two years.

The Saga of the Middle School

We were driving down Kirkwood Highway in Newark, Delaware, on a house hunting trip with our realtor, Charlie. As we passed Shue Middle School, he pointed out that it was a National Model School, and it would be one of the schools our children would attend. The realtor was starting to get on our nerves. Our time was limited, and our oldest child, Kelly, age five, was a long way from middle school. Besides that, we would only be in Delaware for a couple of years; it was merely a stepping stone. But eight years later Kelly was entering Shue Middle School as a seventh grader! Wow! How did that happen? Charlie was clearly more optimistic about our stay in Delaware than we were, but back to Shue.

Unfortunately, it was no longer a National Model School—National Model Zoo maybe, but no model for education. This situation is a perfect example of how quickly an outstanding organization can slip to mediocre or below. It is also an excellent example of the positive effect a truly good leader can have on an organization.

To set the stage, several years before Kelly's arrival, a new principal was hired who simply did not have the skill set of his predecessor. His lack of leadership skills slowly but surely eroded the excellent reputation that the school had enjoyed. He frequently waffled on decisions, student discipline was not effectively enforced, teachers did not feel supported, and in general there seemed to be a growing malaise surrounding the school. Parents were upset and wanted a change. We were among those parents who lobbied hard for new leadership.

Here was our first born going into the clutches of middle-school tyranny where the hormones rage and attention is easily distracted. It is a time when strong leadership is essential. Our concern was multiplied as our second child, Meredith, would be at the same school the following year. Two girls in middle school at the same time at a school where control and academic excellence were hard to find—these are not pleasant thoughts for parents.

Fortunately central office administration responded to our pleas, and a new principal was hired. Hope grew among the parents and faculty, but the jury was still out. To his credit and our relief, the new leader, Bob Adams, took control from the first day. He restored order and pride—no easy task. He demanded academic responsibility and respect—maybe an even tougher task. There was a feeling emerging that Shue was off to becoming a National Model School once again!

How did this "miracle" occur? The very first thing Bob did was to gather the staff together and ask for their views on the issues. He formed a faculty committee to make ongoing suggestions for school improvement. He met with parent leadership so they could voice their issues. He made an effort to get acquainted with staff individually. He talked and listened to students. Most important, he sifted through the information quickly because his instinct told him that he needed to do something visible and do it fast.

Bob told me, "I do a lot of watching and listening, and when I am new to a school, I want to understand the culture and what is valued. I ask lots of questions for the purpose of finding where the staff wants to go and how they want to get there. I find lots of half-formed ideas, and I help shape them into fully formed ideas, and we are then on our way." This was his style of leadership—very relational.

The key words that Bob spoke were as follows:

■ Watch
■ Listen
■ Question

Bob spent lots of time in the corridors observing mannerisms and behavior of both the students and the staff. He did the same in classrooms. He looked for signs that would affirm what he learned from his listening sessions. What was positive that he was seeing? What were the looks on the students' faces? Did they seem happy and engaged or dull and dragging? How about the faculty? Did they seem encouraging of the students, or did they act like jailors? He gave all the constituents the opportunity to talk with him, and he actively listened to what they had to say. If he needed more information, he asked for clarification. His actions following his initial information gathering demonstrated that what he heard and saw made an impact on him.

He came away from his faculty discussions with a feeling that this was a very experienced and talented group of educators who simply wanted to do what they did best—teach! His job was to remove the barriers that were getting in the way. The most important barriers to educating the students in the minds of the staff were the attitudes and behavior of the students. They were doing what they could in the classrooms and the hallways. They needed the support of the principal. This was an area where he could take immediate action.

Taking action with conduct had a double benefit. Parents were concerned about conduct as well. In some cases, they were concerned for their children's safety. Bullies in the school were intimidating the less aggressive students, and no one seemed to do much about it in the parents' opinion. In their view, administration and teachers just blamed each other while the problem persisted.

So Bob went into action. He had something going for him here that I am sure played a part in his success. He is tall and looks like he has seen the inside of a gym (middle linebacker comes to mind). He visited each classroom during the first weeks of school; he took two things with him: his persona and the Code of Conduct (a document that spells out what is acceptable behavior and what is not and defines the penalties for violating the Code). With an appropriate principal's voice he explained time and time again that "nowhere in the Code of Conduct does it say that you get a second chance!" He would not tolerate bullies or disrespect. His message came across clearly—there was a new sheriff in town, and he was not to be messed with.

One day I personally observed him carrying out his promise in the cafeteria. A student was being pushed around at the lunch table by one of the school's bullies. Bob tapped the bully on the shoulder and asked him to stand. Bob towered over the young man. As he stared down, he reminded the boy about his lack of tolerance for bullies. He told the young man that the student who he was intimidating was from that moment forward in Bob's personal protection. He made an immediate impression on the young man and, as I understand it, a lasting one. His bullying days came to an end in the cafeteria that day!

Bob and his administrative staff were highly visible in the halls and classrooms daily. They were friendly and encouraging but tolerated no misbehavior. No student looked forward to a behavior discussion with Principal Adams. The atmosphere of the school changed rapidly. With behavioral problems largely behind them, the work of learning could begin in earnest, and so it did.

Student write-ups fell to a minimal level, test scores rose, attendance rates climbed, and school pride blossomed. The tension that accompanies an atmosphere of intimidation and fear left the building. It was not perfect, mind you, but totally under control. Behavior was simply no longer an issue at Shue Middle School.

What was the difference? The faculty was essentially the same, more than half the students and parents were the same, and the curriculum was the same. Essentially everything was the same except the principal. Bob Adams was the difference, and his relational style of leadership changed the barometric pressure in the building. Now there was optimism where once there was fear. Order came out of chaos. He created an atmosphere of possibility, and everyone responded instantly. Teachers felt they could teach again, and parents felt assured that their children were in a learning environment.

He was successful because he was authentic. There are few characteristics as reassuring as this one, particularly with a group that has been let down in the past. He just did what he said he would do. How novel! If people are the core of relational leadership, authenticity is the heart.

Think about it: Bob took Shue from the depths to the heights in just a couple of months with largely only one variable—himself. This had meaning for me beyond my children's education. It dramatically demonstrated what I already instinctively knew—leadership is the profound and lasting difference in the capacity to change. When leadership is very good, the change will be very good. In this case, it was just so fast, and it held the entire six years that Bob served as the principal of Shue. He left Shue for Dover High School where he stayed for eight years and where he performed similar "miracles." Currently, Bob is principal of Woodbridge High School, and his formula is still successfully at work. Making people the center of your leadership style works!

Over the years in my position as president of Junior Achievement of Delaware, I engaged every new staff person in a conversation during their first week. Among the things I said to them was this: "I am not responsible for your success. I am responsible for creating an environment in which you can succeed." This is exactly what Bob did for students to the delight of the parents and staff.

> **Tip**
> An Axiom: A dysfunctional organization when tied to outstanding leadership will produce a garden of ideas and productivity.

In the end, Bob Adams succeeded where others did not. He did so because he understood what his constituents needed, and he delivered those needs. The teachers needed vision and support, the parents needed discipline and accountability, the students needed order and spirit, and finally the district office needed teachers, parents, and students who were happy and productive.

While this might seem daunting, the task is made much easier for a leader schooled in relational principles. Bob fundamentally understood that the needs at the core of his organization were about people. People were able to see that his commitment was to their needs. This personal commitment brings about a sense that base needs are being addressed—such as physiological needs, security, and belonging (as expressed by Abraham Maslow's Hierarchy of Needs theory).

The day we talked about his experiences at Shue, Bob left me with this: "Leadership to me is just common sense. Just use your common sense, and things will likely turn out okay." Well, lo and behold, that's what relational leadership is all about! I knew I liked Bob!

The Saga of the Start-Up Bank

Years later I had the opportunity to connect with a start-up bank at a time when the U.S. was in the midst of a banking crisis coupled with a full-blown recession. A friend of mine created an idea for a credit card bank that was different, bold, and right for the times. I actually lent him an empty desk in our offices at Junior Achievement so that he could polish his idea and build his business plan. Boy was he right on the money, so to speak!

He was able to attract capital based on some aggressive forecasts involving number of groups, number of accounts the groups would generate, and projected profit. He teamed up with another friend of mine who had experience in business start-ups as well as banking. Then he brought in the rest of his senior management group—all of them young and still maturing on the job and most of them with experience at his former employer.

The idea was simple, like so many good ideas. In this case, go after small- and medium-sized organizations with an affinity card proposal, but treat them like they were a big player. Bank of America, Chase, and others of their size already tied up most of the big organizations, colleges, and universities. They marketed the product for the high-potential groups like the Boston Red Sox, Notre Dame, and National Education Association on whom they devoted their energy, time, and resources. The idea of the start-up was to target the market that was underserved, provide superior service, innovative products, highly competitive rates, and an excellent credit card reward program.

NOTE

An *affinity credit* card allows an organization to offer its members and supporters (those who have an "affinity" for that organization) a credit card that promotes the organization's brand while paying the group for the member's usage of the card. Typically, the members access a rewards program based on net spending on the card.

Further, the strategy was to target these organizations with great marketing tools, on-site professional support, and money to market the credit card product on their own with enough left over to make a tidy profit for their institution. Thus the bank's cost was reduced substantially, enabling profit capability for the group as well. Understand, however, there was much more that enhanced the overall program for the customer. This had all the signs of a winning twist in a saturated market.

The leader's job, first and foremost, is to relentlessly promote and reinforce the vision of the organization—in this case, the vision that my friend created. The vision gives purpose to the organization. If it is easily understood and embraced by the team, it becomes an energizing and driving force. It is commonly believed that allowing staff to participate in the creation of the vision enables the buy-in process to ferment to its fullest potential.

This was not the case in the bank's situation. The leader brought the team into the idea and sold them on its probable success. While there was probably no other real option under the circumstances, the team was left out of the creation process. Yet the management team did buy the concept and accepted senior positions in the company. Most left positions of importance with their employer.

The marketing process meant attracting groups who would project well in the bank's financial models. Important characteristics of a "good" affinity group include the following:

- Sufficient numbers of members and supporters
- Solid demographics
- Commitment to marketing the card within their group

Numbers mean that there were enough people with affinity to the organization that would produce 1,000 accounts, which meant a group needed 10,000 to 15,000 members. Demographics looks at your income, credit history, stability on the job, and residence among other items. Commitment to marketing the card means that you have lists of members readily available and will approach them by multiple means to sign up for an affinity credit card.

With the promise of joy and a strong wind at their back, where did this team of talented, well-financed bankers take this exciting idea? Cutting to the chase (no pun intended)—nowhere! The machine was not yet dead, but the cylinders were definitely puttering, and the gas gauge was reading close to empty.

Affinity groups were signed according to the model. Unfortunately, they were, by and large, the wrong groups. They were small. Their affinity members and supporters were not like the die-hard New England Patriots fans. They had little capacity to market the card themselves due to their own internal limitations. As time moved on, leadership didn't have the cash to provide on-site support; in the cases they did, the individuals were not always the right people to move the programs in their care forward.

Where did all this fresh thinking go awry? Sadly, the answer is in leadership and some less-than-stellar business decisions. Regarding leadership, the CEO portrayed the style of "the King" is in the house and the hammer is always nearby—old-style management of command and control. He mimicked the CEO/leader that populated our institutions during most of the last century and still pops up all too often today. People were not at the core of this business.

The cracks in the foundation began to show early on. The number-two man who was supposed to operate the business was never given the authority to do so. This was actually more of a chasm than a crack. Groups were signed that had a high cost of acquisition and not enough potential for profit even under the best of circumstances. Hiring decisions put people in positions that they did not have experience in or the expertise to perform.

The company began to miss its targets by large margins. The country's economic systems kept collapsing. The principle investor began to pull back on financing (his own businesses were being challenged by the economic climate) while simultaneously demanding the bank shift toward larger groups outside the established model.

With a vacuum in leadership, it opened the gates for the youngsters on the team to undermine the leadership that *did* exist. Belief in the plan was just about gone at the senior staff level. The leader began to allow the team to take the organization off course—his course. And that was the fundamental mistake. The model was not given the opportunity, money, and time it needed to bring the plan to fruition.

What ensued was one mistake after another, further eroding the confidence of the team, pushing people into opposing camps, and creating an atmosphere of chaos. Marketing plans changed regularly, and underwriting standards did the same. A sale offer, good one day, was pulled off the table the next. The CEO regularly overruled his senior staff, sometimes publicly, when he didn't like their positions. All the while, financing from the investor was clamped down even further.

The principal characteristics of the vision were completely lost or misunderstood in this organization. Disorder was rampant. Respect for and support of the individual were virtually non-existent (lots of yelling, swearing, and belittling by leadership). Arrogance abounded in the face of increasingly poorer decisions. Leadership was nowhere to be found (no real listening or observing). Many staffers described the office atmosphere as a morgue (fun and celebration had left this group a long time ago, replaced by gloom). The early energy that once was evident was clearly gone.

A relational organization is built upon a great idea, an energizing vision, and a well qualified staff. Realistically, great ideas and vision will only go as far as the people who are in place to drive them. Regrettably, several key staff positions were filled with people who were not competent in the particular role in which they were cast. Therefore, important business functions were subject to both poor leadership and poor management.

What we have here then is a great idea with a vision that is faltering and an organization suffering from several poor personnel choices. That situation was compounded by a senior management team that was not on the same page and a CEO who was often out of control. The inner conflicts of the senior management team spread to their direct reports. The evident conflict brought about confusion in the ranks as to who was leading and in what direction. Changes in policy and strategy were frequent visitors to the office, producing more and more tentative results among the workforce. Associates learned to expect the unexpected, which produced a destabilizing effect.

TIP

An Axiom: A great and timely idea, when met with ineffective leadership, will most often produce a dysfunctional organization.

It would be unfair to say that everything was wrong in this organization. In fact, there were lots of good things. Nothing is totally bad or good. There were even times when there was a relational feel to leadership's actions, but it always seemed to fall back to command and control. The fun and celebrations seemed to fall a tad short of where they could have been. They lacked the energy that is brought about through sincerity. It could be argued that a fully implemented relational style would have smoothed out some of these internal challenges.

Still, the strongest piece of this business group was its core vision. At its creation, there was thought given to the potential for government intervention in the credit card business. That is what made the concepts of structure so enticing. The vision was right for the times, and there always remained the possibility that its great potential would rise to the top.

Comparing the Middle School to the Bank

You see two very different types of organizations described here. They are opposing images—what you see in one, you don't see in the other.

The essence of relational leadership is found in the Middle School. It embodies these characteristics:

- Trust
- Fairness
- Respect for the individual
- Appreciation of the value individuals bring to the organization
- Consistent and worthwhile goals
- Standards
- Dedication to the vision
- Listening
- Celebration
- Laughter
- Encouragement
- Ethical behavior

The characteristics of the bank as they compare to the relational style are different. They include the following:

- Lack of trust
- Arrogance
- Dictatorial manner
- Inconsistency

- Distorted vision
- Somber feelings
- Telling approach
- Standalone mind-set
- Disconnected thinking
- "Me first" attitude
- Profanity and inappropriate behavior
- Insincerity

When shown in this light, it is easy to pick which organization (if you had the choice) you would like to work in and give your best effort. The principles of relational leadership apply to any type of setting where people come together for a task under a person designated as the leader. Therein lies the power of the model—it can be applied anywhere with a strong degree of certainty that it will be successful.

Summary

Relationalism is a very versatile model. It calls upon common sense as a prime driver of your actions and holds you to high moral and ethical standards. With people as the focal point, it assures that you are working on the predominant critical success factor in your organization. After all, everything begins and ends with people, hard-working and well-motivated, to ensure that your business plans come to fruition.

People are not just your employees. They include all your stakeholders, internal and external. This broader organizational view makes it possible for you to impact all areas of your operation to the exclusion of none. If you apply your relationship skills universally, you increase your probability of success substantially.

People, whether one of your employees or a vendor, are going to respond when they are treated with respect and when they know that their value is recognized. The relational leader fosters this type of atmosphere; therefore, he is able to count on maximum cooperation in pursuit of the vision for the organization.

You saw how two different organizations operated. It is easy to appreciate how one succeeds over the other! People are at the heart of relational leadership. In this framework, the organizational environment supports the needs of the individuals, first and foremost. With these needs in tow, the company or organization has the wherewithal to implement its plans and strategies with the greatest possibility for success. Specifically, a relationally led group will experience an atmosphere where there is trust, fairness, ethics, fun, celebration, attentiveness, and purpose.

Over the course of this book, you will delve into relational leadership. You will see real-life examples of the success of this strategy, see how to implement it for yourself, gain some tools to assist you, discover how to continually improve your capacity to be a relational leader, and finally, find out how to improve your home/family life by using many of its principles. You will come away with a set of strategies that you can implement immediately with your work team. The principles are effective in all work situations, business, social, government, or nonprofit.

KEEP IN MIND:
- Leadership is the profound and lasting difference in the capacity to change.
- Just use your common sense, and things will likely turn out okay.
- Leaders provide the atmosphere in which the organization's people can succeed.
- A dysfunctional organization, when tied to outstanding leadership, will produce a garden of ideas and productivity.
- A great and timely idea, when met with ineffective leadership, will most often produce a dysfunctional organization.
- The leader's job, first and foremost, is to relentlessly promote and reinforce the vision of the organization.
- People in the relational model include all stakeholders.

Chapter 2

The Might of Mentors

> "Even if you're on the right track,
> you'll get run over if you just sit there."
> —*Will Rogers*

- Enhancing Your Personal Leadership
- The Casting Director
- A Cast of Thousands (Not Really)
- Summary

Every great story has a great cast. Becoming a relational leader was the defining success story of my career, and it can be for you too. To help you along the way, I have assembled a cast of characters who played a role in my personal journey. They are people I learned from—examples of the types of individuals you could seek out in your own environment to help you learn and grow. They appear in this book to help me share my insights of *relationalism*. Being *relational* means that you value people. This is an important first step. You need to acknowledge that no one goes through life alone.

As you begin (or perhaps alter) your journey, you will be well served to bring together a solid supporting cast as you move through your career. So throw your net wide and see what it brings in. Use your attentiveness skills as you learn from all of your encounters, positive or negative. The more styles, attitudes, and skill sets you have to observe and listen to, the greater the opportunity you have of finding the right examples for yourself.

There are many influences in our lives. You also know that influence has an impact upon who you are. The environment in which you exist affects what you say and what you do either by design or by choice. It can be a person, place, or thing. You seek it out, or it seeks you out. Understanding the effects of environment is a very useful tool for your workbench.

Enhancing Your Personal Leadership

The interesting part of the relationship between me and my characters is that I never asked them, nor did they offer, to be mentors or advisors. I just hitched my wagon to them. They were smart and successful. They seemed to embrace the principles that I believed in, and they were stimulating to be around. I paid close attention to what they did and how they did it. I asked them lots of questions and engaged them in conversation, often career-type conversation, whenever practical. They were always responsive to me, and I am thankful every day of my life for their willingness to help, push, tutor, and be a friend to me. These are people who always understood instinctively and practically that giving and getting are part of life's success plan.

TIP
An Axiom: Those who give usually get much more than what they gave.

The people I discuss in this chapter are all relational leaders. They all have achieved great success in the business world and in their personal life. All are blessed with sound management and business skills. Fundamentally, though, people are the core of their thinking as they applied it to their business ideas and tasks. The same is true of their home lives, as each is in the midst of a lifelong relationship with their spouse.

It is my belief that you are fortunate to have people you trust who can provide perspective for you. You are always approaching new challenges that require new skills and insights. Leaders, particularly relational leaders, are confident and self-assured, but they are not full of the hubris that befalls so many cast in the role of leader. Just as compassion is not a fault, life-long learning is not a cliché. You must ever be ready to learn something new, particularly from a person whose experience validates the outcome. Mentors don't give the answers—they give alternatives; they cause us to think and, often, to act.

There is a viewpoint held by many people who believe that you have to be a hard-nosed bottom-liner to lead. This position suggests that leaders dictate by command and control. As a commander, people's circumstances are not your concern; you, the leader, are the driver. Similarly, as the leader, you have the answers. Advice is okay but overrated. You're the decision maker and the vision developer. How will anyone follow you if you aren't strong and able? In our complex, world these "attributes" are overrated—seriously overrated!

Today this style of leadership is on the wane, although there are still plenty of examples of it around. The workforce of the new millennium wants to feel valued. They grew up in a different society, where norms were challenged and people had different expectations. Our global economy is demanding that leadership be smarter, and by the way our world is turning today, we have a long way to go.

TIP

An Axiom: Seeking the wisdom of experience, observing the path taken before you, and absorbing the attitudes of people you respect are not only right, they are absolutely right.

You can learn from any situation that you encounter, be it positive or negative; however, it is very important that you understand the difference between the two! Lots of what I learned from others over the years was from the negative side. You see people's actions, and you understand that they aren't the right approach, at least not for you. This is why it is so important for you to understand as soon as possible who you are and why you are that way.

Over time, if you are an active listener and observer, you will compile quite a long list of things that you should not be or do. This enables you to look at the other side and develop a positive twist to the negatives you've encountered. This piece is vital. You don't want to build your belief system on negatives. So if this is wrong, what makes it right? This strength provides a much stronger foundation for your actions and future decision making.

The Casting Director

Before introducing the players, I first want to introduce myself, as authenticity is the heart of relationalism. It is important that you understand who I am so that you have a better appreciation of my perspectives.

Most of my career was spent in the non-profit world, but I also experienced life in the for-profit environment. I have always maintained that the major difference between the two is tax status. Just how many years do you think that your average non-profit executive can go to the board and announce that the organization had another non-profit year and do so without consequence!

Relational leadership (even though I didn't understand it by that name in the beginning) worked for me and led me to a highly successful career in the non-profit world where I spent 25 of my 36 years as the President and CEO of Junior Achievement of Delaware. I also held senior management positions in Boston and Denver.

During my time in Delaware, I took the JA organization from a teetering, unfocused, parochial entity to a thriving, vision-driven, risk-favorable one. We regularly produced revenues at a rate of four to five times the national average (per capita) and energized the support of senior leaders in business and education throughout our territory. Along the way, we influenced the lives of hundreds of thousands of students.

I provided advice and consulting services to colleagues across the United States and helped open or enhance the JA organization in many parts of the world, including Ireland, Africa, the Middle East, and Central Asia. My business and community activities resulted in my election as the 38th Laureate to the Delaware Business Leaders Hall of Fame in 2008.

An Early Lesson

How did I come upon this relational strategy to lead an organization? Actually, there is no good answer to that question other than to say, it made sense to me. It was simply common sense. I did learn an important lesson early in my career that I believed pushed me in this direction. Let me tell you about it.

I was 21 years old, just married, had my own office, my own secretary (whom I could dictate letters to—that's how long ago it was!), managed a fairly large building including four tenants, and had five part-time people reporting to me, one of whom was my father. How cool could you be! I was successful beyond my imagination, and I had just barely started my career. I must admit, I was a bit full of myself.

I knew my way around town and already had quite a few contacts. One day my secretary, Jean, asked me if I could help her out with something she needed; I can't remember exactly what it was now, but it was something I could do. Well, I filed her request someplace in my brain (but it clearly wasn't in the frontal lobe) and went about my very important business, whatever that might have been at the time. A while later, I noticed a chill developing between the two of us. I tried to figure out the reason. If there was ever a door I was sorry I opened, this was one (well at least at that moment in time).

She was very upset with me because I never followed up on her request that I promised I would take care of. In turn, I was very upset and embarrassed because I knew I let her down. I had known Jean for years, as she was in her position during my high school and college years, and I was a frequent visitor to the Junior Achievement office. She was always very nice to me.

Jean was counting on me to help and apparently had told others that she would be able to resolve whatever the situation was. I hurt her deeply. At Jean's expense, I learned a great lesson about people and how you treat them. I learned never to promise something that I wasn't prepared to deliver. I learned to examine myself more carefully. Finally, I learned that this job was not as easy as I thought it might be. I am so thankful that I learned all these things when I was 21 and could still do something about them.

TIP

An Axiom: Never promise something that you are not prepared to deliver.

Highlights of My Journey

As a youngster, I always admired Abraham Lincoln. I was impressed to learn that he was self-taught, read by the light of the fireplace, and failed many times before finally becoming the President of the United States and one of our most beloved and respected leaders. He was a practical man who demonstrated lots of common sense. He possessed a deep belief in people and respected them for who they were. I thought I could be like that too, but to be clear, I never wanted to be President of the United States.

I am a keen observer of people. How people act interests me. As I moved along in life, I began to see a connection between what I saw in others and how I could improve who I was and what I could accomplish. I realized that we are the sum total of our experiences; thus we are not just our self but a compilation of all the people and things that we come into contact with during our day-to-day living. I reasoned that if I could become purposeful about my collection of data concerning my surroundings, I could take from it what worked best for me, and I would begin to possess the strength of those people I admired the most.

I had no strong business background, although I was a business major in college until I discovered that a course in statistics was on the horizon! Considering I struggled through Accounting II, this new challenge seemed to be one that I might just want to avoid.

It made sense for me to head back to my initial desire to become a teacher, and soon I was an English major, minoring in education. Not long after that, I was student teaching at Brown Junior High School in Malden, Massachusetts. It was here in my senior year of college I discovered that, while I loved teaching, the rigid environment of a teacher was just not for me. The constraints of classroom walls and school bells were not part of my persona. The end of your first semester of senior year is not a good time to learn that you are in the wrong major! Well, what to do now?

Fortunately, I had distinguished myself in Junior Achievement in high school. There was a new executive director in Boston, and he needed a manager for the North Shore programs where I lived. Before long I accepted a job as a program manager for Junior Achievement of Eastern Massachusetts. Life was good!

At this time in my life, my business acumen was gained largely through my association as a student and volunteer with Junior Achievement, not through college training per se. One very important part of my maturation in college was learning to think and communicate skills that were directly applicable to business.

I recall vividly my freshman English composition professor, Dr. Joseph Williams. He taught us to write, at least that is the impact he had on me. (I'm hoping you agree!) He also taught me that whenever you can, make your mistakes in a non-threatening environment. Let me illustrate both points.

He required us to write 500 words per night seven nights a week on the subject of our choosing. His standards for grammar were loose; his primary objective was to get us to put thoughts on paper that made sense and to do this with regularity. It was a daunting task; most of us had never come close to this much writing. I mean, really, coming up with the subject matter alone started to get tedious after a while. As they say, "necessity is the mother of invention," so on we went merrily making up new topics, night after night.

He also required a weekly 1,000-word essay. While he never actually said it, I believe that the daily activity was just a tune up for the real task, which was the essay. To be truthful, I didn't come to this realization until many years after graduation. In the essay, he did not tolerate mistakes in grammar or sentence structure. If you made the same mistake twice, you received an F for the essay. After the first four essays, this standard was applied backward. Therefore, if you dangled a participle in essay #2 and did it again in essay #7, you got an F for essay #7 automatically. As I recall, the student population was not as enamored with this policy as he was!

It was the nightly work that prepared us to do the hard work of the essays. The nightly work didn't count for much; the essays counted heavily. Dr. Williams gave us the opportunity to make our mistakes in a non-threatening environment, and he taught us to write by making us write and write and write! The concept of learning in a non-threatening environment was to become a critical piece in my development. Make your mistakes and build your capacity as you move along in environments where the personal stakes are not as high as they might be on your job. I drove this point home constantly in discussions with business executives and potential volunteers for Junior Achievement.

While Dr. Williams was certainly a task-master, he was also a very capable teacher. During that time, I didn't fully understand the profound lesson of learning in a non-threatening environment. I did appreciate it later, however, and used the lesson successfully throughout my career.

There will always be opportunities like this to absorb information that you don't need right at that moment, but may someday. Think of it as stockpiling wood for the fireplace. Your woodpile will have all different types of logs—some will be thicker, others harder, and you will even have kindling. Because you have a variety of wood samples, you will have maximum choices available to you when you build your fires in the winter months. You will be able to select the wood most appropriate for your situation, and so it is in life. The more experiences you have to draw upon, the greater response capacity you will bring to problem solving and the more value you bring to your team.

Junior Achievement was where I came to appreciate the excitement of business, the interaction with people, the creation of ideas, and the identification of markets to deliver the ideas. JA taught me the framework of business and its potential, but it was going to be up to me to figure out how to make it work.

I have always been a self-taught type of person. I taught myself how to type, how to hit a baseball, how to play tennis (once I discovered that my future wife, Carolyn, was an avid tennis player), and now I was going to teach myself how to be a business person. I had to put a stake in the ground somewhere, so I decided to inventory what I knew about myself. People make more sense to me than rules. I believe fiercely in fairness. I believe it is important to be sure my words and my actions are aligned. I knew that you could learn a lot about a situation if you carefully observed what was going on. I am very competitive.

So with this list in mind, I began my career at Junior Achievement in Boston. It was a good thing that I was of the self-taught mindset because the organization was a bit short on training; more to the point, there was virtually no training. So I developed in my own mind what I thought would work and tried to judge its success by how other people reacted to what I was doing.

Later, one of my mentors developed this process for me a bit more. In those days, he called it the Average Man theory. Here is how it works. Our means of measuring action shouldn't be by what was intended (good or bad) but by what the average person would infer from the action. We are responsible for preserving a fair playing field within our sphere of influence as judged by the "average man's" perception. This means that occasionally we have to go out of our way to avoid the appearance of favoritism. In life (and business), we sometimes get carried away with the will to win and forget that principle is more important in the long run than momentary glory (or success), and that life's lessons will endure after the glory fades and the dollar is spent.

Early in my career, I learned the value of examination of my personal actions. Today we call this *self-observation*. Every time I was on a sales call or attended a training session or participated in a meeting, I took the time to assess my role and its relative level of success. I asked myself many different questions: What could I have done differently? Why did I say this one particular thing over another? What seemed to excite my prospect and why?

This introspection enabled me to continuously add to my business success inventory. Every important decision I made, I reviewed to be sure that made sense. Was it fair? Ethical? Did it help the business? The people? I was usually quick to admit mistakes when I made them, and I learned that co-workers respected that attribute.

It was from these early experiences that I learned the power of relationships and their impact on the effectiveness of leadership. Junior Achievement provided one more aspect to my maturation as a business person. I was soon to become exposed to some of the great business leaders in America. I was going to be able to observe what they did and talk with them about why they did it. What an incredible advantage to a young guy with no formal training!

My sainted mother-in-law once remarked to my spouse, Carolyn, "I know Frank has this job with Junior Achievement, but when is he going to get a real one?" It turned out, as Madeline came to understand, to be the perfect job for me to develop my talents and to succeed in the world of business. So with this background in mind, it is my intent to introduce and define for you a leadership style that is right for our times and right for your time. It worked for me, and I didn't even know that it was called relational leadership. Imagine what it can do for you when you are able to look at the whole structure, all at once.

Leading Characters

Early in life, my dad, Howard, made a big impression on me. He taught me what it means to be a good person. He was always there for people in need, and it never mattered if he knew them or not. I vividly remember him collecting money from his co-workers to buy television sets (they were relatively new then) for the sick people at the TB (tuberculosis) hospitals, and then going out with some friends to deliver them and set them up. He drove a big gasoline truck for Atlantic Refining Company (later ARCO) and was constantly being recognized for his kindnesses to fellow travelers on the road. He had a wonderful spirit that resonated with everyone he came into contact with.

The following people (particularly the first four) played a significant role in my adult life. I am an amalgamation of who they are. In my case, I was able to pick and choose what was best about them that fit into what could be best about me. I think you will find their stories interesting and enjoy learning some highlights of their careers.

Bob Albin

Bob Albin, Co-Founder of American Salesmasters, was an early influence. I met Bob when he was 38 years old and had just sold his company to a conglomerate. He served on the board of Junior Achievement in Metropolitan Denver. I figured anyone able to retire at his age was worth staying close to. Good decision, Frank!

The idea of Salesmasters was to provide sales training and motivation to large groups of people in an auditorium environment with some highly effective, known speakers. In the mid-1960s, this was a high-risk business, but it worked. Bob brought the likes of Dr. Norman Vincent Peale, Zig Zigler, J. Douglas Edwards, and Napoleon Hill to audiences across the world. At its peak, American Salesmasters operated in 35 major American cities and 17 foreign countries.

The company started operations in 1964. There were seven principals at the outset led by Hal Krouse. Within a couple of years, Bob and Hal bought all of them out and Salesmasters became their company. This business was no slam dunk. Several times early on they almost went bankrupt. At one point, the two of them went out for a "big splurgy" dinner on their American Express cards, feeling it would be the last time they would be able to use them. Credit cards were not so well established in those days!

They had to go into cities where they had never been before, put together an organization of people they didn't know, and sell a concept that people were unfamiliar with and weren't even going to use until the event occurred six months later! They called on car dealers, insurance offices, and retail outfits—places that had lots of salespeople. They were selling the messages of these great (some not quite great yet) inspirational speakers who, they claimed, would make their sales team more motivated and better producers.

Eventually, maybe by the sheer force of Bob and Hal's will, they turned the corner. In the late 1960s, Bob made a sales call on Dean Darkow of Northwestern Mutual Life. Up until that time, Salesmasters sold records of the speaker's talks. Darkow wanted to know if Bob could put the records on cassette. If he could, he would buy 900 sets of 12 tapes each at $290 per set. Wow! This was big money. The only problem that Bob had at that moment was he didn't know what a cassette was!

Well for that kind of payday, he was sure going to find out. So he told Dean he thought he could do it, but he would have to go back to Denver and work with the production crew to be sure. He found a studio in Los Angeles that had started to make cassettes for music in stereo and was sure they could do the same for mono. American Salesmasters was now off and running.

A new division of the company was started called TBM (The Better Mousetrap). It made custom training programs for companies. The buyer could pick any number of tapes they wanted in their set, and American Salesmasters would logo the product in their name. They began selling 20, 50, 200, and 1,000 individually designed sets to companies across the country. It truly opened and expanded their business.

As successful as this venture became, they reinvented themselves once again in the early 1970s by going to film. They stopped doing sales rallies. They took their one-hour sales talks and condensed them to 20 minutes. Essentially, they went out of the sales congress business and went into the film business. Companies would sign a one-year contract. Customers would receive their film on a Friday, and a salesperson would pick it up on Tuesday and then deliver it to someone else. At this point, the Salesmaster's engine became unstoppable.

I asked Bob when he knew they'd made it as an ongoing entity. He told me that he and Hal were going on a trip together around 1970. It was the first time that they had gone together on a business trip. It was also the first time that they were away from Denver and not worried about running the business the next day, as they had hired someone to do that job. It was at that moment they realized that they were a viable company.

Bob claims that a good leader is effective because he is a magnet for surrounding himself with people who admire, trust, and believe in him and what he is trying to achieve. I can certainly attest to Bob's magnetism!

For Bob, it all started with relationships, which were formed through shared experiences (see Figure 2.1). "We don't become friends because we are alike or different; we become friends because we shared some experience. Surprisingly, often the most unlikely people become friends when they share crisis; and the more profound the experience, the deeper the relationship," says Bob. Figure 2.1 shows how the shared experiences work.

American Salesmasters catapulted into phenomenal success because of shared experiences, first between Bob and Hal and then among Bob, Hal, and their team of associates around the world. Bob in particular was highly visible with his staff. He knew them and their families, he knew their work records, and he knew their likes and dislikes. He knew all of this because he shared himself and his trials and tribulations with them. From this intense belief in people and their abilities, he created a company that knew no bounds.

Basis of Relationships

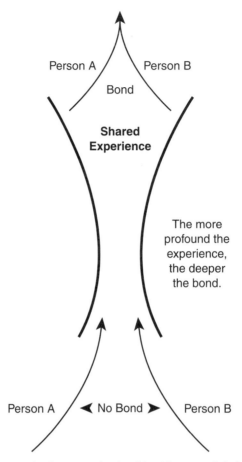

Figure 2.1 *The progression between no bond and bond in terms of the interactions of people based on their shared experiences.*

As I was leaving Junior Achievement Denver on my way to Delaware, I asked Bob for advice. I respected Bob's ability to get outside of his own universe. He was really good at it. I was interested in his opinion about the one thing I could do that would make a difference in my job performance.

His view was that the board of directors was the most important aspect to a non-profit organization. He said that when you are picking your board members over the coming years, make this your most important activity and recognize that it is an ongoing activity. Be active enough in the community to know exactly who you want on your leadership team and then go after them;

most important, don't accept anyone but the person you want. Sometimes this was hard counsel to follow, but it was one of the best pieces of advice I ever received. Because of it, the JA Delaware board was one of the most influential and revered boards in the region, one that community-minded individuals sought out.

Bob's business life was augmented by a recognition that leaders are part of a bigger system, and unless they encompass this bigger system within their own day-to-day existence, they are really not leading at all. Perhaps Bob's greatest accomplishment was not building his extraordinarily successful business, but as the linchpin in the creation of the new Denver Airport. He was asked to lead an exploratory committee for the Denver Chamber of Commerce into the construction of a new airport for the Denver area. From that early volunteer appointment (and subsequent higher-level committees thereafter), he dedicated the next 10 plus years of his life to the creation of the airport. Along the way he persevered over numerous political and practical obstacles to make the airport a reality—all in a volunteer capacity!

What Bob did in his capacity as a volunteer, supporting the construction of the airport, was to develop his learning and, ultimately, his personal influence in a non-threatening environment. Imagine what this sustained effort did for Bob's leadership inventory. Think about the new contacts and friendships he added to the growing list of people who admired him. Picture how he was able to hone his skill set without hindering his personal business activity. Ultimately, this is the personal value of volunteerism that goes beyond the altruistic nature of the effort.

Through volunteerism, shared experiences can become even more intense. This is because of the nature of the effort. The gain is not for the individual; it is for the cause. Bonding together to achieve a worthy altruistic end is a powerful magnet producing life-long relationships. Figure 2.2 demonstrates the concept of shared experience in a different way.

So then, what is Bob's greatest accomplishment as a leader? Is it that he built a company that provided sales and motivational training for hundreds of thousands of people in 35 urban centers across the United States and 17 countries around the world? Or is it that his perseverance with the airport project led the citizens of metropolitan Denver and the state of Colorado to new-found, sustained economic success?

Could it be that one fed the other? You know that leadership is something that you develop over time. Like most aspects of our lives, the more you do something the better you get at it. I have always believed that it is best to make mistakes in a non-threatening but real environment. It just makes sense that

The more profound the experience, the deeper the bond.

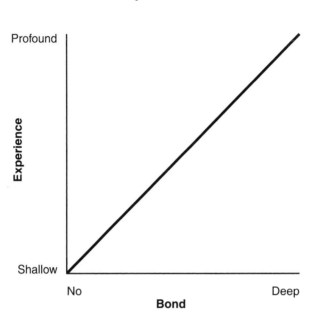

Figure 2.2 *The more profound the experience, the deeper the bond will be, creating life-long strong and meaningful relationships.*

volunteering helps build your capacity as an individual. It is one thing to lead the troops who report to you; it is something entirely different to lead a group that does not. This tests the true measure of your effectiveness. Plus, it has the added benefit of not reflecting directly on your real job performance. You can take chances on improving areas of deficit that you have without as much concern; you can experiment with your thinking. It's like an injured baseball player being sent down to a Triple A league to do a rehab assignment before being recalled to the major league club. Bob not only understood this, but he practiced it regularly, and it elevated him among his peers.

By the way, if you remember the huge problems that were experienced with the baggage and handling system as the Denver airport opened, don't blame Bob. His committee rejected the baggage idea because of cost but more so because it was just too experimental. As a precaution and thinking about the future, his committee built in the capacity to install the system later. However, political powers, greater than the committee, wanted it and wanted it now. Unfortunately, they got more than they bargained for; they got a baggage disaster from an experimental system not quite ready for prime time.

Mark Suwyn

Mark Suwyn, CEO of Louisiana Pacific and New Page, now retired from both positions, picked up where Bob left off. As I arrived in Delaware, it was clear that development of the board was going to be one of my early challenges, so Bob Albin's advice turned out to be almost prophetic. Mark was the first person I added to the JA board.

At that time, Mark was the youngest vice president in the DuPont Company and was marked for major success, perhaps even the CEO's job. He ran the Imaging and Medical Product businesses and was the only VP up to that point who had ever operated two business groups simultaneously. Mark also had the distinction of being a student member of Junior Achievement in Colorado during his high school days. Better yet, he really liked JA! How could you go wrong with a person like this, I ask you? Mark truly believed in people, particularly the power of diversity. He believed in and championed the major precepts of relational leadership.

Several years after coming onto the board, Mark was installed as chairman. One of his first discussions with me involved the organization's roadblocks to strategic success. He challenged me to identify what I believed was the primary barrier to our success and to devise a plan to turn it into an asset. He added one critical proviso: "Don't worry about how much it will cost; I'll take care of that end!" What more could you ask for in a chairman? We never lacked for imagination, so we were able to create a plan that forever changed the fortunes of Junior Achievement of Delaware.

One of Mark's great accomplishments was his work as a volunteer with Junior Achievement International. Shortly after the fall of the Soviet Union, JA took on more and more responsibility to broker the understanding of business, economics, and finance on the world stage. Mark was in the forefront of this activity, serving as the chair of the international board and its true leader for many years, guiding it from its infancy to what it has become today—an organization serving more than 4 million students in over 100 countries.

Mark capped his distinguished business career with his service as CEO for both Louisiana Pacific and New Page, both paper companies and both very successful under his leadership. He carried much with him from his earlier experiences at DuPont and International Paper, particularly about the importance of people and diversity in the business. He says, "If you are in an emerging-maturing business where the issue is how well you compete with other businesses, the only thing that really distinguishes you over the long term is your people and the environment in which they operate."

The multi-faceted question that dogs the leader is this: How do you create an environment where people are engaged and excited, where they can bring their own personality to work and in so doing, bring a level of emotional energy, commitment, and drive that will solve problems, get over hurdles, and move the organization from one place to the next?

While still at DuPont, Mark began a series of diversity efforts, forming core groups and making slow but steady progress. This pursuit began after an encounter he had while on a career development stint in Human Resources. Two high-profile women left the company, and it was said they did so because of personal reasons relating to their families. Mark knew the women and didn't think that was the whole story. He asked to meet with them, essentially conducting an exit interview. What came out was that they could no longer stand the hostile environment they were forced to work in. Life was too short, and they were just not going to put up with it anymore.

Doing a little self-observing, Mark came to understand what disturbed him, perhaps the most, from this discussion. As a white male with a Protestant background, he thought DuPont was a pretty nice place to work. What these women described to him was an environment that was very hard to work in if you weren't white, male, and Protestant. The clarity that hindsight brings us tells us that this situation was not unusual in those days of the 1970s and 1980s.

After about two years of effort and a promotion, he was able to bring in some of his peers at the group VP level, and they began to explore the issues of race and gender, among others. The company began to experience a dramatically raised level of awareness. Large numbers of DuPonters began attending week-long sessions aimed at helping them to understand and be more aware of the new environment that was being fostered by senior management. Doors began to creak open that were never before unlatched. The dawn of a new era was underway, ultimately leading to the appointment of the company's first woman CEO, Ellen Kullman.

The second part of Mark's equation regarding business success focuses on making people aware of how human beings think, act, and feel so that it is possible to identify the fundamental changes that need to be made in the work environment. The process of identifying fundamental changes in the workplace continually evolved over 25 years at all of Mark's companies. He claims that they got really good at creating the environment of excitement, engagement, and drive. What took time was to understand that this environment wasn't enough. "Everybody is excited about everything, and you wind up with chaos. What was missing was an agreed-upon direction, a business model that people understood, and commitment to a continuous improvement process that enables you to point the energy where it is needed," says Mark.

What this meant to Mark was, establish the vision and mission of the organization, determine a business model (how you are going to make money), and then install a continuous improvement process (Lean Six Sigma). With this three-step process in place, managers and employees could get as excited, engaged, and thrilled as they wanted to because they now had boundaries on where the energy is going to be focused; not boundaries about how they were going to behave necessarily but on where the focus should be. After 25 years of evolution, this is a very workable model.

NOTE

Lean Six Sigma is a process designed to improve quality at maximum effective speed. It provides users with the tools needed to analyze process flow for each activity within that process. It attempts to eliminate non-value-added work. It grew out of the Six Sigma process but keys in on speed as the major differentiating factor between the two systems.

A recent example of the results of putting boundaries around where to focus your energy occurred at a New Page plant in Maine. Mark invested heavily in the Lean Six Sigma process, allocating as much as 20 million dollars per year in training designed in large part to help his people think differently about problems.

Remember, New Page is a paper company, and that paper is made from logs. Crushing and grinding the logs is a very important aspect of their business. One of the functions within the plant is to run logs down a chute, smash them into stone, which in turn grinds them into fragments. About once every three weeks, the plant had to close down the system to clean out the water the logs ran and were crushed in—a very costly proposition. Leadership challenged the workforce to improve this process by cutting the downtime. Workers came up with a plan that cut the downtime from one day to eight hours—a massive improvement. Everyone was quite pleased with this result except one fellow who thought they could do better. He suggested that they "gate" the water. His system called for installing gates in the water; when it got dirty, you put the gate down and then ran the logs backward, cutting downtime to zero! This new process saved the company millions of dollars.

Mark reasons that these ideas were always out there. What it took to unleash them were people who were emotionally invested in the business. They understood that if the mill ran better, they would have a job longer. They may have understood that before, but there was no means for them to express their thoughts. By creating an environment where the workers were either comfortable or compelled to think of ways to help the business, Mark opened the doors to 60 to 70 million dollars of improvements every year—all because New Page was engaging its people!

Nathan Hill

Thanks to local legislation, Delaware became a banking Mecca in the mid-1980s. Enter Morgan Stanley and its upstart credit card operation called Discover Card. Nathan Hill was a member of the launch team, and to the good fortune of the state and Junior Achievement, he was named the second president of Discover Bank about three years after it began operations.

Nathan came to Delaware from Columbus, Ohio, and was favorably impressed with the JA organization there. His predecessor at Discover, Ron Cahill, was a member of the Delaware JA board, so signing Nathan up was one of my easier tasks in board-building. Under Nathan's leadership, Discover Card burst out and gained more and more traction each year to become a fully recognized entity in the credit card arena.

Nathan's passion was for volunteerism. He believed that when Discover Card volunteers came back to the workplace, they were inspired to do a great job. "The more people got involved outside, the fewer problems we had with employee morale and motivation inside," says Nathan. "The staff didn't mind working because they were happy. If we have happy employees, we will also have happy customers. The customers feel it; it's a win-win for all."

Nathan took on the task of leading volunteerism for JA, and through his strategies and actions, we were able to serve thousands more kids each and every year. He clearly demonstrated how a passion and belief in people can move mountains. I should point out that Junior Achievement was not the only organization that benefited from Nathan's benevolence. He shared his organization's resources with many worthwhile community groups across Delaware.

Recently, I had the good fortune of working with a couple of young women who were formerly members of the Discover Bank team. I asked them when they worked for the bank, and when they told me, I commented that they must know Nathan Hill. Did they ever! They jointly exclaimed that "Nathan was the best person they had ever worked for and we just loved him to death—everybody did!" I related this story to Nathan, and I was struggling to remember their last names. I did remember that they were credit analysts, though. I would have gotten their last names; I'm just not as quick as I used to be. Nathan didn't need my foggy memory to clear; he came up with their full names almost like he was just with them the day before!

Now here's what you have to know about this story: Nathan had retired five years before (in 2004) and had spent the five years before that getting the International Consumer Banking Group up and running in Europe for Morgan Stanley. The last time he could have possibly encountered these individuals was more than 10 years previous, and they were among the 2,000 people who worked for him at the time! It is no wonder why he was loved. Nathan truly paid attention to the people he encountered in his daily life.

An interesting fact about Nathan Hill is that he is African-American, born in Boston, Georgia. I have always joked with him that at least he got the city right! (If you haven't already guessed, I'm born and raised in Boston and a devout Red Sox fan!) Boston, Georgia, was a town of 2,000 people, so everybody knew everybody. If you got out of line, someone was going to tell your parents, and it didn't matter if you were black or white.

Nathan spent two and a half years in the service and did a year-long stint in Vietnam. He graduated college with degrees in biology and chemistry and was leaning toward being either a doctor or dentist. Along that path he wound up taking a part-time job with Sears in their credit department where he captured management's attention. They wanted him to go into their management training program. However, Affirmative Action was very big in 1972, and Nathan wasn't interested in being a statistic on Sear's charts, so he declined. His bosses were not to be deterred. They didn't see Nathan as a statistic. They told him that he commanded attention, that his presence attracted people to him, and he was really well liked. "Just take the test and see where it goes," they said.

Well he did, and he went far. He climbed the ranks quickly, receiving one promotion after another, and finally winding up in Delaware as president of Discover Bank. From Discover, Nathan had one final promotion ahead of him. Morgan Stanley was intent on sending him to Scotland to become head of operations for Stanley's new International Consumer Banking Group. This assignment could prove to be his greatest career challenge. Nathan said that you could, seemingly, count the number of blacks in the country on one hand! Those blacks who were there were largely Africans, not African-Americans.

So the big day came when he was to be announced to the workforce. All 800 staff from Scotland, Ireland, Wales, and Great Britain were assembled for Nathan to address, and not one of them was black. Nathan recalls thinking to himself, "What have I got myself into here!" I have already said that Nathan was very personable, had a strong presence with people, and he is very quick witted. One aspect I have not mentioned is that he has a terrific voice and he is able to sing *a cappella*. He was aware that Scots were loyal followers of American music, and they particularly liked Motown. So early in his presentation he stopped and sang "My Girl" by the Temptations, and he brought the place down. This gutsy move opened doors and enabled him to do things that might otherwise have been difficult. The organization picked up his positive, thoroughly relational theme and turned a profit within three years, well ahead of the schedule that Morgan Stanley had in mind. These many years later, he is still a friend to many of his associates in Scotland and a welcome guest in their homes.

When Nathan's name comes up in conversation among people who know him or know about him, the most common character trait that is said about him relates to his enormous success with people. It is through this tremendous capability that he achieves such great outcomes in the business world.

I mentioned how he communicates with his senior staff on a regular basis. He reminds staff that they are in this business together, and whether they succeed or not is not about "me" against "you," it's about working together to achieve outstanding results. Discover (or wherever) has to be a great place to work for everyone and this has to be foremost. Each person must bring something to the table to make this happen. It might be

- Enthusiasm and spirit
- Attention to the training to do the job
- Budgeting to provide the proper tools to get the work out
- Building a level of trust
- Recognition for the work both in and out of the company

Nathan knows that enthusiasm and spirit engender an atmosphere of fun and purpose in an organization. When you invest in people's capacity, they appreciate it and work harder to hone their newly acquired skills. It is vital to ensure that you have the financial resources allocated so that the physical assets are available to do the job well. Trust is built by consistently doing the right things, being fair, and demonstrating concern for your associates. While people say they don't do things for recognition, what they mean is that recognition is not the motivating force. When you take the time to celebrate accomplishment, little and big, everyone feels better.

Finally, Nathan reminds his staff to think every day about the five or six things that they must always be conscious of in order for the company to be a great place to work. That ever-present thought is a powerful tool in making it a reality. I believe it was Napoleon Hill who said, "Whatever the mind can conceive and believe, it can achieve!"

For Nathan, his greatest challenge boiled down to people, that is getting people to appreciate and believe the fact that he genuinely wanted to help them. For the most part, in past lives, wherever they were, there was usually nothing to believe in. Other leaders just didn't give them a sense that helping them was all that important. For them, it was all about the leader, not about the people. Time and time again, Nathan had to overcome this mistrust of management and leadership. This was even more of a challenge with, in his own words, "people who looked like me." With these folks, he faced his greatest challenge. He had to make sure they understood that he didn't owe them anything "just because they looked like him." He would tell them what they should be doing in order to challenge themselves to reach for higher levels of performance. "Don't come to me with your hand out," he'd say, reiterating that I don't owe you anything. What he committed to was being fair and being a great coach. His view of himself, which he projected to his people was this: "I can quarterback, I can tackle, I can help remove obstacles—I can be a cheerleader. It's up to you—use me." How many of us would die for a teammate like Nathan Hill?

Bob Brightfelt

My career was moving along nicely, entering its final phase, when my last mentor brightened my life in the person of Bob Brightfelt. Bob was president of Dade Behring and one of its founders. It is a medical equipment manufacturing company. Prior to his position with Dade, he was a career-long executive with the DuPont Company, last serving in the Medical Products Business unit. When DuPont decided to spin off the business, Bob was retained by Dade to head the group. Under his dynamic leadership, Dade Behring (he later acquired Behring, a Germany company) became a leader in its industry. Bob's people strengths along with his business acumen developed a following that was truly dedicated to both him and the company.

By this time in his career, Bob had already been recruited to the JA Delaware board. He served as chairman and led a strong strategic effort that repositioned the organization, creating a new and compelling vision with powerful drivers behind it. Anyone who spends any time with Bob realizes one thing: He has a "bias for action." So it didn't matter if it was at Dade Behring or Junior Achievement—the way to Bob's heart was action. If whatever you are doing isn't working, fix it or move on, but always move toward the doing stage. He infused the Junior Achievement organization with this attitude, pushing JA to heights never before dreamed of.

Bob was influenced by a management expert at DuPont, Walter Mahler, author of many management books. Walter discussed at length his Power Structure and Results theory. He suggested that you first need to know where you are, or your current state. Once you know this, you then must know where you are going—your vision and how you want to achieve that vision. With this knowledge in hand, you could then determine what structure would be best to get you where you want to be. This theory, which Bob subscribed to, was that the organization as a whole had to know where the power was so there were no conflicts on a day-to-day basis competing for power.

Walter was an influence on Bob, yet Bob had his own ideas about business operations. He advocated a flat organization structure. Bob's philosophy encompasses making sure that goals are clear and that he is personally willing to spend time communicating them to staff. He believes that staff should know where they stand within the structure, and then let them loose to do their job.

Bob is not a believer in large staff organizations that have multiple layers of management. He believes that the less interference the better between him and the people in the field getting the real work of the company done. Bob wants folks who are managing on the production line, doing the job, and making things happen. The managers are the people responsible for their employees; they take care of the human resource issues on a day-to-day basis. You need a workplace where the decisions can really empower the organization and its people to take action. When you manage by fear, no one wants to make any decisions or take independent action. Decisions need to move very fast. Keep the organizational structure as close to functional as possible.

Clarity, communication, shared values are tenets of the Brightfelt creed. He is all about telling the truth, fairness, action, teamwork, and diversity. Bob's very nature is to be positive and totally inclusive. He likes being on the floor and with customers and believes that people should be happy on the job and have fun. Being accessible to staff and customers, listening, observing, and taking action on their suggestions whenever possible helps build a team and supports a flattened organization.

Moving along in his career, Bob came to understand that all too often in performance reviews, the manager focused on the weaknesses of an individual and not their strengths. This resulted in action plans designed to shore up the weak parts of their performance. It made them feel bad about themselves, and most important, it rarely worked. He admits that until this epiphany, he did pretty much the same thing in the reviews he personally conducted.

The eureka for Bob was the concept of matching the strengths of the individual to a job that required those strengths. He began to focus reviews on employees' strengths and discuss career paths that built on those strengths. When you think about it, it is easy (or at least easier) to take something you are good at and get you to do that even better. You understand the fundamentals of your strong points, so when suggestions are made to increase your efficiency or improve your application, you get it and feel like you can do something about it.

Bob's frustration (and mine too) with trying to fix people's weaknesses is that a lot of effort is put into a task that just doesn't move performance very far along the line. There is a reason why it is a weakness, so get over it. Lots of times, the weakness doesn't even materially affect how well the total job is done. Don't waste your time on it. If the weakness impacts the capacity to do the work, then find a job for the individual that matches the strengths he exhibits. If you don't have one, then you might have to move on without the individual.

This idea of "fixing" seems to be part of the male genetic makeup. So, if you're a guy, beware—generally it doesn't work! Certainly you can make adjustments. It is not an either/or situation. However, turning a weakness into a strength is costly and with a high degree of sureness, it will fail.

Bob uses a concept developed by the Salt Water Institute out of Kennebunkport, Maine, called One Level Up. Essentially it is a system of cross-functional teams at multiple levels of the organization. Figure 2.3 shows a typical organization chart in a manufacturing environment.

Typical Organization Chart

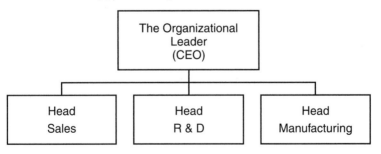

Figure 2.3 *This chart represents a classical organization in a manufacturing company and would certainly represent other departments if it was extended, like Supply Chain and Finance.*

In One Level Up, it is Bob's job to engage his direct reports to help him do his job and for them to learn his job, increasing their capacity to be promoted. They are predisposed to do their personal job well, and that is where their focus is centered. Practically, they are also required to help their peers do well, so they must work across lines of responsibility. If there is no cross-functional accountability, they have no incentive to do their best to ensure other functions do well, too, in a way that maximizes the whole. One Level Up, therefore, enables people at lower levels to experience portions of the work that are done at the level above them while working across lines to ensure that the team is working as a whole unit in pursuit of the company's goals.

The president is responsible for the vision, strategy, investor relations, performance goals, quality, customer satisfaction, cash flow, sales growth, and so on. The leaders of the various business areas agree with the objectives of the president because they helped create them as a team. The idea is to have the leaders take on certain aspects of the president's job. As a result, they are moving their focus to work in part at Bob's CEO level in addition to ensuring that they do their own job. In order to do this, they have to work laterally and as a team with their peers to make the optimizing decisions themselves as opposed to going to Bob with the trade-offs. Bob is making his direct reports think about what needs to be done and then make the decisions required to do it. He wants to minimize the "trade-offs," or decisions that come to him, particularly when they could be made at a lower level. Because Bob's direct reports are participating in the process, the decisions are better because they are closer to the action. Implementation strategies involving the decision then become easier because the team of direct reports are "all in." Plus they learn how decisions are made. Figure 2.4 graphically shows you how One Level Up works.

The next step is to push the management concept down yet another level (for example, to optimize the outcomes of the manufacturing head). This practice begins to change the way everyone in the organization thinks about work and decisions. It is no longer the leader saying, "Give me your recommendations, and I'll make the decision." The leaders of the company are engaging people at all levels in cross-functional activity, which tends to strengthen the whole organization. Figure 2.5 demonstrates how the concept works at the next level down from the CEO/president.

In addition, it is a powerful learning tool because everyone is learning about what it takes to succeed at the level above them. They become more and more capable of moving to the next level. Some, of course, are not able to work at the multiple levels required by One Level Up, but for those who can, it is a very effective method of moving forward successfully within an organization.

One Level Up Concept

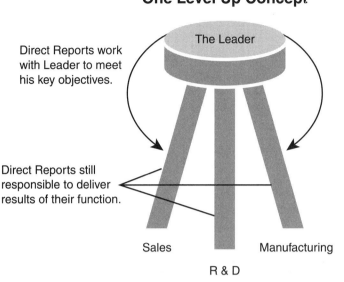

Direct Reports work
with Leader to meet
his key objectives.

The Leader

Direct Reports still
responsible to deliver
results of their function.

Sales   Manufacturing

R & D

The Leader's Direct Reports

Figure 2.4 *One Level Up: The leader working with his direct reports to develop their capacity as leaders.*

One Level Up Concept
Second Level

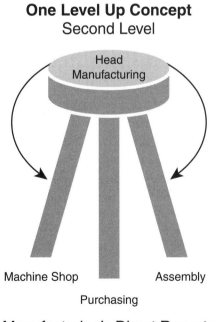

Head
Manufacturing

Machine Shop   Assembly

Purchasing

Manufacturing's Direct Reports

Figure 2.5 *The head of manufacturing works with his direct reports in a similar fashion to the CEO depicted in Figure 2.4, but is also responsible for working with his peer group laterally.*

To this point, I have spoken almost entirely about Bob's business activity. But he has many dimensions, including a strong sense of public service. Following is what I believe to be a remarkable example of his concern for the world outside of his direct business life.

Bob is a devoted graduate of the University of Nebraska. He loves to make connections to amplify his work. Let me give you an example. Several years ago Bob asked me to help him on a project that he was working on with the University's engineering (his college) students. He wanted them to experience engineering as it was practiced. He proposed to bring a group of freshmen to Delaware and wanted them to see engineering in the workplace.

I arranged for site visits to W.L. Gore and Associates and the Chrysler assembly plant in Newark. He took care of Dade Behring. He also wanted his students to experience Junior Achievement, so we set them up to do our interactive Economic Simulation exercise. All too often engineers get very little practical experience in business, and this was an excellent opportunity for them to take in some of the basics. As a topping for the cake, he added in a Philadelphia 76ers game and a few other amenities.

What an incredible undertaking for the students! He recreated this skill-building excursion in several other cities across the country in subsequent years for freshman engineering students with the help of some of my colleagues.

Wrapping Up the Mighty Mentors

In introducing these four gentlemen to you, I have given you a glimpse of their business acumen and their social commitment. Each believes deeply in supporting his community, be it local or national, or even international; it is vital to the business of being a leader. They believe in it for themselves, and they believe that the leaders of tomorrow must subscribe to the same course of action.

TIP

It seems that great business leaders are not only capable of leadership within their own companies but seek to share their resources in the communities where they live—an attitude to emulate.

Mark Suwyn was always concerned about his scientists not understanding business. His belief was that until they came to grips with the business aspects of DuPont, they couldn't fully contribute to the overall effort. Nathan Hill felt that volunteerism was a business strategy for Discover Card. The two

Bobs felt similarly. All understood the powerful concept of learning in a non-threatening environment.

These four men entered my life at different times and provided me with perspectives that were essential to my success. They distinguished themselves both in business and in Junior Achievement. Bob Albin was a dynamic leader and chairman of JA Denver, and through his efforts he revived an organization that had fallen on bad times to become one of the most successful in the country. Mark Suwyn was a National Silver Leadership Award winner, a member of the national board and chairman of the international board being the driving force behind the international expansion of Junior Achievement and the emergence of JA Delaware as a force unto itself. Nathan Hill set the standard for volunteerism in Junior Achievement of Delaware; he too was a Silver National Leadership Award winner and a member of the national and international boards of JA. Bob Brightfelt was honored with the Gold National Leadership Award, one of only 12 in the world for his remarkable leadership efforts. He opened the gates to another rebirth of our organization.

A Cast of Thousands (Not Really)

Remember the old movies from the 1950s and 1960s with their casts of thousands? *Ben Hur, Lawrence of Arabia, Spartacus,* and so on. You needed lots of bodies to fill out the massive landscape and story line that the movies depicted. Some were headliners (the leading characters), many filled secondary roles, and finally hundreds (and sometimes thousands) of extras filled up the screen. Together they made the film successful.

Your business career is going to have, as well it should, many more than four people of influence (my leading characters) affecting you, just probably not thousands. I have six more that made a significant impact on my relational growth. Their thoughts and actions are also captured in this book as examples of relationalism. Let me briefly introduce them to you.

Alan Burkhard, Jim Kelly, Ed McKenna, and Russ Owen all served on the JA board with distinction. Ed is retired after a very successful career in banking. Alan, Jim, and Russ are still very active in their worlds of entrepreneurship, banking and technology, and are the essence of relational thinking and acting.

One other, who somehow escaped being elected to the JA board, is Skip Schoenhals. He recently stepped down as CEO of WSFS Bank but retains the position of Chairman of the Board. He took this small community bank, on the verge of bankruptcy in the early 1990s, and turned it into a power-house. His relational leadership skills and his strong business acumen were the key ingredients in the turnaround. I once described WSFS Bank in a letter to the editor as "the little bank that could!" Skip is a Laureate in the Delaware Business Leaders Hall of Fame.

Representing the government viewpoint is Christopher Coons, County Executive, and Mike Kozikowski the Register of Deeds, both for New Castle County, Delaware, the state's most populous county. Chris has a strong background in business and law from W. L. Gore and Associates, where he served as in-house counsel, ethics trainer, and government relations coordinator. Mike has served many terms in office as register and revamped the way the office operates during his tenure.

There is a clear advantage to having access to the people you admire; you can approach them, observe them, question them, and listen to them. But people of influence are sometimes far away or even in the past. However, you can still study them and incorporate their thinking in your being. I have mentioned Abraham Lincoln as such a person in my life. There is so much to respect in him. His ability to overcome adversity, a spirit that kept him on track even under the most challenging of circumstances, his belief in people (their worth and capacity), and his ability to build alliances. There are stories upon stories about Lincoln being out among the troops, the Congress, and his constituents. These were his public opinion polls, as he was known to refer to them. It was remarked that he spent more time out of the White House than he did inside. Whatever else is true, the people knew that he cared about them and their well-being. He would often stand on a balcony of the Willard Hotel or some other such place to greet and salute his troops. One particular time, it is said, he stood at the Willard in a torrential rain storm as the troops marched by. His aides suggested that he come inside and he reportedly said, "If they can stand it, I guess I can."

So much of what makes a relational leader is considered the sum and substance of Abraham Lincoln. For certain, he held a strong belief in people; he always tried to lift them up. He demonstrated absolute strength of character, fairness, and trust, and he spent much time observing and listening to those around him—you could say attentive. He led a life of purpose and held the nation to purposeful actions. Finally, he considered fun and celebration to be important characteristics in the somber times of his presidency. In fact, these character traits that have been observed as the essence of the man are the very essence of relational leadership.

It is easy to see why Lincoln captured my imagination. All the character traits that I believe are important were embodied in him, the manner in which he conducted himself, and how he treated the people who surrounded him.

Summary

To a large extent, I believe that my life represents the best of the "American Dream." I came from a middle-class family. My dad drove a gasoline truck most of his life, and my mom was a homemaker for most of her life. I went to the local state college, and studied to be a teacher. Events occurred that enabled me to reach well beyond where my early dreams were taking me. I was able to lead a very successful organization, hold leadership positions within my community, travel the world, and interact with business, political, and educational leaders from across the United States. With the help of a talented and enthusiastic team, I assisted hundreds of thousands of young people to shape their future with an ethical grounding. This was made possible because of the people I had the honor of associating with over the course of my career. You met some of them in this chapter, and you will hear from them as you move through the rest of this book.

The story of this chapter is about using your powers of attentiveness to build a better you through the people you associate with in your life. Adults are always admonishing their children with the warning that "you are who you hang around with." I believe that!

KEEP IN MIND:

- Seeking the wisdom of experience, observing the path taken before you, absorbing the attitudes of people you respect is not only right, it is absolutely right.
- Always be prepared to learn something new, particularly from a person whose experience validates the outcome.
- Be both an active observer and an active listener; apply this not just to others you deal with, but even more importantly to yourself.
- It is much easier to build on people's strengths than it is to neutralize their weaknesses.
- The act of volunteering enables you to learn and grow in a non-threatening but real environment.
- As a leader, be a teacher, too.

Chapter 3

Getting Started

"It is not good enough to do good things;
you must know why you do them."

—*Al Boyce*
Branch Manager, Sun Life of Canada

- Exploring and Assessing the Basic Framework
- A Sad Story Without a Fairy-Tale Ending
- A Story with a Better Ending
- The WHY in the World
- Assessment, Compromise, and Focus as Leadership Traits
- Summary

This book is intended for leaders. It does not matter what you are leading. Any person currently leading a team of individuals, be it in the private, government, social, or non-profit sector, will benefit from the principals of relational leadership. An effective relational leader has the best of all worlds: the probability of personal success in the work environment and the inner feeling of satisfaction that comes from extending yourself and enabling others to achieve their desired levels of success. For those of you considering adopting this model of leadership, I suggest that you follow these five steps:

1. Read this book.
2. Assure yourself that the model makes sense for you.
3. Be certain that your nature is compatible with the concepts.
4. Be sure you are fully versed in the fundamentals of your organization.
5. Create a plan for introducing the model to your team.

It's very important to have the whole picture before making a decision to move forward. The relational model of leadership is designed to be fully implemented. Having said that, it does not have to be implemented in its entirety all at once; it can be implemented over time. I will discuss this in detail later.

Relationalism is a wonderful, robust concept of leadership. Those who practice its principles are very happy with it. They often comment, "I like what I see when I look in the mirror at night." Nevertheless, take the time to review the entire model and think about all of the implications and how they will impact you now. It is better to put it off than to start when you are not ready. It is hard work, particularly if you are shifting from a style that is more directive and controlling.

It may be that after reading this book, you will be concerned that this is just too much of a shift for you. This could be a big red light. If you don't think you align very well with the precepts of relational leadership, do not attempt to implement them. It will not work well, and you will probably do more harm than good. Having said that, it just may be that you need more time to evaluate the pros and cons or to get your mind in a position that you are ready to make a significant shift in how you operate.

A relational leader is very comfortable in her own shoes. She has grown through the ranks and understands the fundamentals of the business she is in. This is critical because the building blocks of the model stem from the basic beliefs of the organization—what it values. Make certain that you can comfortably say you are in touch with the core processes of your organization. Do not discount this important aspect of leadership.

Finally, you will create a plan to introduce the model to your organization. It does not have to be done all at once. You might even consider making some implementation moves before you announce any changes. This subject will be dealt with in some detail later. For now, understand that it is okay to implement over time; for many, that is the only way to go.

Exploring and Assessing the Basic Framework

This concept of relational leadership, easily understood yet not so easily practiced, is meant to fully embrace common sense. Discipline is the key to practice. The cornerstone of relational leadership is as old as the ages, the Golden Rule: Treat others as you would like to be treated. Other aspects you have heard as well, like fairness, trust, character. These attributes, among the other pillars, will not be new to you but will be presented in a manner that makes their interconnectedness come alive through both the narrative and examples. Applying all of the attributes of this leadership model will provide you with a very powerful framework. Seen in this new light, you will be able to effectively implement a leadership strategy that makes a difference.

As you think about this framework, you will want to be sure that you are prepared to succeed. There are four points to consider:

- Being authentic
- Knowing yourself
- Developing a knowledge base
- Timing career moves

Being authentic essentially means that you do what you say you are going to do. *Knowing yourself* means that you understand where your strengths and limitations lie. *Developing a knowledge base* is about fully understanding the essentials of your business and the customers you serve. *Timing career moves* means that you have balance between short-term gain and long-term results.

Being Authentic

If people are the soul (referred to as the *core*) of relational leadership, then authenticity is the heart. Without it you have no real chance to be relational; you may not have any real chance to be a leader period. Being authentic is a qualifier. It's go or no go. By *authentic* I mean you can be expected to say what you do and do what you say. You are consistent. Your beliefs and mannerisms, your method of dealing with people and events, and your demeanor and attitude are constant. You are reliable. You're trustworthy. In the vernacular, you're the "real deal."

> **TIP**
>
> An Axiom: Being authentic means you are true to yourself and are trustworthy; you can be expected to "walk the talk."

Without authenticity, how could you possibly hold up the pillars of relationalism? Therefore, before you commit to this concept of leadership you must look within yourself. Do you see someone who can stand up to the rigors of the model? If not then you might want to rethink how plausible it will be for you to move your organization in this direction. Relationalism is born of a moral and ethical compass. There is no escaping this fundamental reality. You would have more success as an uncaring tyrant than to set yourself up as a relational leader and be exposed as something far different. People would be able to adjust to the tyrant much faster than they would or even could to a fraud.

When Chris Coons assumed the office of County Executive for New Castle County, Delaware, he replaced a controversial and controlling individual. So from the very first moment of his tenure, he needed to put a stake in the ground around this subject of authenticity. People had to know that he meant what he said and would stand behind it. When he said to his permanent staff, "You are all welcome to work with me as long as you are ready to work hard and serve the public," he meant it. His job then became one of proving it, which he did. And he keeps proving it daily in every facet of his work; and now over five years later, he has gained authenticity in the eyes of his staff.

Normally it wouldn't take so long, but Chris was fighting long-held beliefs about how leadership operated in the system he was heading. Therefore, it is important to practice patience as you strive to attain authenticity. The key is to stay on your course, take no side trips, and never say you are going to do something that you can't deliver or don't want to deliver.

> **TIP**
>
> Patience is a virtue that will serve you well as you try to establish authenticity with your team or organization.

Knowing Yourself

To succeed in any form of leadership, you must have a clear understanding of who you are and what you need to do to improve who you are. You may already have a handle on this aspect of your life, but if you don't, you need to do something about it.

There are lots of strength inventories available to you at nominal cost. Your co-workers or supervisors can certainly help you understand yourself better. Go over your performance reviews. Self-observation can give you lots of information all by itself. Break down your success stories and figure out what you did that made a difference in the result. Do the same where you didn't achieve as much as you desired. I will delve into this area deeper in Chapter 7.

Skip Schoenhals, the great leader of WSFS Bank in Wilmington, Delaware, and a member of the Delaware Business Leaders Hall of Fame, learned about himself through his mentors. He greatly admired but never met Walt Disney. Disney said, "If I can imagine it, I can make it happen." Disney's creativity was so impressive, some of the things he did probably haven't been equaled to this day. When he built Disneyland, it served as a tremendous inspiration to Skip both to himself and about leading others. It is important to note that you can find yourself in many places—you just have to look.

Success as a leader is not a series of sprints—it is a marathon. It requires careful and thoughtful preparation and a gradual building of endurance or personal capacity. Sprints are high energy, and they are over before you know it. They provide quick highs, but they do not give you the wherewithal to compete in the long haul that a career requires. A leader is constantly "on" and constantly challenged, so stamina is important.

Developing a Knowledge Base

The strength of a leader is his depth of knowledge about people and the ability to turn that knowledge into effective motivation for his associates to do their best. The most successful people I know are ones who started out learning their craft at the most basic level and worked through a series of steps, climbing the ladder and building upon past successes. They understood their business fundamentally, and they understood themselves and how they could contribute to the business.

> **TIP**
>
> An Axiom: Knowledge of the fundamentals is a powerful tool for a leader; without it, the leader is a disaster waiting to happen.

Some of the least successful people I know skipped steps along the way. Usually, a leader in the organization where these not-so-successful people worked recognized them as having talent, perhaps some charisma, some early successes, and so on, and as a result, promoted them to a position that needed to be filled. The problem was that they were not ready for it. They didn't yet understand the business or how their talent (still developing) would play out in the environment. However, they were ambitious, and we're taught early in life to take on all challenges no matter what; that was the path to success.

Getting ahead of ourselves happens more and more often, as our world moves faster and faster. No wonder we have seen so many blunders in all aspects of our society. People are just not prepared to do what they do, and no one will take the time or exert the fortitude to stand up and say, "You're not ready yet." In fact, very often we say the opposite: "Get going, and don't stay in any one place too long."

> **TIP**
>
> An Axiom: In the desire to succeed, be sure that you are carrying the knowledge of a step skipped forward with you.

Alan Burkhard, entrepreneur, talks extensively about gaining a knowledge base. It is the backbone of his business philosophy, and it doesn't matter what the business is. His new hires are always challenged to learn the basics of the business before they even start the work they were hired to do! What is this business about? What does it value? He wants you to know what the customers think of the business and what they want for themselves. He wants employees to know as much as they can about the fundamental systems and beliefs of an organization. He believes that is the only way someone can contribute to the long-term health of the company.

Timing Career Moves

What it comes down to is timing. Do you know who you are and what your strengths look like? Have you put in the requisite effort to learn the fundamentals of your business? Do you understand the plan? What are you able to contribute to the plan? Are your skills currently transferable to the next level? How do you know that? What do you know about leading? What do you know about managing? Do you have a track record that demonstrates you can do either consistently?

What is absolutely true is that each person is going to answer these questions differently. There is no reason to stay in a job when you are clearly ready for the next rung on the ladder. The trick is to identify when that time is right for you. So answering these questions honestly and assessing their meaning for you is an essential skill. Your ultimate success depends entirely upon the choices you make in the early years of your career as you move from one position to the next.

TIP

Time your career moves so that you can say with confidence that you have mastered all you need to know at the level of your current position and that your skill set is well matched to what is needed at your new position.

Don't let your ego get in the way of your future. A career is a long time in the making. It may involve many moves, new companies, new positions, or new skill development. You are hampered if you haven't yet mastered the requisite skills of your current position while you are moving off to a new one.

A Sad Story Without a Fairy-Tale Ending

Over the course of my career, I saw one example after another of moving people to the next level too quickly. Rarely did it work out well. I can recall one person in particular who was an excellent example of moving too far, too fast. He had very good tutelage from his leadership, and they were considered to be top-flight individuals in their profession. Leadership's problem, while they knew their craft well, was that they were not very good judges of individual potential. What they did came easy and natural to them—but not so much with this particular young man.

What he was good at was mimicking leadership's behavior, but he lacked the skill set to perform "outside the womb." So he showed well, and senior management took a liking to him without really studying his record very closely. After all, he acted just like they did. How could he not be good? How he felt about himself personally I do not know, but I do know that to the outer world, he was full of confidence. So he climbed the ladder quickly, so quick that it was hard to see what he was leaving in his wake. Unfortunately, because he was considered a big-time player, the folks who had to clean up his messes did so without exposing him.

TIP

You can't just show well; you have to be able to do well—so be sure that your strengths match well with job ahead of you.

Before long, he took a significant headquarters position. By then he was fully enthralled with himself (some might even say narcissistic). He was good— look at what he accomplished at such a young age! He ran well ahead of the pack. He believed his own press releases, but what he built for himself was a house of cards just waiting for a strong wind to kick up.

He was like a Double-A pitcher coming up to "The Show" (the major leagues). Any baseball player who signs a contract is a professional, by definition. The hitters at the major-league level are the best in the world, even if they fail around 70 percent of the time (and those are the top hitters). What major-league hitters are able to do is hit the mistakes a pitcher makes. A Double-A pitcher still make lots of mistakes (usually) that he can get away with at his level, but not in The Show. There is no room for error.

This young man's skill set was weak because he never fully learned his business. Sticking with my baseball analogy, for most pitchers, it takes quite a long time (five or six years) for them to learn their craft sufficiently to even moderately succeed at the major-league level. But this man was, quite simply, imitating what he saw others doing who were deemed to be successful. He was very good at imitation, but fundamentally he did not understand the building blocks of the business he was in. When put in this position, it is difficult to make effective decisions, particularly when the call is a close one. It is that deep-seated storage chest of knowledge that enables you to wade through the murky waters to gain clarity in the assessment process.

> **NOTE**
>
> As an aside, I know a person who was highly regarded in a major industrial company who was climbing the ladder, making continuous progress toward his goal of being CEO. Along the way, after having exhibited great success in the profit centers he was assigned to, he was given what he thought was a totally off-the-wall assignment—Human Resources, albeit as its head.
>
> At first it was a big letdown for him, and he thought he had done something wrong; his career was over. Essentially, he was told the opposite by a confidant, more senior than him. Senior management felt he needed this experience to round out his background so that he would make better decisions later when they would count for much more.
>
> Thankfully for him, he had the maturity to appreciate what the opportunity meant to him. He gave his all to the assignment for the two years he was there. His career catapulted from this experience. By the way, this person I am speaking of was one of my mentors, Mark Suwyn. Mark would tell you today, it is all about the fundamentals!

For the young man, the other very damaging piece for him was the exalted opinion he held of himself. He was suffering from the sin of hubris. He did not fully calculate the extent of his exposure once he was in a headquarters position, gone from the protection of the womb. The more he was exposed, the less he was revered. His communications and his actions just didn't make much sense. His feelings about himself led him to take questionable actions, both strategically and ethically. His life became a "sticky wicket" as our cousins "across the pond" might say.

His career quickly unraveled. Everyone (well not everyone, really) was shaking his head and asking, "How did this happen?" The answer was pretty easy—moving up too far, too fast. Not enough exposure to the fundamentals of the business. No commitment to understanding the basics. He manufactured a career based on fraud, and he wound up going down in disgrace. A true tragedy, as it could easily have ended far differently and better for all involved, including the company.

How could the ending have been different? Well, of course, many things could have happened. Senior management could have taken responsibility and looked beyond the façade that he placed in front of them. They could have been less absorbed in their own day-to-day existence and seen him for what he was—a person with potential who wasn't applying discipline. They could have held him back and tutored him in the underlying "secrets" of great leadership. They could have done their jobs. However, they did not. They turned out to be less-than-stellar leaders. They failed in one of their fundamental functions—to identify and nurture their direct reports. Failing him, they failed the company and they failed themselves.

More to the point, the young man did not understand his own failings. He did not self-observe. He did not criticize his own work. He built a false picture of himself, and no one (whom he cared about anyway) did anything to dispel that sense. He did not understand that the responsibility for his success was his own. He thought because his managers passed on his record, that he was okay. That tacit approval by his bosses led him to believe that he was doing the right things to succeed. He never took the acid test, meaning he never looked in the mirror and analyzed his own actions. He never knew why he did the things he did. He convinced himself that he was the right man at the right time.

Unfortunately, his performance did not square with his thinking. At some point, it seems to me, he had to realize this bad turn of events. People were criticizing him, which had never happened before. Even his friends were suspect of his capabilities, and many privately told him so. He was lost in his own persona. He did not know how to change his operational style, as by this time it was deeply imbedded. I have to believe that in his own mind, there was no turning back. He could only hope that something would happen to save him, although I doubt he actually knew what that might be. By now, he probably understood the implications of starting over. He would have to give up the "high life" that he had become so accustomed to enjoying. He would have to learn the fundamentals of the business and reapply his skills in a new environment. He would have to admit that he moved too far, too fast. In the end, he decided to "roll the dice," hoping he might somehow continue the way he was going and survive. Of course, he didn't, and in the end he lost.

So roll back your clocks for a minute. Did you ever create a "cheat sheet" in school? The people I know who did spent an enormous amount of time getting all that information on that small piece of paper. There is no doubt (in most cases) that the same amount of effort going into studying the material would have produced better results. Cutting corners usually does not work out very well. Cheating indicates that you lack confidence in yourself to do it the right way. The young man in this story cheated when he mimicked leadership, which was no different than making a cheat sheet. Honesty about who you are and what you are currently able to do is a critical success factor in your career ladder.

A Story with a Better Ending

Contrast the previous story with another: One of the business leaders I admired was my wife's Uncle George. Uncle George owned a small oil company in Miami. A large part of his business was servicing cruise liners. Now you know a cruise liner needs a heck of a lot of oil and you can imagine, George's business was very profitable.

This story is not about the long hours, scary days, and sleepless nights that he endured while building the business; but you know (good reader that you are), it took all of that and more to become successful. This story is about his son-in-law, whom he took into the business long after it had become a thriving enterprise. Michael was a very successful executive for Chrysler in Atlanta and was to serve as treasurer of the oil company. Today we would call him a CFO.

On his first day of work, Michael showed up in a suit and tie. No one told him that was the dress, but it was what he was used to wearing to work. Seeing this, George wondered why on earth Michael would wear a suit to the office. I'm guessing he was chuckling a bit to himself as he caught up with Mike at his desk. He was quick to let Mike know that while he was indeed the treasurer of the company, he would be working in the warehouse moving barrels of oil around and other such everyday jobs until he understood the business. When he was through with those tasks, he could pay attention to the company's finances. There would be plenty of hours in the day for both!

The great lesson that George was teaching here is this: You are not going to be an executive of any business that I am involved with unless you know the business from the ground level. How else can I truly trust you to make good financial decisions? We can extend this beyond the oil company to any work situation. If you don't understand the basics, you are probably on a collision course with career disaster.

Well, Michael did get it. At first he grumbled a bit, but he understood the point. Besides, George was not a person you argued with very often! Mike had the skill set to do the CFO's job, but he knew very little about the business he was now in. Surely, there were going to be financial issues that would require a thorough understanding of the oil business and more particularly, the oil business as it pertained to the cruise ship business. Eventually, Mike acquired the knowledge of the business and successfully transferred his skills from Chrysler to be an effective CFO.

I have retold this story countless times when doing career counseling. Sometimes it resonates and sometimes not. To a large extent, it depends upon the maturity level of the individual. In the end, as I have said, shortcuts rarely work out. If you doubt that, next time there is a tie-up on the highway, take the side roads that everyone else is taking to avoid the highway traffic. You are likely to find that it will take you longer to get where you're going than if you'd stayed on the highway. Investing time in your career is the best long-term investment you can make for yourself and your family.

The WHY in the World

It is not enough to be talented. It is about continuing your learning tactics and cycles so that you are always defining who you are and how you can improve. When you know *why* you do something, you are in control. It becomes relatively easy to shift positions or strategies if you know why you do what you do in the first place. You can improve incrementally by adding features or additional benefits to your routine. Your methods may change because of circumstances in a changing world. You will make better decisions because you are working from a position of strength. You not only know what you do, you know how you do it, and most important, you know why you do it.

During a sojourn from Junior Achievement, I was employed as a sales representative and sales manager for Sun Life of Canada. As a representative, I was regularly ranked in the top 10 in New England and in the top 25 percent in the country for sales volume. One day after a sales call that my branch manager, Al Boyce, attended with me, he debriefed the call on the way back to the office. He told me all the good points that I demonstrated in the interview, and then suggested that I take the counselor selling course offered by Wilson Learning. I asked what the course entailed, and he said that it focused on all the good things he talked about me doing in the interview. I must admit, I went from feeling pretty good to feeling insulted very quickly.

I was a bit confused; why would I waste time and money taking a course about things that I already did and did well? I related these thoughts to him. His response was to become one of the most profound insights of my life. His message to me was simple: It's not good enough to do good things, you must know *why* you do them; otherwise, you will never be a true professional. He said that once I learned why I did what I did, my performance would be greatly enhanced. He was right, I rationalized, but I sure was not giving that up while we were sitting in the car.

> **TIP**
>
> An Axiom: In order to be considered a true professional, you must know the "whys" of what you do—they are what make you a success.

I can honestly say that I was still a bit of a skeptic as I listened to his reasoning. I mean what about all those little award plaques I kept getting? What did they mean? In my mind, selling was about being in the field talking to prospects and turning them into customers. It was not being a student in a classroom trying to figure out the esoteric "why" question. We all go through a maturing process in life, and this predicament was certain to be part of my growth.

He must have appreciated my continuing reticence. So, much to my dismay, when we got back to the office, he invited me to share some time with him in the training room. What was wrong with this guy? He had no personal life, that was for sure!

In the training room, he explained to me the theory of the true professional—something he called a Conscious Competent. Well that was a new one on me, so I paid attention as he laid it out. The following is a derivation of the popular model of Conscious Competency; in this scenario the concentration is on the *why*. Not to mention, the modification of the theory suited Al's needs quite nicely. There are four stages to the Al Boyce version of the theory, as shown in Figure 3.1.

The term Unconscious Incompetent means that your performance at tasks is not good, and you do not have any idea why this is so. The Conscious Incompetent doesn't perform tasks very well but has figured out why this is the case and can do something about the situation. The Unconscious Competent seems to be able to perform tasks well but doesn't know why; actions seem to be intuitive. Finally, nirvana, the Conscious Competent—this person performs tasks given to him at a high level and knows beyond instinct why he does what he does.

Al suggested that I was a Conscious Competent in waiting. All I had to do was take the course he was suggesting, and the "keys to the kingdom" would become mine to use! Of course, being a rookie in the business and having your boss's boss suggest that you do something was not lost on me! I was clever, even at an early age.

Stages of Consciousness

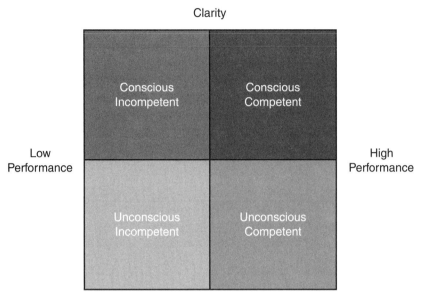

Figure 3.1 *The Conscious Competent performs at a high level and is clear about why.*

> **TIP**
> Strive to become a Conscious Competent, a person who gets things done well and knows definitively why she does what she does.

As I am sure you have already surmised, I took the course. I even liked it. I did learn why I did what I did, and it began to make even more sense to me once this happened. There is a certain amount of comfort in knowing the why of something. It enables you to make shifts in strategy more fluidly. It gives you confidence and builds your personal esteem. This is all good.

By using the same theory and applying it directly to relationalism, you can see the four stages that the relational leader moves through. The chart in Figure 3.2, called the Stages of Relationalism, demonstrates where you are at in the process.

You can place yourself in one of the stages through your answers to the following questions. Are you *exploring* the idea but generally acting non-relational? Are you *practicing* the concepts but not getting too far with them just yet? Are you *acting* relational but have no framework for why you do so?

Stages of Relationalism

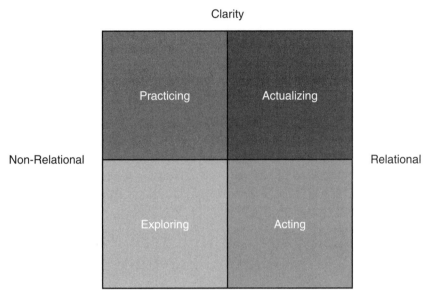

Clarity

Practicing | Actualizing

Non-Relational | Relational

Exploring | Acting

Ambiguity

Figure 3.2 *The relational leader understands and is clear about the concept of relationalism and follows the model.*

Are you relational, understanding and employing the model successfully? Or put in another way, are you able to *actualize* the concepts into action and know why you are doing so?

I have always found it's best to understand where you are in any process that you are involved in. By possessing this information, you are able to plan your next growth steps effectively.

Assessment, Compromise, and Focus as Leadership Traits

Chapter 1 introduced you to relational leadership and gave you an opportunity to read about two organizations that achieved very different results because of their leadership. In this chapter, you've learned about the critical success factors that prepare relational leaders to succeed. More importantly, you are putting order to some of the fundamentals that you must possess if you are going to achieve success as a leader.

Ideas stem from knowledge, which is one of the keys to leadership. Testing your ideas and assessing their results adds to your knowledge base, which enables you to see how those ideas work in real environments. Testing ideas is a good way to add to your leadership knowledge because it gives you data points to compare. You just can't have enough knowledge. The more of it that you possess, the better you are able to make decisions and to back them up, if challenged. I am talking about gaining a fundamental foothold on the business and then using your skills to build that business.

My friend Bob Adams introduced a most controversial idea as an outgrowth of a teacher school improvement committee he formed to help keep Shue Middle School on track for excellence. The idea was school uniforms. I said "controversial," but I could just as easily said "courageous." Courage is an aspect of leadership that people sometimes forget but appreciate when they see it. The firestorm that ensued was a sight to behold. Keep in mind that this was his team's idea, not his. It was the result of two to three months of research on the subject that suggested the uniforms would cut down on the distractions that a middle school attracts. No more "gang gear." No more sloppiness. No more clothes competition. Students could concentrate on school work and develop school pride.

He believed it was his responsibility to "ride point" on this idea. As the leader he took the hits, not his teachers, and the hits came from every direction. One time a parent stormed his office with an armful of clothes and dumped them on his desk saying, "You pick out what he can wear!" She was referring to her son. Boy, that would have been a sight to see, one of those times you would have liked to be the proverbial "fly on the wall"!

Bob's overriding premise as a principal was to act in the best interest of the kids. He saw the dress code issue in this light, and through several hotly debated public meetings and many less-public meetings with parents and district officials, he persevered. Parents and students argued that this rule took away the students' individualism. They compromised along way but got their dress code into the school's code, where it remained at least through Bob's departure several years later. Much knowledge was gained along the way about how students responded to the new rules.

People respect and follow leaders who are able to stay on task, even if the end result is delayed. Sometimes it is important to just stay in the game until you can achieve the end result.

> **NOTE**
> Compromise as I describe it here is like a middle relief pitcher in baseball. The plan is for the starting pitcher to pitch into the sixth or seventh inning, but sometimes he gives up runs early. The manager's job is to give the team a chance to win the game, so he brings in a "middle reliever" to hold the other team at bay, giving his offense time to tie or move ahead in the contest.

Compromise without losing sight of the long-term objective is a talent that many people miss in life. It is an aspect of leadership that is often overlooked. People who comment on Ted Kennedy's career in the Senate always point to the incredible ability he possessed to stay focused on the end result, even through compromise. He knew that some issues were just going to take time to bring to fruition. Kennedy's belief was that the compromise kept moving the issue forward yet another step. Every step forward brought him closer to his goal. He was truly focused.

For Bob and his team, the dress code was a piece of the ever-increasing test scores the students were achieving under his direction. He believed that putting the dress code system in place at any level would enable him to put forward the larger agenda of student academic performance and a safe environment for learning that was being developed jointly by the faculty and administration.

If you consider just some of the ingredients that make an effective leader— like ever-increasing knowledge, experimenting, compromising, protecting your staff, and maintaining focus—it is easy to understand why there are so few of them. Leading is a lot of work—hard work. It takes time and effort over the long haul. Each day's lessons build upon the next day's efforts, and those efforts produce more lessons. The study of leadership is never finished, and what is touched upon in this chapter is essential to building your effectiveness as a relational leader.

Vince Lombardi was a great football coach and a quote machine! He once said this about leaders: "Leaders are made; they are not born. They are made by hard effort, which is the price which all of us must pay to achieve any goal that is worthwhile." Words to take to heart!

Summary

It is important that you understand what it takes to become a relational leader. This chapter gave you insight into what you need to think about and what you should be prepared to do physically and mentally. You must have the right mindset to embark. Specifically, you have to be willing and ready to change. In Bob Brightfelt's words, you must have "an unwillingness to stay where you are!" This translates to a fair amount of determination and commitment on your part to become relational. In my opinion, this is the most important step in your journey. If you have the resolve, I am confident that the other pieces will fall into place, perhaps not without effort but you will get there. The mind controls your actions. Remember what Walt Disney said, "If I can imagine it, I can make it happen."

Once you are past the commitment stage, the next big hurdle is authenticity. This is particularly true if you will be making a major shift in how you operate, but it still applies regardless of the degree of change. People by their nature resist change and can be quite untrusting of change agents. So that leads you back to the determination piece and introduces the virtue of patience.

I had a nun as a teacher in sixth grade at Sacred Heart School in Lynn, Massachusetts, a Sister Odilla. She reminded the class about patience, almost daily, with these words, "Patience is a virtue, possess it if you can, seldom in a woman, never in a man." I don't know how much she knew about people, or patience for that matter, but I do know that is the only thing I remember from sixth grade! I also know that I agree with patience being a virtue and that you should possess it if you can; the rest I'm not so sure about.

By switching your style to relationalism, you are absolutely becoming a change agent. Therefore, the virtue of patience must become your best friend. Your staff will watch your actions closely, always testing for alignment between your words and your actions. They are leery of trusting even you, when you are touting some new "panacea," promising great days ahead for the organization. Their attitude will likely be, "We like it just as it is, thank you very much!"

Understanding the why of things is vital to making you competent and having others view you as competent. You know that statement can be mutually exclusive. It doesn't matter what you think of yourself; if the folks you are leading aren't buying, then you have a big hill to climb. Invest whatever it takes to understand the why of you. Instinct is good, but alone it's not enough. I would certainly rather have it than not, but if you truly want to be the best, you have to know why you do what you do.

If you are talking to the troops and telling them you have decided to send them into battle based on your instinctive reaction to the battle conditions, you better have a darned good track record. When you put people at risk, they want assurance that you have been careful about the plan, and have weighed the consequences, and are putting their best interests first. If you have a reputation for knowing the whys of things, you will greatly reduce the tension of change.

The bottom line in this discussion is you doing your due diligence. Make sure you understand what you are getting into and commit to making the change happen. Relational leadership will open many new opportunities for you to make a difference in your life, your organization's life, and your staff's lives— all good!

KEEP IN MIND:

- Being authentic means you are true to yourself and are trustworthy; you can be expected to "walk the talk."
- The cornerstone of relational leadership is as old as the ages. The Golden Rule: Treat others as you would like to be treated.
- Success as a leader is not a series of sprints; instead, it is a marathon requiring thoughtful planning and gradual building of personal capacity.
- Understand the basics of your business before moving to the next step.
- The strength of a leader is his depth of knowledge about people and the ability to turn that knowledge into effective motivation for his associates to do their best.
- Self-observation tells you how you are doing and enables to you make adjustments to your style.
- Understanding why you do what you do enables you to make effective strategic shifts when the situation calls for them.
- Time your career moves so that you can say with confidence that you have mastered all you need to know at the level of your current position and that your skill set is well matched to what is needed at your new position.

Chapter 4

What Does Relational Leadership Look Like?

"Those leaders who achieve something at
the head of one group will eclipse those
who do nothing at the head of a hundred."

—*Abraham Lincoln*

- An In-Depth View of the Relational Leadership Model
- Summary

Perhaps you have heard the story of Greg Mortenson, the K2 climber who, on his way to the summit, was stranded in Korphe Village in Pakistan's Karakoram Mountains. He was impressed with the people and their culture. He wanted to do something to pay them back for their kindness, so he decided to build schools for the children.

We can learn much from a mixture of cultures. Mortenson's book, *Three Cups of Tea: One Man's Mission to Promote Peace . . . One School at a Time* (by Greg Mortenson and David Oliver Relin, Penguin Books, 2007), is the story of the impact the children of Korphe Village had on him and what he did about it. A passage from the book goes as follows: "Haji Ali taught me to share three cups of tea, to slow down and make building relationships as important as building projects. He taught me that I had more to learn from the people I work with than I could ever hope to teach them." The message is clearly about valuing people.

I was in the Middle East at the request of the U.S. Embassies in Oman, United Arab Emirates, and Bahrain representing Junior Achievement. The objective was to open JA operations in these locales as part of our ongoing international expansion and America's mission of educating the world about our free market economy. There I learned the same type of lesson about valuing people.

Every meeting that I can remember began with coffee or tea and the exchange of pleasantries. It is in this manner that you get to know each other so that the discussions may proceed at a higher and more effective level.

Establishing a relationship is very important in the Arab world. Without a relationship, I am not sure that much of anything happens. In fact, even being late for a meeting is considered rude almost to the point of an insult. Oftentimes in the U.S., we don't put quite so much stock in either relationships or punctuality. We frequently over schedule our time, and when we get to the meeting, we want to start. The culture in the Middle East is not so frantic, and connections between people are highly valued.

Your own business culture must support the values you want your associates to espouse. ING Direct is an extraordinarily successful Internet bank. It has created a culture that is unique in the industry. Virtually no one gave them a chance of succeeding. The experts responsible for the feasibility study back in the mid-1990s said flat out—no chance. Well the company launched anyway with a different approach to banking that has captured the imagination of its customers. Beginning in 2000, its rise to the top has been amazing. Savings deposits increase by one billion dollars per year, and more recently the same is true for mortgage loans.

One of its leaders is Jim Kelly, the chief operating officer. Jim is a member of the JA board and a past chairman. He also was awarded JA's Gold National Leadership Award, one of only a handful in the country to be recognized. He believes that for your culture to be pure, it must be relational in nature.

Jim says that "You have to be consistent and keep hammering away at the culture. If you don't do this consciously, you will get one anyway." ING has its "codes," and they are what govern the culture of the company. You have to talk about what you believe in. At ING, the codes are featured in the orientation of new employees and reinforced time and again through "reorientation." Kelly adds, "We call the career path your 'Orange Journey'—it's not just about today but all the days you spend at ING. You can't let elements of another company's culture work their way into your system. People who do not subscribe to your culture will try to subvert it." There is no short-term thinking at ING. People—staff, customers, shareholders, and community—are central to its culture. Leadership at the company focuses its efforts on the long term.

Alan Burkhard, entrepreneur supreme and former board member and National Leadership Award winner approaches life a bit differently than most. His philosophy of business is culturally driven. By that he means a way of thinking—how you think and how you act. His way of thinking is through information, and information is customer-driven. For anything to be accepted in the company, it must demonstrate value by passing a simple test: Ideas must have value to the internal customer (meaning staff) or the external customer (meaning consumer). If the idea has value, then we do it; if not, then it doesn't apply, whether it is planning, structure, roles, or responsibilities.

Culture to Alan is a list of traits that have meaning for both staff and customers. This is what we "do." If we live by the traits, it would equal a way of thinking. What are the traits that enable this customer-driven culture to work? They are things like trust, truth, sharing, and being direct. Alan says, "My goal is to create an organization where everything we do is a value to the employees and a value to the customers."

People are always at the center and are the core of a relational leader. People are more than the employees; they are everyone who is a stakeholder to the organization. People interconnect with all the elements and attributes that will be discussed later in this chapter. It is the connection of one to the other that provides the bond that makes this framework so powerful. When the attributes work in consort with each other, a harmony is created that produces a tremendous force of positive energy within an organization.

> **TIP**
>
> An Axiom: Applying the attributes of relational leadership across the organization creates a harmony that will produce a tremendous and positive energy force.

An In-Depth View of the Relational Leadership Model

What then are the attributes that relational leaders believe in, think about, try to improve upon, and drive home to their workforce or teammates? You will be able to tell an organization that values relational leadership if you are able to observe the following characteristics on a regular basis. People are at the center of the organization (see Figure 4.1). It's almost as if you can feel

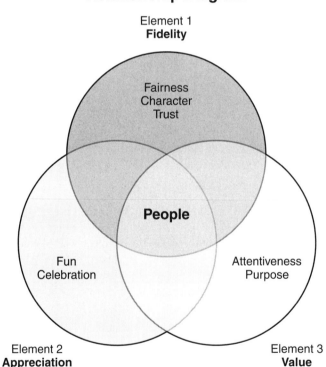

Relationship Diagram

Element 1
Fidelity

Fairness
Character
Trust

People

Fun
Celebration

Attentiveness
Purpose

Element 2
Appreciation

Element 3
Value

Figure 4.1 *This diagram shows the relationship of the core to the elements and the attributes they represent.*

it when you enter the door. If you pay attention to the actions of the organization and the principles that guide the actions, you will be able to see relationalism at work.

Three important elements surround the core of people: fidelity, appreciation, and value. These encapsulate the important attributes that are the foundation of relational leadership and what makes it work. The attributes are the working parts of the engine of relationalism. They are what leadership drives in motivating its people to achieve the anticipated results of the business plan.

In my reading over the years, I have always appreciated books and articles that not only deal with the *what* of a subject but also the *how*. In that spirit and in order to fully explore the core and elements of relationalism, I will share with you not only my own experience but that of other relational leaders. The purpose is to give you a deeper understanding of the components and a wide a range of possible strategies that you can employ in the many dimensions of the relational model.

Understanding the Core and Elements

While it is perfectly acceptable to introduce the model piecemeal, particularly if you are making a major shift in your operating style, it is important to note that the model performs at maximum when all of the component parts are engaged and working in unison. To that end, it is vital that you appreciate each of the pieces individually so that the puzzle becomes a mosaic. After all, it will be your artistry at bringing the pieces together that connects your people to the new world of relational leadership.

Core

Organizations are built around people. Valuing and respecting people can be demonstrated in many different ways. I will explore some of them in this section. It is critical that you understand the people piece of this model in order for you to apply the elements that support it.

The core is the central part of the model. It is like the sun in that it supplies energy to all the elements that interact with it. The core is the people—they are the key to the success of the organization. Without them, nothing happens. It is their energy and enthusiasm that create results that are above average. They are valued because they make up the team, and individually they bring their strengths to the team's success. Each individual provides worth in the pursuit of the overall team objective. Each person is recognized for the level of expertise she possesses at the development stage she's at.

> **TIP**
> An Axiom: When people are valued and respected, they will always try to put forth their best effort and demonstrate a strong work ethic.

Valuing and respecting people requires leadership to step outside of itself. The leader must recognize that each individual has a perspective. People see life through their own prisms, their own experiences. Just because your employees don't live in your neighborhood (assuming that's true), it does not follow that they are clueless about the world they do live in; it's just different from yours. That's the good news.

One of my truly outstanding board members from Delaware was Russ Owen, also a Junior Achievement National Gold Leadership Award winner (one of nine in the country that year). Russ is President of Managed Services Sector, CSC (Computer Sciences Corporation). He says, "The true element of leadership is not just about picking and guiding exceptional people; it is more about getting a large collection of average people to do above average things."

Just how important are people to an organization? Mark Suwyn found out through research while working at DuPont in the Corporate Plans business unit. He and an associate were tasked with finding a solution to a problem that the executive committee was facing: Where do we allocate funds for projects that come before us? They did not have a good reference point, strange as that may seem. Owing to a faltering economy, funds were tight for the first time in quite a while.

After looking at 75 to 80 business units internal to DuPont and a similar number externally, there seemed to be only one good correlation. Mark noted, "If you found a group of people who were invested, not money-wise but emotionally invested, in the outcome of the business and how it was operating, that business tended to be successful. The people environment that you created and how people responded to that environment was the only correlation that we could make about successful businesses." His finding underscores the importance of the people equation in relational leadership.

Successful organizations, particularly if they are relationally based, promote harmony among their associates. The leaders understand that a certain amount of tension among staff is good, but it must be controlled. I am reminded of a story that serves as an example of how an organization can keep its focus on the importance of people. I once had the opportunity to attract two young and very high-potential people to my team in Denver. One,

Pam (Van Dyke) Seaholm, was a local Denverite who distinguished herself in the JA program while in high school. The other, Michele Hollandsworth, was a fresh transplant to Denver and a freshly minted program volunteer. Pam was a recent college graduate, and Michele was starting her first job as an engineer at Martin Marietta. Both of these women were quality individuals—honest, hard working, friendly, and personable people.

Their relationship got off to a shaky start. Each individual was thinking one had an unfair advantage over the other, stemming from their particular backgrounds and hiring circumstances. You can guess that the uneasy feelings turned into real relationship challenges between them. It became emotional. Their attitudes were sure to cause problems with the volunteers and students as they went about their business, and in fact, it was already showing.

One day, after a particularly exhausting coaching session that went pretty much nowhere, I decided that the situation called for a new approach. We talked about how their trouble still existed because neither one was willing to commit to the hard work it takes to identify the problem they were experiencing; they were merely identifying symptoms, and thus not making much progress. We discussed guidelines that would help them resolve this symptom versus problem dilemma, and I kept digging to get at the root of it all. They had to approach the discussion rationally. After setting up the best possible scenario, I then left them to themselves to work out a solution.

Well that exercise took a while, but they finally got it. They realized that their challenge with each other was based on pettiness and misunderstanding, and in actuality, there was no substance to it. When you are embroiled in an emotional situation, it is often hard to see beyond your own viewpoint, particularly if you are not addressing the problem. Given their epiphany, they were then able to work effectively as a team. It was hard work, but once the problem was identified, the solution was relatively easy.

As a leader you must be able to separate the symptoms from the problems and enable your associates to do the same. Solving symptoms only guarantees the problem will be back with more intensity. Effective leadership focuses on solving problems, not the symptoms. Leadership that addresses relationship issues with staff is demonstrating value and respect for its people.

Remember the story of the ill-fated Titanic? Think of the tip of the iceberg that was visible to the captain of the ship. The tip was in effect a symptom of the impending problem (AKA disaster). What was below the sightline under the water was a significantly larger mass of ice. That was the problem. By steering away from what was visible, the symptom left the ship in peril because the problem, the true mass of the iceberg, was still close at hand. We all know what happened to the Titanic when the ice mass below the sight-line ripped the ship apart.

While Pam and Michele have parted ways with Junior Achievement, they remain close friends to this day, some 25 years later, in spite of their rocky start. Building relationships has to do with getting to the heart of the matter if you have an issue with another person. Solve the problem (rather than the symptoms), and you create a long-term solution. In the case of Pam and Michele, attention to their issues with the goal of fixing the problem is an example of an organization that focused on people.

TIP

An Axiom: Until you identify the problem, you are always trying to solve symptoms and the problem never goes away.

Another means of demonstrating value and respect for your associates is to get out among them—talk to them, listen to them, get to know them. This principle of interaction is generally referred to as "management by walking around." It is very effective to get out among the people who are actually doing the work because it gives you direct feedback on the what's and how's of the current projects. Nathan Hill did a lot of walking around, and it was very purposeful. However, he did not walk around at random; he planned how he approached the task and what he wanted to gain from it before ever leaving his office.

He would always ask, "How are things going for you?" He would study people and their facial expressions to validate their answers. If he sensed there was a problem that they did not want to bring up, he would encourage them to talk with him over coffee in his office or the cafeteria or some other such place. I asked him, "How did you know something was wrong?" He responded, "I pay attention; it's not just lip service. I wanted them to know I really did care; it was not superficial."

Wherever Nathan went throughout his career, he was noted for his skills with people. That he cared for them and their well-being was obvious. His staff would do anything for him in part because they knew he would do anything for them.

Just as important, this practice kept Nathan in touch with what was happening at the ground level in his organization. How critical is that? Surprises are not very welcome in the executive suite. You can't always rely on your direct reports to give you all the facts (particularly while they are trying to fix a problem). It behooves a leader to observe and listen. By doing so, he learns what is really going on in his organization without the filters that often accompany the reports he may receive from subordinates.

Bob Brightfelt reinforced the importance of observing and listening when he said, "When you are out among your associates or customers or vendors, you get the 'real' reality. Maybe not the first time, but if you do so regularly, people will observe your behavior and will begin to trust your motives. You get the good and the bad. Eventually you are going to get the bad anyway; I want to get it as soon as possible so I can do something about it."

Before leaving the example of "management by walking around," let me emphasize that it must be sincere. I am thinking about a person who is not committed to this interaction but does it because he wants people to think he cares. When he walks around, his eyes rarely focus on the person, and if they do they invariably wander fairly quickly. He always gives the impression that he is moving on to the next cubicle so he can put this bothersome task behind him for the day. For the leader, it becomes counterintuitive. Unless you are sincerely interested in connecting with your people, you are better served by just staying in your office. Otherwise, you run the risk of being seen as a fraud. If you're not sincere, walking among your people will have the exact opposite effect from what you think you are getting. It will not engender loyalty or dedication to the mission. If anything, it will challenge your leadership and perhaps damage your entire capacity to lead. And not only that, but you will never get a true feel for your organization. And if this is true, how can you lead anyway?

People in the relational model do not just represent the employees of the company. People are your vendors, your customers, your community. All add value to your operation. To only concentrate on the people within to the limitation or exclusion of outside influences is a big mistake. A vendor or customer who feels valued is much more likely to go the extra mile for you when you need it. The following example demonstrates how important the vendor relationship can be to your business.

A few years back, Junior Achievement of Delaware was engaged in a major new building project that would have an enormous impact on the future of the organization. I know a lot of things, but engineering and construction are not among them! Our task was to create a multi-dimensional, real-world environment for the students to act out—two "hands on" models that JA produced to teach business, finance, and economics. There was nothing available to draw upon, as this was the first of its kind to be constructed in the country.

Well, not knowing much about building projects, I had to rely on what I did know—people and relationships. I knew I needed a team, which had to begin with someone who knew about construction and was willing to volunteer time to advise me. Enter Sal Gioia. The next important piece was an architect who understood the value of the project to the community and would value his services appropriately (in other words, at a significant discount). Enter Jim Nelson and Phil Conte. With these three guys, I selected the rest of the team that would do the work. In the selection process, I always placed a high value on how much passion the contractor displayed for what we were undertaking.

The next step was to make all these disparate groups and companies into a team that shared our dream. We did this by how we treated them, both professionally and socially. We made them comfortable in our environment. We sold them on Junior Achievement's importance to the children of our community. As a result, the team wanted to do the best job possible, to the extent that they went beyond the letter of the agreement time and time again to make this a top-flight production.

From our realtor, Phil Hoge, to our muralist and set designer, Chris Kanienberg, to our general contractor, Dave Hall, the project supervisor, Bill Micheline, and all the workers in between, there was an energy and commitment to doing something special. What ensued was a huge success. By most accounts, it was the best facility in the country and arguably still is today, six years later. Hundreds of JA colleagues from across the United States visited to get ideas on how to build their own, many of which bore a striking similarity to the Delaware facility.

From my perspective, the success of the project emanated from taking all these workers and making them part of the Junior Achievement team. They became as vested in the end result as much as I was, and it showed. This is an excellent example of extending the concept of people beyond your employees or members of your team, and it demonstrates how vital it is to hold this broader viewpoint. Whether it is a sensitivity to your associates needs, management by walking around, the positive treatment of outside vendors, or arbitrating disputes among staff, you as the leader must be active and involved. The examples in this section were meant as a guide to give you a sense of how others have prioritized people. If there isn't an absolute commitment to people, the core, then the relational model falls apart. However, if you get this right, the elements of relational leadership will fall into place.

Element 1: Fidelity

Relationally led organizations do not necessarily do extraordinary things; they do the right things for their people and their customers, shareholders, vendors, and so on. We are living in a time when doing "the right thing" seems like doing something extra special. The principles of relational leadership are *fundamental*, but they are not *fundamentalist*. It is very important to separate the two concepts because they are very different. Turning to a model that changes the nature of how organizations and teams are governed and lead will have a profound effect on the immoral and unethical behavior that surrounds the world today.

The relational element of fidelity (fairness, character, trust) is like the trees in a forest—the trees support each other and gain strength from their relative positions to each other. When trees fall or are taken down, the remaining trees simply are not as strong, and over time, they too will fall. Therefore, for fidelity to falter, you don't have to stop being fair altogether; all you have to do is not always be fair or not always demonstrate character. If you do this, trust will certainly topple.

Of the three elements, fidelity probably speaks the loudest; it represents the *soul* of the elements. This is so because the attributes of fidelity are so critical to the relationship between people and leadership. It is in this element that leadership often fails. You see in Figure 4.2 the attributes that fidelity embraces, and in the text that follows, each will be defined and demonstrated in real situations.

Relationship Diagram Components

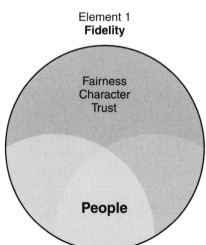

Figure 4.2 *Relationship between the core and fidelity, comprised of fairness, character, and trust.*

Fairness

The first attribute of fidelity is *fairness*. It is here that leadership balances the difference of what is best for the company and what is best for the individual. Fairness is a fundamental principle that all people should expect. It is not about what is right or wrong, necessarily; it is about what is right at that time and circumstance. Most people recognize that they are not always going to get their way; they just want to know that their side was heard and valued. There are many reasons why something goes a different direction, and it might not have anything to do with the individual. In an organization that values fairness, people understand that they will always be given a chance to state their case. If they don't win their point, they will, as best as possible, understand why their case didn't win.

Non-profit organizations often have to adapt to their world in ways that they would prefer not to. In the early 1990s, the U.S. was experiencing a major downturn in the economy, particularly in Delaware. The well-known leader of DuPont, Ed Woolard, an elected member of the United States Business Hall of Fame, announced that the company was going to cut 2 billion dollars in expenses out of its budget. Now this was in the days when 2 billion was 2 billion. I doubt if there was another company in town (in that era) that had as much in assets on their books! This was a big deal.

It was clear that JA was going to have to cut back its own expenses, as DuPont was our biggest contributor. So was this fair? What did JA have to do with DuPont's woes? The answer didn't really matter because the situation was still starring us in the face. I had to determine how JA was going to make this adverse circumstance work (or be fair) to our organization. I was determined to do this without cutting back on our programs, which were catching the imagination and support of our constituents and were a critical part of our strategic planning.

We researched and adopted a management style that would enable us to compete, even in light of DuPont's cutbacks. That became what was fair to us—we adapted to the new world and didn't bellyache about the loss of the old world. We adopted a strategy called Self-Managed Teams (SMT) as our operating system. SMT suggested that business teams working together could and would solve their own problems, and the company would get more efficient output. SMT proved to be a very taxing concept for us, but we survived in a terrible economy.

One challenge we faced was also an example of fairness. One of our very capable staff members, Betty, was outstanding at her job but did not care too much for this teamwork business. Her style was to fly solo! We helped her to adapt in every way we could imagine, but to no avail. In the end, Betty's "will" to be an individual could not overcome our efforts to bring her on board as a team player. She was given every opportunity to adjust, but in the end, I had to let her go.

Fairness is an interesting concept. JA could have claimed that DuPont treated us unfairly but, right or wrong, we would have lost. I chose to take a different path, to tough it out, and the organization survived. Betty, on the other hand, didn't want to change how she operated; she lost her job but not because the organization was unfair to her.

Another example of fairness comes to mind involving Bob Adams and his introduction to the ROTC program at Woodbridge High School shortly after he arrived there. The ROTC director came by to see him. He was a Marine. Bob described him as a "hard-core guy." The director wanted to make some changes in the program and wanted to know how Bob would deal with ROTC. Bob simply said, "It's your program—tell me what you need, within reason, and I will get it for you. If there are obstacles in your way, let me know, and I will remove them for you. You take care of the kids and make sure the program is moving in a productive manner. I'll trust you to do that until you show me otherwise." The director's response was "No problem, here," to which Bob responded, "So we're good."

What could be fairer? I do my job by ensuring you have the resources you need to do your job; you do your job by making sure the students receive what they signed up for in the program. Bob stated the ground rules and the consequences clearly and concisely, and by doing so, removed any possible problem with interpretation.

So fairness really comes down to making sure that people understand what is expected of them and that the expectations are reasonable, giving opportunities for people to express their viewpoints on matters that affect them, not playing favorites, making the rules rational, and sometimes even bending the rules. In other words, it's really okay if it is not always your way!

Character

Character is the second attribute associated with fidelity. It is critical to the relational model because it enables people to enjoy the security that decisions are borne out of principle. People want someone they can look up to, someone they can count on, someone who personifies ethical behavior.

Unfortunately, our society is character-challenged. I don't know when it started, but it seems to me that when we stopped teaching it in school, we began to lose our way. The problem is that our faltering expectations regarding character are beginning to have profound effect on our lives. The ethical flaws regarding Enron cost thousands of people their jobs and their pensions.

Enron pales by comparison to the maladies of the financial world in 2008 and 2009 and the impact felt by the world economy. However, it is unfair to single out business as the culprit in the ethical decline because there are examples everywhere, from religious people to politicians to athletes and extending even to Little League treasurers! "Let's get what we can and do what we want" is the new mantra.

Regardless of your political persuasion, your ideological leanings, or your religious beliefs, moral and ethical behavior transcends all these ideologies and tends to be relatively constant. It seems to me that we should not excuse a president's immoral behavior. A person in this position must be held to a standard; it doesn't necessarily have to be a higher one. In this country, the generally accepted norm is that it is wrong to cheat on your spouse; it is also wrong not to tell the truth. Yet President Bill Clinton did both when he said that the allegations about a sexual relationship with Monica Lewinsky were false—and he said this emphatically and repeatedly. His answer ultimately was, "I need to go back to work for the American people." Does that mean that living a moral life is not a part of working for the American people?

The prevailing sense in America during this period was that Mr. Clinton was doing a great job as president and that this was a personal matter affecting only him and his family, so he should not be judged. Wrong, wrong, wrong. The actions of your president affect everyone. He sets the tone for the country. When we allow this type of behavior without retribution, we create an atmosphere of permissiveness, and as a nation, we begin to crumble. In time, if the crumbling is not repaired, we will fail.

Let's change the situation. Think of the anger that wells up in parents when a ball player refuses to sign an autograph for their child. They ask, "What kind of role model is he?" He is nothing more than an overpaid bum! Mind you, he is a private citizen, and his true accountability is to the owner of his team to play up to the potential he possesses. Yet we are willing to vilify him for not signing an autograph. Maybe it is okay to feel that way, but how does that reaction square up with our acceptance that President Clinton strayed from his marriage vows and then excused himself on flimsy grounds.

If a ball player is a role model, what does that make the president of the United States? He was not held to any standard. Is it possible that he created a new standard? I really don't know. What I do know is that the breakdown in our society's morals and ethics is at epidemic proportions. I also know that leadership—good or bad—produces followers. We just have to get a handle on this issue and stop it. We can, if we have the will to do so.

Some of you reading this book might be old enough to remember the meat shortages of the 1970s, government controls, dramatically rising prices, and so on. Rising out of the protest generation of the 1960s (from civil rights to Vietnam to feminism), it was not surprising that a furor erupted among the American people. They seemed to speak with one voice—thou shall not take our beef away! The people boycotted beef, and the effect was a drop in prices back to normal levels. Wow, the price of beef—more important than the ethical and moral behavior of our president?

My point is this: If we have the resolve to come together to bring down the price of meat, why can't we do the same for the far more serious issue of character and ethics? We can and we must. Creating societal norms that fly in the face of a reasonably acceptable sense of morality send us down the path of perdition. When the society allows a disregard for the common good, when it abandons its values, its roots start to wither, and it begins to disintegrate. It is not someone else's problem; it is society's problem, and we must address it as a people. So we must be clear to stand our ground on the beliefs that were inherent in the founding of our nation. We must demonstrate our character.

There are laws and systems that define what society considers acceptable behavior. The United States Constitution says that no one person is above the law. However, it often seems that certain classes receive benefits that other classes do not. This sows seeds of unrest, which can result in situations deleterious to the people as a whole. Lack of character undermines people's sense of fairness and trust, and thus creates havoc with the element of fidelity.

The rules that govern our institutions favor the people who are in power. Lest you be mistaken, this statement applies to all institutions. I could be talking about the local PTA president or the police chief in your town or the director of a government agency. It is hardly confined to CEOs of major corporations or business people in general. All these people hold power, regardless of the size of their dominion. Exercising their power ethically demonstrates how the leader interprets the rules for himself and the organization he governs.

Finally, I want to be clear about this: It is pretty hard to be a relational leader and be dishonest. Your commitment to relationalism and its concepts would have to be at a surface level to perpetuate dishonesty. I guess you could do it, but you would really have to work hard at it. And if you did succeed, you would be a fraud.

Fixing this ethical dilemma must involve the youth of the country. Junior Achievement is one organization that is addressing the issue from a youth standpoint. Several JA programs deal with character and one in particular addresses it exclusively. It is interesting to me that students seem to truly enjoy getting into discussions that involve behavior (as long as the discussion is not about them!). In part, I believe this is true because it does not take any special intelligence to do so. They are on a level playing field with their peers. Reasoning helps for sure, but knowing the difference between right and wrong is often obvious, particularly in a guided discussion.

NOTE

The one difference I would state here has to do with culture. Right and wrong can be different when comparing American culture to other countries' cultures. Sometimes cultural differences lead us to judge others unfairly. It is important but often difficult emotionally to understand why actions that seem abhorrent to an American would be okay to an Asian, for example. For the purposes here, I am talking about cultural norms in the United States.

We need more education on this topic for our young people and our not so young. Over the years, I regularly addressed students on the subject. I told them that it can be pretty easy to figure out what was right or wrong. The litmus test was how you would feel if your actions were on the front page of the paper the next day. Would you be proud to read about it with your family at the breakfast table? If not, then don't do it—pretty simple when you break it down in those terms.

TIP

An Axiom: Figure out what you stand for before you are placed in a crisis situation; then you are much more likely to make the right decision.

Trust

Trust rounds out the troika of attributes that make up fidelity. I believe that where trust exists, you know that character and fairness have preceded it. Trust evolves from the environment in which it exists.

Nathan Hill maintains that a leader must be genuine, and he talked with me about assessing staff performance in this light. The bottom line is that you must be honest. Some leaders will not tell their staff the hard truth about how they are doing on the job. First of all, this behavior simply is not fair. They will eventually learn that they are not performing at the level of expectation (and they probably know it anyway). Second and just as important, when you are honest with your employees, you build trust. Because you have been fair with them in the trusting environment that you are creating, they can do something to change their performance or at least find some other way to contribute to the organization's overall good.

A man I greatly admire is Alan Burkhard. Alan distinguished himself on the JA board for many years. Over those years, he built many dynamic businesses oftentimes without any real knowledge of the particular industry when he started out. Currently, he owns two popular restaurants, one in Newark, home of the University of Delaware, and the other in Wilmington, close to a very trendy neighborhood called Trolley Square. These restaurants were suffering a downturn at the time he bought them a couple of years ago. Today, both have doubled their receipts under his philosophy of leadership, which he calls "Outside In." Trust and truth are important elements of his philosophy. Alan sums up his thoughts on trust like this: "If an employee believes and trusts that they are going to get value beyond what they are paid every day, they will come to work with a song in their heart. People value trust and respect. For example, I took all the cameras out of the restaurants. I trust you, you trust me. Trust begets trust."

He believes in no limitations, openness, and sharing. These attitudes and ideas create trust as well. Everyone who works in the restaurant gets a copy of the monthly P&L, and everyone gets information on productivity. He will share anything and everything with his employees. "I don't care where it goes. What are they going to do with it?" Alan believes that over-sharing helps people to trust him more. The opposite, under-sharing, makes people believe that you are better than they or that you are hiding something from them, which tends to defeat trust. He told me once, "If I share one ounce less with you than you expect, then I might as well not share at all. If I share one ounce more with you than you expect, you will love me forever!"

So, with regard to trust as one of the pillars in a relationally led organization, you must exhibit the other pillars too because otherwise it creates a disconnect with trust. If trust doesn't exist, the other pillars are compromised. Also, if you haven't already noticed, it all starts with people. If you get that right, the other pillars all flow from the fundamental way that you treat people. It is the strength, the center, of the relational universe.

People seem to be able to smell sincerity easily; therefore, insincerity bursts out like 3D on a home theater screen. Or maybe, insincerity has a certain telltale stink to it! Folks are just not fooled for very long in this basic relationship matter. They look for alignment between what you say and what you do. Leaders often miss this very salient point. If people sense sincerity, they will believe that they can trust you.

Element 2: Appreciation

Appreciation is the second of the three elements, and it represents spirit. This is so because the attributes of appreciation are so critical to the vitality of the organization. Appreciation brings life and excitement to the team and an element that leadership often ignores. You see in Figure 4.3 the attributes that appreciation embraces, and in the text that follows, each is defined and demonstrated in real situations.

Relationship Diagram Components

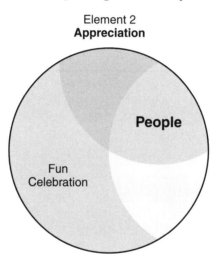

Figure 4.3 *Relationship between the core and appreciation, comprised of celebration and fun.*

Celebration

Celebration is the first attribute of appreciation. Who doesn't like to celebrate? In this country, we'll celebrate just about anything. Celebrating can be lavish or simple. Many times lavishness is called for because of the significance of the event. However, what gets lost sometimes are the little opportunities that are in front of you every day. Often if you drill down far enough, you will find that it is the sum of the little things that forms the fabric of an organization.

Bob Albin talks about the importance of celebration. What is celebrated is what gets noticed. He tends to keep it directed toward the individual or small group, which was better suited to the way his company was organized. Before visiting one of his many sites, he always took the time to get fully briefed on the activity of that business unit. He believed in working from people's strengths. He wanted to reinforce the point for them that it was their strengths that were making their efforts worthwhile. He would pick out the activity that was helping to drive the business plan, and then do something appropriate on behalf of the individuals who were making it happen.

Maybe it was a lunch, or a dinner with spouses at a fancy restaurant, or a ballgame, or other special activity that was in town. He wanted to express personally that they were making a difference and that he appreciated it. Just as importantly, the celebration itself demonstrated that the leader was paying attention, and I can't emphasize enough how important that is to the people in the trenches! Celebration in a relational organization is about creating a culture where the little things are noticed and appreciated. It focuses on the core—the people. Not everyone can do big, fancy celebrations, but everyone can do the small stuff that has impact over time.

Over the years, I have been blessed to have many administrative people on staff who paid attention to the little details that can cost the company money and, sometimes, a lot of money. They regularly went out of their way to get the best price or an extra service. They were proud to make this type of contribution to the business's success. These were contributions worth celebrating, and we did. My recurring message to staff was to be mindful of the little things because over time they become big.

At Junior Achievement, I used a technique for celebrating that was widely successful. I had a habit of writing an e-mail about a person on their employment anniversary and sending it out to the entire staff so that they could all congratulate the individual. It required me to think about the individual and identify what they did day in and day out that helped our business grow and prosper. By involving the entire staff, it invited them to do the same thing—reflect on the individual's contribution and comment on it. What an impact this had on staff morale! It demonstrated in a very real way that you were special and that your peers knew what made you special. Individuals can't get enough sincere recognition; it lights their fires and encourages them to do more.

I know this because even after I retired I still sent a few more of these e-mails to folks whose anniversary was relatively close to my retirement date. In these cases, it was just sent to the individual. (I had to remind myself that this wasn't my shop anymore!) Well, in each case the person wrote back to tell me how much that meant to them. They always looked forward to these messages and thought they would not get another one.

It is easy to celebrate if you are committed to doing so, and it doesn't have to cost a lot. Actually, I think our best celebrations cost very little or nothing at all. It is rarely about the money; it's about being appreciated. It's about someone actually paying attention to who they are. This is a powerful motivator. Lots of people don't have that feeling in their lives; leaders sometimes forget that!

Fun

Fun is the second attribute of appreciation. People like to be in places where they have fun. One of the guiding principles of my life is, "If it's not fun, then why do it?" Even the most serious people want to have some fun in their lives, particularly their work lives. After all, having a bit of fun makes the day go by faster, releases stress, creates a congenial atmosphere, promotes loyalty, and good dental care. (Only kidding—see that's fun!)

What you find a lot in the workplace are cynical and sarcastic actions that pose as "fun." These are destructive and counterproductive to any relational leadership organization. The leader must squash this kind of environment in favor of good, clean fun where people can laugh from the belly. However, fun isn't just about telling jokes or even being funny, but it does help! Fun is about letting your hair down, poking a bit of fun at yourself over some past or current incident. Or it could be taking someone out to lunch or doing something out of the ordinary. I can think of several examples of creating a fun atmosphere at JA.

There is a place in Salem County, New Jersey called Cowtown, just across the Delaware River from the JA office. Cowtown is a local landmark, which hosts a Saturday night rodeo and Wednesday flea market. It attracts thousands of people. One day I declared an office holiday for a morning. I closed the office and off the staff went to Cowtown to experience a different atmosphere and to take our minds off of the stress of the work environment. People talked about the morning for years afterward, always with a certain sparkle in their eyes. Some even got some pretty good bargains! It was different. It was fun. It was remembered. It marked our organization as a neat place to work. We lost a half day's productivity, but what we gained was well beyond that.

And we also had parties. St. Patrick's Day was considered a national holiday. We did Secret Santa during the holiday season. Staff had a breakfast club on Friday mornings. All of these activities involved anyone who wanted to take part, and everyone contributed, creating an atmosphere of shared experience where people got to know just a little more about their co-workers and could appreciate them more as a result. Shared experiences create strong bonds among people.

But fun for us at JA wasn't just activities focused on ourselves. I believe that all organizations have an obligation to their community that goes beyond themselves. Just because you are non-profit doesn't exempt you. We selected Meals on Wheels as the official charity of Junior Achievement of Delaware. Staff would deliver meals to the needy in our city. We also participated in a holiday food donation and other such contributions as appropriate for the organization. This was fun for staff (not every time, mind you, but generally so). They got to share time with each other off the job doing something worthwhile, and they came back to the office feeling that they had made an important contribution to someone else's life. Maybe this is the true meaning of fun.

Fun can be aimed at work processes as well as activities. Delivering the annual corporate plan doesn't sound like too much fun, but Bob Brightfelt had a way of doing it that made it fun and kept the staff's eye on the plan throughout the year. The plan was delivered in the form of a Monopoly board—the team had 12 months to get around the board and collect their $200. Interim objectives were laid out by quarters. Communication centers, each with its own objective, were found around the building. If they were colored green that meant everything was allright and on schedule for that objective. Yellow meant that it was the right idea, but there were some problems; red meant things were not working so well, and there was need to replot the course. Simple, illuminating, fun, and on target for accomplishing the objective— what's not to like? Fun can come in many different forms.

Finally, there is a body of research out there that says that smiling produces positive results. Folks who smile a lot, first of all, look better, but more importantly, they do better. Let's face it—it's hard to be nasty (although I have seen it done!) when you're smiling. When you create an environment where people smile, it is a better place to work. It is a wonderful motivator for staff to come to work prepared to do their best.

Element 3: Value

Of the three elements, *value* is the bedrock of an organization. It represents the will of the elements. This is so because the attributes of value are critical to the fundamentals that keep the group on task. It is in this element that leadership often gets confused. You see in Figure 4.4 the attributes that value embraces, and in the text that follows each is defined and demonstrated in real situations.

Attentiveness

Attentiveness is the first attribute of value. It is a quality that most people admire. Attentiveness shows that you respect the individual or group by actively listening to what they have to say. Everybody likes a good listener, particularly the ones who like to talk a lot! Attentiveness extends to observation as well. Active observation gives you the clues to follow up with an individual or group; it gives you the sense of how an organization is responding to the current environment. Observation is both external and internal to you.

Relationship Diagram Components

Element 3
Value

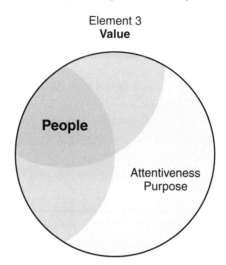

Figure 4.4 *Relationship between the core and value, comprised of attentiveness and purpose.*

Are you actually walking your talk? You may not get that feedback from staff, but the mirror doesn't lie!

When people are not attentive to you, it can be disturbing. Perhaps you have a story like this one. I was in a restaurant one day with a potential new board member, a senior executive from Avon. Hand-helds with e-mail capacity had just come out, and he was having just a great time playing with his—thumbs going a mile a minute while he was presumably carrying on a conversation with me. He even acknowledged what he was doing, being careful to let me know that he was a superb multi-tasker! I considered this rude at best. No need to drag this story out, he was never invited to join the board. By the way, multi-taskers are starting to lose their glow. There is a growing body of research that suggests multi-tasking is inefficient and produces lots of flawed results, not to mention that it can be just plain impolite.

With attentiveness, the point is to pay attention to the speaker, and if observing, to take in the details of what you see. Typically, listening will tell you all you need to know about a situation. A salesperson will find out the objections and the "hot" buttons of her customer. An interviewer will learn the strengths and weaknesses of the candidate. We reveal a lot about ourselves when we talk, so there is a very solid business reason to listen. I would often take calls from salespeople just to hear what they had to say about what they were offering. We can really extend our knowledge base just by taking the time to listen.

> **TIP**
>
> An Axiom: Everyone has something to say—listen to them carefully, and you will become enlightened, regardless of how much you know.

There is no doubt that applying this listening skill to the people around you will mark you as a leader, particularly in your employee's eyes. Remember in the relational model, it all comes back to the core—people. Active listening is not easy to do when you first try it, but it is certainly worth the effort. Have you ever heard someone say, "I have such a problem with Caitlin; she's such a good listener"? Of course not. People love someone who will listen to them. People gain a sense of self-worth when they perceive that others care about what they say. What greater compliment could there be than to honor a person by listening to and considering their opinion?

Attentiveness is certainly about listening, but it also goes beyond listening. In a greater sense, it is having an awareness of your surroundings. The relational leader will always know when the environment is changing before anyone else, unless, of course, he has elevated the organization so that there are many relational leaders within it. You develop a sensitivity to the world around you, which causes you to understand when something is just not right.

Listening will give you information that you can act on to improve the effectiveness of your organization. For example, as a non-profit executive I had to know when a board member's interest in the organization was peaking because, once this occurred, the downward slide was fast. To be aware of this was crucial because, first, I wanted the members to leave the board with a sense of fulfillment, and second, their belief in the cause must remain unwavering. I could only make this possible while they were still happy. While they were at their peak, I still had an opportunity to re-energize the individual and start the climb toward the sublime all over again. I made sure to facilitate an exit strategy for the board member that made them feel valued. My experience with boards is extensive, and Junior Achievement of Delaware was noted for the strength of its board. In the end, understanding through listening and observing is what enabled me to weather the storms in challenging environments and push to great heights in the good times.

Here's another reason why attentiveness is important. Had I been more attentive one of the biggest mistakes I made during my long career in Junior Achievement would never have happened. One of my best and most trusted board members and a JA student in her youth, Sue Linderman, was stepping down by her own decision. She had served on the board for many years, including as its chair. I did not anticipate her leaving, and I was very busy at the time it occurred. Here's the bottom line: I failed to recognize her many contributions as she was leaving. I hurt her, but I honestly believe that I hurt myself even more. I failed to perform one of the most fundamental principles of the style of leadership I espoused—valuing people. I did all that I could to make up for my transgression, but I still have a hole in my heart for my misdeed. Sue deserved more from me and I did not deliver. To make matters worse, the situation was revealed to me not by self-observation but through a candid conversation with Sue after the fact. I finally caught her tone in a conversation we were having, and it dawned on me that something was wrong. It took very little prodding to get Sue to open up about how upset she felt. My only consolation was that I did get it eventually, which is not much consolation.

NOTE

Here's a note to non-profit executives and people who deal with boards: It is never bad to lose a board member who is happy about their association with the organization. Oftentimes, there is a tendency to try to hold onto generous and influential board members, even after they have gone past their prime. Big mistake! Send them back out to the world at large with your appreciation and the appreciation of the organization. Above all else, your objective must be to keep them as your friend. This is why observation is so critical. Their past contributions demand it. Friends do things for friends. You never know when you will need them again, and surely you will.

Active observation is an important component to attentiveness. Bob Brightfelt talks about self-observation in these terms: "You must be able to observe yourself in all environments; you are continually seeing what you are saying, what you are doing, and how people are responding to it. Self-observation will add to your authenticity if you pay attention to what you see. By making it a part of your personal behavior, you will be able to align your actions with what you say, you will observe your shared values and be better able to define them for and with the whole organization." Paying attention to your staff and noticing a shift downward in performance may just be a temporary blip that everyone goes through, or it could be something more serious. Either way, you need to be prepared to address the change and support the recovery.

Being adept at noticing shifts in trends is a very useful skill. Being ready to coach and support is vital to the ongoing success of your organization. It works two ways. The person having trouble appreciates what you are doing and will respond by applying more energy to their tasks. Just as important, your other staff will know that you pay attention to the needs of your people. They know if they ever get into that situation, you will be there for them, too. Not only is that comforting, but it is also energizing!

Being attentive applies across the entire organization. Sometimes it not only reveals a staff member who is having trouble performing their job, but it can also reveal a staff member who can't actually do the job. When leadership does not recognize this situation, it has a tendency to cast a pall over the entire organization. The leader must move quickly and decisively. The following example will help you understand how your observation can work to your organization's benefit.

I recall an individual who worked for us in a sales capacity. He was an outside salesperson, yet I always saw him in the office. I questioned his manager about this and got the old "I'm working on it" response. Shortly after this conversation with his manager, there was a networking event that we were scheduled to attend. I pulled aside the three people who were going with me and went over the strategy for the evening, which included each person taking the opportunity to "work the room" alone. My two program managers did a great job, and in fact, I received several comments about what a good impression they made. My salesperson wandered the room, doing his best not to make eye contact or to stay in any one place very long. It was clear to me after the event that this person, a good person by the way, was just not cut out for this job.

A few weeks later, I noticed that he was not at his desk anytime I was in the office. Maybe I misjudged. I went to his manager, excited to comment on this change and was informed that he was on vacation. Talk about deflation!! It wasn't too much longer before we acted. He was disappointed but at the same time relieved. He understood that we provided support to him, but he was not able to respond in kind. Even after his departure, I continued to counsel him because I cared about him. It was an amiable separation demonstrating the power of relational leadership in yet another way.

Attentiveness is vital to the well-being of an organization and to your personal growth. Accumulating data from listening and observation, and then taking action on your findings, makes all the difference in your relations and your results.

Purpose

Finally, *purpose* is the last of the seven attributes. A relational leadership organization is purposeful. I think of it as the glue that holds everything together. It is the substance that gives meaning to all the work and efforts of the organization. When your purpose is clearly defined for your associates, it makes getting the work done possible. The leader invests in people and creates an environment of success that includes trust, fun, character, attention, fairness, and celebration for one primary reason. All of this ensures a purposeful entity—people who are committed to achieving goals and objectives. The vision and mission of the organization lives for the staff in a relational team.

When Mark Suwyn bought New Page from Westvaco in 2005, he had to craft a compelling vision and purpose for the organization. He says, "I had to create an environment where associates were excited about new opportunities, where they felt they were listened to, and finally, where they were committed to the Lean Six Sigma program." When Mark took over, the training budget for the company was $100,000. Today the training budget is between 15 and 20 million! All of this money is aimed at getting everyone engaged and focused on using their new skill sets to help the company.

Everyone at New Page goes through the Sigma training, all 8,000, at their appropriate level—some at black belt or higher levels, but everyone goes through the training. Two-thirds of the training is focused on how to build an environment and to give participants the skills they need to engage in the process. They also learn about barriers to this particular thinking process and how they can break though the barriers that keep them from wanting to be engaged and helping. Further, they learn to notice how people around them think, feel, and act so they can be more positive in their interactions with co-workers. Finally, they learn how to build the emotional intelligence of everybody in the organization. The other third of the training focuses on the skills they need to collect and analyze data to identify issues and solve problems.

At the supervisor, manager, and VP levels, the training is more intense. The first reason for the extra training, interestingly enough, is that people at this level are more apt to be resistant to this process. More practically, they have to use the skills at a much higher level so that they are able to see, anticipate, and be proactive when engaging their staff in the process.

Overall, this is a truly significant investment in the human resources of New Page. Are the millions of dollars invested in the people of New Page paying dividends? Mark believes it is worth every penny, and the results are starting to roll in. By December 2007, the company had doubled in size, due to both acquisition and improved productivity. New Page has a completely different culture, values, and thinking process. "In just 15 months everything changed, but only because we were willing to put the time and effort into training and practices that utilized the techniques and technology that was available to us. The company is taking off!" Mark's team at New Page understands what their purpose is and also knows that their needs will be met as they travel down this new and exciting road.

Bob Albin took a different slant to the same attribute of purpose. He had a philosophy about coming into a new business setting. He assumed that the people there were successful and knew what they were doing. "The organization was successful, which was the only reason why I was attracted to it. My bias was taking the people who were there and have them adapt to what I wanted to do while they continued to do what they were doing operationally. It created a great deal of loyalty." Purpose implies importance, and people like to do important things when they can. Relational leadership sets the table so that the people can see the outcomes have meaning. The staff knows that what they do makes a difference, and they are proud of that.

My experience is that with purpose, people work more and gripe less. They are seemingly healthier, at least compared to the amount of sick days they use, and stay on the job longer. They believe in what they are doing, and they feel really good about themselves. So you wind up with a more efficient, effective, and energized organization that is committed to you, the leader, and to the company. Productivity is higher because people are happy and want to be on the job. Their greatest fear is letting you down.

Bob Brightfelt, an extraordinary relational leader talks about a purposeful organization in these terms. He says that in order to make a change in what you are doing or to take an organization anywhere at all, four things must be in place:

- A vision of where you are going
- An unwillingness to stay where you are
- A path forward with the first few steps of the process
- The tools to get the job done

People will go where the leader takes them. Just how they go there is vital to the success of the organization and squarely in the hands of the leader. An energizing vision that captures the imagination of the organization is a sure way of bringing people along willingly and with dedication to the cause.

A purposeful organization recognizes that staying in one place is like being on a death watch. You know what is going to happen, but you don't know when. It is a letdown. There is no force, and there is no desire. There is always competition and sooner or later, no matter how good you are, the competition will pass you by if you don't continue to grow and develop new ideas.

As the ship needs a navigator to get out of the harbor, an organization needs a plan to move forward toward its vision. In Bob's mind, you don't need everything set down, but you do need to get the engine heated up. You will add to the plan as you see how it is developing. The leader is responsible for making sure that roadblocks are removed and resources are acquired that are necessary to achieve the end result. Get the right people in place and then get out of their way so they can get their job done.

Summary

To sum up, relational leadership is a framework superimposed on a functioning business that enables it to perform at the highest and most productive levels. Strong business tactics and strategies, product or services in demand, appropriate training, and excellent financial oversight are all factors that make an organization work effectively and profitably, combined with its commitment to people, the core element of any enterprise, is the winning combination. The relational leader keeps people at its center, surrounded by the three core elements of fidelity, appreciation, and value. The elements encapsulate these attributes: fairness, character, trust, fun, celebration, attentiveness, and purpose.

The relational model will work at peak efficiency when it is fully implemented. At the core is an organization's people—think of this as its heart. Fidelity is the soul, appreciation is the spirit, and value is the will. If you think of the organization in these terms, it is easy to see how important the interconnections become. The heart provides the lifeblood of the organization—the organization cannot exist without the heart functioning effectively. The soul provides the organization's emotional and moral compass, enabling it to survive and prosper in a noble manner. The spirit provides the enthusiasm and energy that lift the organization as it pursues its purpose. The will provides the understanding and determination of the needs and destination of the organization. They all stand together, united in the pursuit of relationalism.

When embarking on this journey, particularly if it is a shift in operating procedures, you must take it slowly. In future chapters, I will deal with the impediments to success that a group faces when changing directions. In this case, it is appropriate to bring on the elements in a predetermined order. The greater the shift, the slower and more deliberate you should go.

KEEP IN MIND:

- Applying the attributes of relational leadership across the organization creates a harmony that will produce a tremendous and positive energy force.
- If it is not fun, then why are you doing it?
- When people are valued and respected, they will always try to put forth their best effort and demonstrate a strong work ethic.
- It's hard to be nasty when you are smiling.
- Until you identify the problem, you are merely solving symptoms, and the problem never goes away.
- Figure out what you stand for before you are placed in a crisis situation; then you are much more likely to make the right decision.
- Everyone has something to say. Listen carefully, and you will become enlightened, regardless of how much you know.
- Relational leadership is a framework superimposed on a functioning business that enables it to perform at the highest and most productive levels.

Chapter 5

Breathing Life into a Relational Organization

> "A long habit of not thinking a thing wrong gives it a superficial appearance of being right."
> —*Thomas Paine*

This chapter will explore many different aspects of creating and maintaining a vibrant and successful relational organization. No one piece will do it. It becomes a lifestyle change in how you treat people, and the importance of your commitment to this change cannot be emphasized enough. As you plan to form your own relational structure, you will find the points in this chapter to be very helpful. Here's what will be discussed:

- Important components of a relational organization
- Adopting a new way of dealing with people
- Maintaining the model once in place
- Understanding your role of leader in a relational organization

Key Components of a Relational Organization

Now that you know the components of the leadership model, it is easier to appreciate the nuances and situations that will make it work. The relational model is in effect your people plan—how you will treat and motivate your staff, vendors, customers, shareholders, and community.

This is not window dressing. If you don't commit to certain actions or attitudes, the relational model will not be effective. The model works best when all the attributes are in play and integrate an expanded viewpoint of the business or mission of your team. By committing to become a relational leader, you are also committing to a whole system of leading your team.

Figure 5.1 demonstrates how the model works at its full implementation. The components of the model represent a system that governs how your business plan is implemented through the people of your organization. At the core is people—the system's heart and lifeblood. Fidelity is the soul, appreciation is the spirit, and value is the will. Heart, soul, spirit, will—easy.

The heart is the lifeblood of any organization, and for the organization to function effectively it must work properly. The soul provides the organization's emotional and moral compass, enabling it to survive and prosper in a noble manner. The spirit provides the enthusiasm and energy that lifts the organization as it pursues its purpose. The will provides the understanding and determination of the needs and destination of the organization. They work together cohesively. As the elements circle the heart, they radiate energy to maintain the vitality of the core.

The Essence of Relationalism

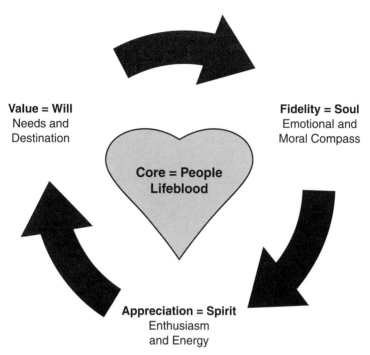

Value = Will
Needs and
Destination

Fidelity = Soul
Emotional and
Moral Compass

**Core = People
Lifeblood**

Appreciation = Spirit
Enthusiasm
and Energy

Figure 5.1 *A representation of relational leadership working at peak efficiency. It is the fundamental nature of the components working in unison.*

When you look at your business/team holistically, there are five basic components that must be addressed to support a relational organization. They are as follows:

1. Having an effective business plan in place
2. Appreciating the value of common sense
3. Hiring the right people
4. Accepting the need to change or improve
5. Embracing people inside and out of your organization

The Business Plan

I cannot caution enough that relational leadership is a framework superimposed on a solid business model. Keep in mind that the relational model does not deal at all with your business structure or most of your business issues. It is about people, motivation, ethical behavior, organizational environment, authenticity, and a clear understanding of mission. Diagramming this relationship would look like what you see in Figure 5.2.

Relationship of Business Plan to Relational Model

Figure 5.2 *This chart shows the relationship between the business plan and the leadership model. Relationships fuel the plan, enabling the functional structure to work at maximum.*

Essentially, the case for relational leadership is that it will make your organization function better. The people are motivated to work harder and smarter. They think of the company when they make decisions. They are happy, and happy is good in a working environment. It brings the best out in people.

This book is not about business planning. However, it shouldn't be left out of the discussion completely. There are a couple of business structures that have worked for my mentors that I will present as an overview so you will get a general idea of their thinking. Bob Brightfelt and Mark Suwyn lived by these as they achieved their business goals.

Brightfelt believes that top leaders in a company must have the following: a vision for where you want to go, an unwillingness to stay where you are, a commitment to recruit and employ great people, a strategy for how you will achieve the vision, and a formula for assessing your competition now and in the future. I want to underscore that *there must be an unwillingness to stay where you are.* You don't hear that thought phrased in this manner very often. It is a powerful force for change.

Mark Suwyn also places vision as the number-one activity for a leader. Second is utilizing a model that tells management how the company is going to make money, and third is a continuous improvement process. (At Louisiana Pacific and New Page he used Lean Six Sigma.)

> **NOTE**
>
> *Lean Six Sigma* is a process improvement strategy. It seeks to achieve a fast rate of improvement in key business areas. The areas include customer satisfaction, quality, process speed, cost, and invested capital. It provides analytical tools to assess process flow and delay times in each work activity. It also provides tools that help eliminate the root causes of non-value-added activities and their cost. It is complimentary to Six Sigma, but not the same.

Notice the similarities between the two business plan concepts. Everyone I have talked to about business models named vision as the most important piece. Without it, you can't get anywhere. In my discussions, other pieces of the puzzle differed, but the idea of great people, products, strategies, and research formed one part or another of the formula for a successful business model.

No business can succeed without a solid business plan, regardless of the motivation of its people. Therefore, a viable plan must be in place in order for anything else to happen. When that is in place, the relationship model can then fuel the structural plan to achieve the goals it sets out to accomplish. It does this by providing the motivational force to the employees, customers, vendors, and community to make your company a great place to work. When a great business plan meets a great relational leadership model, excellent results occur.

The Value of Common Sense

A relational leader regularly demonstrates common sense—period! It is an accepted organizational value. When I speak of common sense, I mean the reasonably accepted norms in society—what experience tells us is right—or how the average person would respond. The relational model holds that certain precepts are inviolate. Think about it: What's not to like about treating people fairly and with respect, listening to them in a trusting environment that is rooted in character and ethics, celebrating successes both large and small, and having fun while being purposeful? That sums up what relational leadership is all about—in other words, leadership through common sense.

Remember, people will follow any leader to some degree. We have all sorts of leaders. Some are called good and some bad; some are leaders of good things and some are leaders of bad things. It doesn't matter. There will always be a group of people who will follow the "drink the cool aid" method as it is popularly referred to today.

My belief is that the greater the plausibility of a leader's method, the greater the possibility that she will be followed. The tenants of relational leadership, if consistently and sincerely applied, will produce followers who have a vested interest in the outcome of the leader's plan. Also, they will follow with the knowledge that the path they are on is the right path.

> **NOTE**
>
> An Axiom: When a leader consistently applies the principles of relationalism, employees understand intrinsically that they have a vested interest in the outcome of the business plan and will work toward achieving its objective.

Nathan Hill's dad used to tell him, "It's great to get good book sense, but it's even greater to have good common sense." Bob Adams, a great relational school principal, said, "What I do—it's just common sense." There is no doubt in my mind that the application of common sense in the team setting (as it applies to the relational leadership model) will fortify the members of the team and encourage them to do more. This is so because people understand a common-sense approach to the world more than they do rigid rules made up in the past, often for reasons that are no longer applicable to today's situations. When people experience leadership that values commonsensical approaches to life, they become more comfortable and supportive of the environment they are in.

As a leader, you must always be testing what you do against the relational concept of common sense. How would the average person react to the decisions you make as a leader? If you feel it would be positive, it passes the first test. You must also be sure that the idea has business or people value. With this information in hand, you can move forward.

> **NOTE**
>
> An Axiom: Even if an idea passes the common-sense test, it still must make good business sense in order to be implemented.

If a person's reaction would be negative, perhaps this is telling you that the individual just doesn't have enough information. You must appreciate this and provide the clarity that is needed—this is called *transparency*. Keep in mind that transparency develops trust. Alan Burkhard promotes transparency in his organizations. Wherever you find Alan, you find a sense of openness. If he thinks an employee doesn't understand something, he will explain the derivation of the decision so that the employee will have a better framework to assess the decision. Likely, it will then make sense to him. That's using your noggin or better yet, your common sense.

Hiring the Right People

Hiring in a relational organization is two-pronged. First, the person being considered must have the technical qualities to do the job. Second, the person must have the interpersonal qualities to be a functioning and contributing member of the team. If I am going to err, it will be on the side of the technical. Here's why.

If an individual has good technical skills, I can train him to be better. In the meantime, he will not hurt my team; he just won't be able to contribute technically at the highest level. If I hire a person with poor interpersonal skills, the individual will not fit well with the group that I have assembled, and I may never be able to successfully train him in relational skills. The truth is, it is likely that I won't be able to change how he deals with people. So when I say hire the right people, my focus is on an individual who can function effectively and immediately in a relational organization.

NOTE

An Axiom: Your hiring focus should be on individuals who possess the highest possible relational skills with, at the least, the basic technical skills.

Your job then becomes one of selection—get the right people. Back in the heyday of MBNA America (the credit card giant of the 1980s, the 90s, and the early years of the new millennium) under the legendary Charlie Cawley, the walls of his buildings were full of inspirational, simple messages. One of the ones I liked best was, "Find the right customers and keep them." I would apply that same logic to your work team.

Leadership makes it possible for a team to truly become successful by doing three things:

1. Put a solid plan in place to move the product.
2. Recruit the right people to deliver the plan.
3. Install a relational style to govern the organization's interactions with people, vendors, shareholders, community, and customers.

Importance of Hiring the Right Person

Hiring is one of the toughest jobs there is in an organization. It is worth the effort because of the return on investment (vis-a-vis productivity and bottom-line results). Look at every hiring situation as an opportunity to improve your team.

You mustn't allow the obstacles to get in your way. This is particularly true these days because of the limitations in the types of questions you can ask. It is also a challenge to obtain solid information from the former employer (many times you will just get from/to work dates). Few employers will open themselves up to suits for disclosing personal information (major employers in particular). But in any case, it is time-consuming. Regardless of circumstance—profit, non-profit, government, or social—putting the right team together is a critical success factor that requires the leader's attention.

> **NOTE**
>
> As an aside to non-profit leaders, getting the right person on a volunteer team is even more critical. Oftentimes, people volunteer for something regardless of their qualifications. Because a person volunteers doesn't mean that you as the leader must accept their services. I know this is hard, but, in fact, if the individual does not have the appropriate skills, then it is your duty to reject his service in the nicest way possible. Find some area they can contribute to, but do not allow an unsuitable volunteer to take you off course.

How Active Must I Be in the Interview Process?

You are fortunate if you have a Human Resources department that can do the screening and selection work for you. However, you still must take some responsibility in this arena. This could mean personal involvement or ensuring that key people on your team take personal involvement. There are four areas that the CEO/president/chairman must oversee in the hiring process:

1. Communicate to your team what you value in the hiring process and what you expect.
2. Ensure that there is a hiring plan.
3. Insist that some appropriate leader be involved in the process.
4. Provide interview skills training for all in leadership.

You communicate the type person that you want in the organization. Make sure the team understands that you place hiring as a top-level activity. Let the team know what you think is the level of technical expertise versus interpersonal skills that a candidate must possess. It is possible that the level might be determined by the particular job. Let your team work it out if you are not going to be involved.

A plan for hiring is important. Exactly what minimum technical skills are necessary? What character or personality traits do you want to see in an individual? Who needs to be involved? Who will have final sign off on the offer of employment? Part of the plan should also include post-hiring review. Did you hit the objective? If it fell short, where? How can you approve the process next time?

Someone in leadership must be involved in the process. At the least, a member of the leadership group must sign off on hires within the organization. You do this to ensure that there is fidelity between the hiring process and the business and relational goals of the organization.

All leaders in the organization should have interview skills training, including the senior leadership group. Remember, it's your company, your work team, and your organization. The best plan, product, and culture will not produce great results if the people who are in place to execute the plans are not the right ones. It behooves you to ensure that this skill is always ready to be put into practice.

Acquiring Behavioral Interview Skills

Now here is the conundrum. If you are not doing a lot of hiring, you're also not doing a lot of interviewing. And you know what happens to skills or knowledge that isn't used, and you know that it doesn't take very long.

If you are in this situation, as I was, you have two options:

- You can spend time reviewing your notes from your behavioral interviewing class, if you took one, and brushing up your skills with an associate. This will work, but it doesn't really help you get better at the task; only regular practice will do that. It's like the difference between having 15 years of experience or one year of experience 15 times—two very different scenarios.

- You could use your behavioral skills in your interactions with staff on a regular basis. Become a person who asks a lot of questions as opposed to a person who directs conversations. Be purposeful about how you ask your questions. Make sure they are open-ended and require a thoughtful response. Plan these interactions carefully in the beginning, and within a short period of time, they will become second nature to you. Also (and this is a nice plus), you will become trained as a behavioral interviewer without taking any of the courses!

You will see a lot of results from this new approach to employees, and they will reinforce your persona as a relational leader. The following are some examples of behavior questions that you can engage your team with:

- That's interesting, why do you say that?
- Give me some background on two or three of what you consider the most important aspects of this proposal.
- I'd like to understand more about your point. Please elaborate on the areas that you believe will help our bottom line.
- What are two or three points that make this project vital to our organization?

You get the idea. Make your staff think more when they are in your presence. This may be awkward at first, but in time that will become an expectation. By doing this, you are not only helping to hone your knowledge-gathering skills, but you are sending a clear message to staff that you believe they have something of substance to offer in the conduct of the business.

Thinking about my own past, one day a staff person unwittingly let loose with a piece of information that I was not particularly aware of. Apparently, staff was a bit jittery when they had to travel with me on appointments, particularly those that involved long drives. For myself, I really liked it when I had the opportunity to spend drive time with staff on our way to a meeting. Can you imagine how many questions you can ask on a two-hour car ride? Apparently, it could be uncomfortable, so I decided I would only do the uncomfortable type discussion one way, usually on the way back. I couldn't give it up because of the rich information I received and the insight I learned about the employee. I got lots of information, and ultimately, the individual riding with me had the opportunity to impress me with his thinking. It generally worked out well for both parties.

Tactically then, you can develop interviewing skills while you are enhancing your relational skills. The idea of open-ended questions goes beyond interviews; it provides information.

NOTE

An Axiom: Information is knowledge, and knowledge is power.

More Tactics for Hiring the Right Person

Alan Burkhard has built his business philosophy on getting the right person in place for the job. (Prior to his current entrepreneurial activity, he was CEO of a hugely successful staffing agency.) Some of his tactics are unusual and not for the faint at heart. Try this one on for size as an example. It was a post-selection tactic to better ensure that the right person was hired. Alan's experience (and mine, too) is that, regardless of the hiring process you put an individual through, you still don't know how they will work out until they actually start working.

Alan has been known to hire someone (after a rigorous process), and then tell them that for the first 30 days they didn't have a specific job. They are to learn about the company and present a report to him at the end of that period. Some would ask, reasonably enough it seems, "What do I do?" Alan's answer, simply put, "That's up to you—no limit." End of instructions!

NOTE

Usually, people know themselves and their capabilities beyond any screening process set up to discover their strengths. Oftentimes, people are able to fool what amounts to an imperfect system whose purpose is meant to hire the right person for the job. As a hiring manager, you can often be pretty sure (but never totally sure) that you have *the* candidate in front of you. Alan's method can help you because it reveals a much deeper insight into an individual. For the person being hired, it shows what the company is really like and how they can expect to be treated. It becomes much easier for the candidate to determine if the culture of the organization will actually work for them.

Some would go to clients, some to other employees, and some would spend time observing activity. They would figure it out, and when they came back to Alan with their report, Alan in turn would learn a lot about his company as the individual learned about the company. Then the person would be put in the job they were hired to do, assuming all was still good on both sides. If Alan doesn't like what he sees during the 30 days or when they come to him with their report, he can withdraw the job offer.

It is part of what Alan calls "backing it up"—it's having patience and building a knowledge base. In fact, it is an amazing tactic for building an understanding of the culture of an organization. And on the other side, it gives the candidate an opportunity to experience the culture and determine if it is a culture that they can prosper in. Alan calls his hiring process, "Hard In, Easy Out." If they don't like what they see during these 30 days or they are not comfortable with the environment, they can leave—no problems (easy out).

Alan's post-selection tactic produced good results for him, but there are other means of finding the elusive "right person" for the job. I will give you another example to consider that worked very well for me. My tactic involves attentiveness skills. I was always on the look out for the right kind of person—a person who I could see doing a good job for me because I liked the way they were doing a good job for someone else.

When in social circles, networking events, or frankly, anywhere, I made it a habit to listen carefully to people when they were talking about their work circumstances. People reveal a lot about themselves when they are in unguarded situations. If they didn't seem totally happy, they went on my list of potential employees. If I saw someone doing good work that appeared to be a fit for my organization, they went on my list. Occasionally, a friend or neighbor would tell me about someone who might be a good fit to work in my shop. Once they were on the list, I paid more attention to them. Depending upon my observations, I could move them up or down or off the list. I did this regardless of our current hiring situation.

When we had an opening, I always went to my list first to see if there was an appropriate person on it. If so, they got a call. If they wanted to pursue the opportunity, they got an interview. Oftentimes, they got the job!

Regardless of how you do it, hiring the right person is hard work. It demands your attention as a leader. The opportunity to make your organization better exists every time you have a job opening.

Making a Personal Commitment to Change

As you read this book, you may decide that what is discussed here makes sense, and you would like to try it. I hope you do. It will be one of your best decisions concerning your leadership style. Perhaps you already embrace some of the relational attributes and now want to move toward an expanded implementation of relational leadership. Maybe you have never been on this ship, and now want to embark on this journey. Either way, it will take your absolute commitment.

I am going to make the assumption that either you are at the front end of relationalism or not there at all. I am going to discuss what this commitment will mean and what you have to do to stay on point. I do not recommend that leaders announce a new model to their organization, regardless of how much enthusiasm the leader has for it.

There is no doubt you will be more successful with your commitment if you see results. If you haven't been relational with your organization, there will probably be a trust issue when you announce a new way of doing business. In no uncertain terms I say to you, do not make this announcement—just begin the personal and private commitment by changing what you do and how you act. I say this knowing full well that people like models and structure. I get that! Chaos does not have such a good reputation. However, there is plenty of time to bring on structure.

You need action—not labels, not models. Structure will surely flow from implementing the precepts of relational leadership. Words are meaningless unless associated directly with action. As Bob Brightfelt would say, "I have a bias for action!" Therefore, if you are implementing a relational approach, you don't have to wait until you feel ready to put the "whole enchilada" in place. Put together a plan of implementation, and take it one step at a time.

Be mindful that trust is a huge issue with change. If you announce you are going to change the way you act, your organization will immediately hone in on your actions. Change is difficult, and you will make some mistakes undoubtedly. If you haven't told anyone you're trying to do things differently, they won't judge you when you make a mistake. They will notice that you are doing things differently, though, and likely react positively to what you are doing. You will need all the positive reinforcement that you can get as you move through the process. So give yourself the best possible environment to succeed.

Embracing Staff, Customers, and Vendors

First, remember that in relational leadership, when you talk about people you take an extended view. *People* include not just staff but also your customers, shareholders, community, and vendors. All are central to the success of your team.

While this book focuses on your relationship with employees, it is vital to know and accept that you must treat your customers and vendors the same way. People like consistency in their leaders; they want to know what to expect—it's comforting. When you treat different groups of people differently, it is noticed. Even if you are in the "privileged" group now, you may be thinking, "One day the boss could change how she thinks about me, and I will be treated the way she treats those other folks." That's not the message you want to be sending.

Ultimately, your actions dictate how you are perceived. There are many ways to embrace people. Because attentiveness (listening and observing) is such an important piece of an effective relational organization, I am including some thoughts on the subject of people by leaders who have done it well. You will see that any outside people (customers, vendors, community) work you do will reflect on your inside people (employees).

Practitioners Speaking About People

Following are a few thoughts and ideas from my mentors that are reflective of connecting with people inside your organization as well as outside. Both are important for success. Never doubt that if you treat your people well, they will treat you well.

People like to work for companies that are admired. It reflects positively on them as individuals. Prioritizing your people relationships through the leadership model will have them saying good things about your company. Your employees will be more motivated, your customers will be more loyal, your vendors will work harder for you, and your community will hold you up as a hero. As such, community outreach, or *community marketing*, as Alan Burkhard refers to it, becomes a reinforcing activity for your organization that brands it in a very positive way. When done well, people begin to think of you as the employer of choice. Parents begin to tell their children, "If you can get a job at XYZ, you will be really set." This reputation can take on a life of its own.

Ed Woolard of DuPont included the surrounding community as part of his stakeholders list because that is where a company's reputation starts. Shareholders like this concept because it builds loyalty and increases share prices. There is an ever-increasing number of people who invest in companies that they perceive as community and environmentally conscious.

Community outreach brings publicity to the company in a very positive manner. Businesses like to do business with companies that are perceived as good corporate citizens because they feel that they will be treated in like fashion. At Junior Achievement, I treated vendors as part of our extended family. I worked hard to get them to understand our business and why supporting JA with excellent service was good for them as well as us.

Ed McKenna (the only person elected to two different terms as chairman of the JA board and also honored with the Silver National Leadership Award), who led credit card operations for Corestates, Mellon Bank, and Applied Card, has told me time and again that people and how you treat them is the delta in the success of his business operations. This included his customers and vendors. He says, "People need to be included in the business process at all levels. The foundation of a business, whether it be manufacturing or service, is its people. They need to know what they are doing and why they are doing it, and they need to be able to ask questions. As leaders, we have an obligation to give them good answers."

Ed understands that a business must listen to its customers and respond to their needs, and that can only be done if you are out where the customers are. And the same is true with vendors. You can't squeeze them so much that they can't make money just so you can make more. "You need to create 'win-win' scenarios for all the people in your organization, whether they are inside or out."

Alan Burkhard expends a large amount of energy on customer preferences, interaction, and service. He defines customer service as "the difference between what a customer expects and what they perceive they got. If there is a gap, we failed." He talks about how businesses make customers feel. "Have you ever seen a sign on the door of a business announcing 'No Shoes, No Shirt, No service'? Someone, sometime must have come in without them and caused a problem. Now everybody has to see that restriction—99% of us suffer for the 1% who don't act properly. I refuse to do that. We deal with exceptions as they come up."

When a customer comes into one of Alan's restaurants, they can sit anywhere they like because he discovered that people liked that option. If it causes a problem in some way, it is up to the business to figure out how to make it work. He is constantly building a knowledge base by asking questions and observing the people who frequent his businesses. He turns this knowledge into action by creating a superior customer experience. "If I get the customer experience piece right, I don't have to advertise. The customers do it for me through word of mouth," says Alan.

Nathan Hill's approach to his organization at Discover Card touched on all the tenants of relational leadership, not because he was following a model but because this was his belief system at work. I think it was personified by his desire to encourage his 2,000 associates to volunteer in the community. It was an opportunity to make a difference—working with kids, fixing up homes, working with low-cost housing, and more. He had a large talent pool, and he wanted it to do special things inside the company and outside in the community.

In his own words, here's how the community outreach program at Discover Card paid dividends: "When people could get outside themselves and help others, they were repaid through letters, hugs, thank yous, and smiles—this was an energy transfer from the people they touched. When the volunteers came back to the workplace, they were inspired to do a great job. The more people got involved, the fewer problems we had with employee morale and motivation. They didn't mind working because they were happy. If we have happy employees, we will also have happy customers. The customer felt it; it was a win-win for all."

I never talked with Charlie Cawley (a laureate in the United States Business Hall of Fame) about his corporate strategy for the community, but he certainly had to have one. MBNA America was deeply involved in the community wherever it had an operation. His executives were expected to serve on non-profit boards and to contribute significant dollars as well as their individual talents. Likewise, the company was very generous, making significant financial contributions throughout the community. He embraced organizations that mattered, which he defined as organizations that were changing the lives of people in need.

I recall one particular activity that MBNA sponsored. They called it their "Thanks" night. They invited all the organizations that they supported to a night on the town as their guests. The non-profit could send a specified number of people to the event, usually between five and 10. That evening, they would honor an executive who was doing a great job at serving the underserved. There was a wonderful reception beforehand and some form of entertainment afterward. Every person who attended received a gift as a token of MBNA's appreciation for the work they did every day. They also had a drawing where they gave away dozens of valuable prizes or cash, like vacations packages, Broadway shows, gift certificates, checks for $500 or $1,000 or more, and so on. (By the way, senior staff from the organizations were not eligible for these gifts.) The evening ended with a significant entertainer or personality performing or addressing the group. One year it was Colin Powell, and another it was Gladys Knight.

In the 36 years I spent in the non-profit world, I worked with thousands of companies across the country. I never experienced a company that was as committed to the community as MBNA America. They made every place where they had a facility a better place. Charlie never spoke of his charitable work in terms of return on investment—that wasn't him. But there was certainly a return on investment for MBNA. When people spoke of the company, they did so with a certain awe in their voice. It was the company of choice to work for, and they had lots of jobs to fill. The people who worked there had enormous pride in the company and were happy to be a loyal member of the team. From a community standpoint, it was almost as if you were a very special individual just by being employed there.

MBNA was a different kind of company—unique in the world of corporate philanthropy. All of us in the non-profit world were thankful for their presence, but we also appreciated the community outreach of the other companies around town. They accrued many of the same benefits in terms of employee satisfaction and community esteem. So while we really appreciated MBNA, we also knew that our bread and butter was with all the rest of the companies who generously shared their profits with the missions we pursued.

This expanded view of the people that you pay attention to in your organization is a winning strategy. As a relationally led business, you demonstrate authenticity when you commit to the principles of the relational model in every endeavor. You become a trusted and revered institution that everyone looks up to.

Shifting from Non-Relational to Relational Leadership

How do you make the style shift from non-relational to relational? This maneuver can be touchy. It must be well thought out and executed with precision, and it should not be entered into lightly. I talked already about the commitment it takes. Let me underscore that it requires absolute commitment to the change process and the understanding that there will likely be pain along the way.

Quite likely, the conversion process will test all the trust meters in the organization. When anyone attempts a radical shift in behavior, it is often looked upon as a tactic for some ulterior motive that has little or nothing to do with the people affected by the behavior. Therefore, the leader must understand that people crave affirmation of their value because it gives them a sense of worth. It is this sense of value and worth that drives their behavior and work ethic. They want to know that the leader cares about them, is fair, is willing to listen, and has an ethical code.

What has to happen to make a successful transition? I will begin with a story about an individual I have tried to help over the years who is decidedly non-relational, though he would probably argue the point. He wouldn't win, but he would still argue!

Adopting a New Style for Dealing with People

In this section, you will learn about the effects of treating people in a non-relational manner, and then gain pointers on how to be relational instead. Behavioral change is a process that takes time, patience, and a commitment to seeing the change to the end.

When Commitment Is Soft or Non-Existent

The following story demonstrates what is likely to happen if you are not committed to changing your behavior. It is real, and it is not unusual. It concerns an individual who regularly seeks advice from me. I always agree to talk with him. I do this in the grand hope that one of these days he will actually listen and do something that will change how he acts. So far we haven't quite gotten to that level.

115

Let me set the stage with a little background. His issues tend to stem from his relationships with people. This could be an action that didn't sit well with staff or comments he is prone to make that are "off color" or demeaning. He definitely likes to be in charge. While he likes to be in control, he has no control over himself. Therefore, he is apt to make lots of comments that by most reasoning would be better left off his tongue. He gets so wrapped up in himself that he thinks his comments are witty, helpful, and even encouraging. Mostly though, people don't react well to him telling them that they are "a little big around the butt." This is true even if he tells them about an exercise or two that might reduce their girth! Who'd a thunk that?!

He has no real idea why he says and does things like this. When I prompt him for an answer, he shrugs and admits that it was inappropriate. We then discuss a strategy to extricate him from the situation as it currently existed and talk about how to prevent it from occurring again.

After his "therapy" session is over, he will go back to his workplace and announce, individually and collectively to his staff, that he is a changed man. He now has new insight into his actions, and he actually details the advice given him.

Sometimes there would be a temporary change, but it never lasted. This pouring out of the soul was a catharsis or a *mea culpa*—usually a *mea maxima culpa*! But it wasn't done for the staff; it was, for him, a way of being penitent and, once cleansed, he could go back to his less endearing ways without feeling guilty. He had absolutely no commitment to changing behavior. He was a work in progress from his point of view; from others' viewpoints, he was a perpetual work in progress.

Knowing his proclivity for pouring out his soul after our latest "advice session," my final recommendation to him was not to announce his foibles when he reentered the office. Instead, he was to simply enact personal change in how he handled himself. I promised him that people would notice. While he said he understood and would refrain from his normal reentry behavior, he went right ahead and did it anyway.

He just couldn't bring himself to the "doing" or "action" stage. Thus no one believed that any change was actually on the way. In fact, he was more entrenched in his non-relational style than ever before. For him to become a relational leader would be the challenge of a lifetime because he had trained the people around him not to trust his commitment to change and, as a byproduct of that, not to trust him. This placed him in a very tenuous position. People do not follow someone they do not trust, which leads to the topic of authenticity.

Change Must Be Authentic

To be *authentic* means to do what you say you're going to do and mean it, and then demonstrate it consistently by your actions. People quickly tire of excuses. You might get away with the *mea culpa* once, perhaps even twice, but if there is no change in your behavior, people will blow off your penitence as just so much blather. In fact, if you came back and announced that you were putting in place a new relational leadership model, it wouldn't change the reaction. You have simply lost trust and put your character into question.

So, moving from non-relational to relational is a challenge because the behavior is not something you comport with comfortably. How then do you become authentic? It is wise to think of this phase of style change as transitional. Following are the eight steps you will need to make the shift to an authentic relational leader:

1. Study the relational leadership model elements and attributes (refer to Figure 1.1 in Chapter 1).
2. Rank each attribute according to how well you do it.
3. Solicit help from a trusted co-worker or coach.
4. Begin work on the mid-range attributes.
5. Be prepared to stumble.
6. Take on the really tough attributes.
7. Tell your staff what you are doing and ask for their help.
8. Bring the rest of your leadership group into the change process.

Referring to the model in Figure 1.1, determine where your behavioral characteristics lie with each of the attributes in the eyes of your team. Pick an attribute that is in the middle in terms of difficulty with your *modus operandi*. This gives you a reasonable chance of successful implementation and will be fairly visible to the team.

A trusted staff associate could provide excellent insight on this one. Do this exercise without fanfare. Make it a personal work objective. Monitor what you are doing and mark your successes. It's okay to have a coach and even desirable, particularly if it is someone outside the organization. Once you have your first attribute underway, consider what the next one will be. Again, pick a middle-ground attribute and repeat the procedure.

Depending upon the degree that you must change, accept the fact that you will stumble along the way. Don't let it stop you. Changing behavior is not easy. A coach can be a significant asset to your plan. Always remember, one of the marks of a winner is that a winner gets back up when she falls.

By the way, when I say make it a personal work objective, I mean it. Make the effort to change your own behavior; let people see you're working at something that is different. Don't bring them into the grand plan until you can demonstrate that you are serious and have a track record to prove it. Otherwise, you will find that people will just pass this off as another one of your whims.

Establish the Change Baseline, and Then Ask for Help

You will want to save the really tough attributes until you have built some personal stamina and organizational credibility around your transformation. This will take time, but every day that you stay on point, you build credibility. Eventually, you will have enough credibility to move to the next step, which should coincide with those attributes that cause you the greatest difficulty.

When you get to the big challenges, you can ask for help. Now is the time to talk about what you are doing and why. Get affirmation that you are making progress toward being relational. Let the team know that you want their help and will be willing to listen and act upon their observations in your quest to complete the transition.

The trick is to get people to actually believe that change is underway. When they experience the different you in multiple stages, they may then begin to trust that something good is going on. And so it is; begin with yourself. You become the model. People really don't care how you learned the behavior you're exhibiting as long as it is positive, promotes harmony, and provides forward momentum. That is when you can codify what you are doing and bring them on board. You can use yourself as an example: If I can do it, you can too, and our world will become a much better place.

Teach your direct reports the same type of behavior and expect them to perform to it. Then have them teach their direct reports, and just like Amway, before long, you will have a pyramid with everyone feeding each other positive behavioral actions. It works on the same principles as Brightfelt's One Level Up. You can infuse your organization with the habits of relational leadership by converting yourself to the model, one step at a time, and then injecting it into your system.

Maintaining the Relational Model

Many people believe, me among them, that it is easier to create energy from chaos than it is to sustain that energy once stability takes over. Some people are really good at starting things and bringing them to a level of maturity, but sometimes they have little energy to sustain the effort. An entrepreneur is often like this. He or she is all about blazing new trails, innovation, excitement, and newness. But when the Wild West becomes suburbia, that person often becomes bored. Compared to the adrenaline rush of creating such energy, the job of maintaining it becomes challenging in a very different way and not nearly as much fun. This is a critical moment in an organization's life—just as much effort (and oftentimes more) must be exerted to carry on and improve things as was exerted in the building stages.

Sustaining the Model

First and foremost, the role of the leader is to create (with the leadership team) and drive the vision of the organization. Second, the leader is responsible for ensuring that whatever models the organization is committed to are carried out, preserved, and improved. All the other roles are secondary. The rest of the leadership team is similarly responsible for the vision and models at their level.

Structure and models grow from the understanding of the organizational beliefs and that is the appropriate place for them to sprout. You will put systems in place based on your understanding of the precepts and beliefs, and these systems will undoubtedly change over time. But the precepts and beliefs rarely change. They are deep-seated. Therefore, it is vital that sufficient time and energy be dedicated to identifying these beliefs.

Think about the cornerstones of relational leadership: people at the core, then fairness, trust, character, celebration, fun, attentiveness, and purpose supporting the core. When would you want to throw out trust for instance? It's not a good idea to be fair anymore or act ethically? Systems will change but not the fundamental underpinnings of those systems.

Therefore, the leader becomes something of a sentinel at the gate. Whatever standards you have come to regarding the attributes must be maintained and improved. It is easy to let standards drop on a situational basis. Something comes up that pushes the standard hard, so this one time it's okay to make an exception. But this attitude becomes a slippery slope. The ripple effect can be devastating.

One example of maintaining the model comes from my organization, Junior Achievement of Delaware. It was a small enough organization that I could meet with every new employee. My role in the usually one-hour meeting was to give the new staffer an understanding of the organizational philosophies. It was important from my viewpoint that a new person should have an absolute understanding of what was acceptable and encouraged and what was unacceptable and not tolerated. In my view, they needed to get it from the top and be able to ask questions for clarity.

Rooted in the meeting were all of the precepts. I did not, by the way, go down the list, but instead I talked about how our workplace functioned, what they could expect, what they could challenge, and what would send them out the door without question or recourse. Within that meeting were stories that detailed the precepts in a way that gave them life and meaning. It served to set the stage for a new employee and gave them grounding in what we were about as an institution.

Every organization is different, so delivery of this message may come from different places; however, it must be consistent. An employee should be able to travel to a different work group or location and see and feel the same thing. Regardless of what you do, do something to reinforce the model. People must know that you are institutionalizing this method of operation.

Reinforcing the Model

One way I kept the JA guiding principles alive came from a monthly activity called Cans Nominations. This was undoubtedly the most successful activity I engaged in during my 36 years with JA. It drove home our model without ever mentioning it or telling staff about the importance of the principles. Every part of this activity was upbeat, fun, celebratory, purposeful, fair, attentive, ethical, and trustworthy. Staff always knew what we valued because we talked about it and celebrated it every month.

Here is the genesis of the Cans program. I once attended a JA meeting in Phoenix. One of the presenters, Joel Welding, was fascinating. Among my "take aways" was his business card, which happened to be a small bright orange can. On it the legend said the following, "Success comes in Cans, not Cannots"! How powerful is that?! On the side it listed the ingredients. Some of my colleagues didn't think too much of this presentation, so I was able to return to Delaware with two extra cans that they left behind.

At our next staff meeting, I asked people to submit nominations to me in writing about one or more of their associates. "Tell me," I said, "what you saw them doing that helps us to be a better team. At the end of the meeting, I will read your nominations, and we will revel in our teammates' actions with applause and back-patting. Next, I will select the three most worthy of recognition, and I will give one of the cans to them to place at their desks for the next month."

There was both form and substance to this process, mixed with a bit of humor. For instance, under "pain of termination," the cans were never to be opened as that not only wrecked the can (which was in short supply), but it also lost the magic of the can's ingredients—not to mention, it was my can! I was the sole and only judge of who was recognized with a can.

Rooting for a particular individual's action was jocularly rebuffed. Secretly, if lots of people believed an individual should be recognized, I recognized that this action was meaningful to the team as a whole, so the person would inevitably be recognized. On the other hand, if a nomination didn't rise to the level of reinforcing our models or beliefs, it was not recognized. Over time, people would understand what was important to the organization. It shaped behavior unconsciously and without conflict!

The beauty of this activity is that it served to reinforce the precepts without ever mentioning them directly. People were paying more attention to what their peers were doing, it was a celebration, and it was fun. It supported our purpose. Most important, it showed that people and their actions were valued in this organization. It gave visibility to individuals who most likely would not seek or be in a position to attain such. Thus they achieved standing within the team. More importantly, this was a unifying activity that involved everyone and everything we believed in.

This was certainly one of my more successful motivating activities and very simple as you think about it. Essentially, I asked staff to notice their peers doing things that were moving our team forward. It required the nominator to see, hear, and write about what they observed. Because I read each nomination, everyone on staff heard about the action being nominated, and it gave me the opportunity to reinforce a particular aspect of the action. Taken in totality, this was individually and collectively effective in codifying the fundamental principles that the organization lived by.

Once I considered stopping this, as I was fearful that it was becoming blasé. We had gone through a period where there seemed to be a decline in the number of nominations. My philosophy always has been to leave people with good memories about events or the organization. Dragging something out beyond its lifespan is self-defeating. I certainly was not going to let this happen to the Cans Nominations, which were so much a part of the fabric of the organization for so long. So as part of a survey sent out to staff on office environment, I asked about the cans. Would they like something different? Overwhelmingly no, said they. The can portion of the meeting was a feature they all looked forward to!

Part of the reason for this support is that I institutionalized the system. Once a year, usually in December, I tallied the results of all the nominations by individual for that year. I recognized the top three individuals with a small cash award based on their placement. The check they received was from me personally, not a corporate expense. The amount in total was around $200. Who can't use a little extra cash around the holidays? The amount of the check was not important. It ranged typically between $50 and $100. It was the recognition that was important. Note that I said I tallied the nominations and not the actual number cans that were awarded per individual. I counted those too, but not for the cash award. I was giving value to the people who regularly went out of their way to make our team a better one and that their efforts were noticed by their peers.

Another aspect which I know gained attention when it occurred, albeit rarely, was a staff member "placing in the money" after terminating from the organization. The individual was recognized and as long as he left under favorable conditions, he received his check. Doing this supported the element of fidelity and did not go unnoticed by staff.

Also I produced similar cumulative statistics for every staff person who ever worked in the company. All this information and the reports were managed by me on my personal system. I did not want any staff person to bear the task of the administrative duty.

The idea was to celebrate the history of the Cans program. This included totals and averages based on years of service. It helped us remember people from our past who made great contributions that we were enjoying in the present. It demonstrated that our organizational values had staying power and that all present were part of a rich tradition. Usually, there followed some wonderful stories and remembrances of days gone by. When you left this meeting, you had a very good feeling in your tummy!

You need to find what works best for your personality and the makeup of your team. The important point is that you find ways to reinforce the core values of your organization.

Your Critical Role as a Leader in a Relational Organization

As the leader, there are many success factors that you have to consider regularly. Some are more critical than others, but the following four are at the top of my list. If these factors are not attended to by the leader, the organization will be like a ship taking a torpedo below the water line—it will likely sink.

- Stay on course—protect and promote the vision.
- Be the "keeper of the flame"—enforce the established codes (how you operate).
- Be authentic in your words and deeds—don't deviate.
- Assess the organizational environment—make shifts if needed.

Because the attributes are simple concepts, it is not hard for most people to understand them. Sometimes they need to be reinforced with training, but not usually. Often, it only takes a conversation aimed at illuminating where someone went off track, and then discussing how to correct the behavior. People are, after all, simply that—people. People make mistakes. As a leader, you can't ignore the mistakes; you are charged with bringing the ship back on course.

As mentioned earlier, your role is to be the "keeper of the flame." When training and coaching don't change behavior, your job (or it could be the job of a more appropriate manager) is to remove the individual. People will watch you to see if you will do this. They know full well how the person is performing, and they are looking for alignment.

As a matter of fact, your team is always watching you, analyzing what you say and do against what you publish as the "rules." Remember, most often people have encountered less than authentic leadership in other positions or circumstances. Are you just one more of the many who speak from "both sides of his mouth"? Your credibility is always on the line, so do your best to preserve it.

What Happens If Your Words and Actions Are Not Aligned?

My brother, Howard, once told me a story about a situation where he worked as a production executive. It was a profitable but relatively small truck body assembly operation. The business was in the throes of a pretty bad year financially. It was losing money, and some drastic measures were deemed necessary by the owner. Not everyone agreed that the plight of the business was as bad as it was made out to be, but the owner called the shots. He directed that benefits and hours be cut back, and on top of that, management pay would be cut by 20% and the workers' pay by 10%. The cuts were particularly hard felt by the workers in the plant and administrative offices. The word from management was that what had to be, had to be—times were tough. Begrudgingly, the workers accepted their fate, believing that it was better than losing their jobs.

That very same week, the owner purchased two brand-new Jaguar automobiles with company funds, one for him and one for his wife. And not only that, but he made sure everyone in the plant saw them (apparently, he liked to flaunt his wealth). Understandably, this purchase created very hard feelings among the workers and befuddled the management team. How could he make such a decision under the circumstances the company was faced with?

Immediately, the workers began finding more fault with everything that management did. Why didn't the owner invest in the business? Why didn't he buy new or upgraded equipment that would make the company more competitive if he was going to spend so much money on personal cars? The emotion and tension in the plant was high anyway because of the cutbacks, but this took the stress to even higher levels. Management, principally my brother, was tasked with the job of calming everyone down. Eventually, this was accomplished but at a very high price—trust was destroyed. A wall emerged between management and employees that had not existed before. The message sent by the owner was this: "The business is failing. You have to take cuts in pay and benefits and work fewer hours, but I get to buy two new Jaguars with your money." In a nutshell, the owner's misalignment between his words and actions proved to be the beginning of the end of his company.

Preserving the Organization's Environment

It is your responsibility as the leader to continually check on the environment you are creating. A simple survey, regularly administered and charted, will tell you a lot about how things are going and where changes need to be enacted.

A sample of such a survey is provided at the end of this chapter. There is nothing magical about it; make up your own, if you prefer. The important thing is to regularly administer it—I suggest once a quarter. Keep an ongoing chart so you can see how you are doing over time and make notes about what you discover and how you are reacting to the discovery.

It is also very important to share the information with the staff. Take time at a meeting to go over the results. Confirm what you believe the data is suggesting with the people who are providing it. The comments section of the survey is a critical piece of this discussion. What your staff is saying could be far more important than the numerical value they assign to the question. Assume nothing! The idea here is transparency. Defensive behavior is not welcome or allowed. Your primary objective is to look for means to improve the environment.

Recognize that your best temperature reading for the atmosphere and effectiveness of your workplace exists with your new employees. Find ways to formally or informally do data digs. For the first six months, their perspective will be especially fresh and valuable. A new person will see things that escape all of you who are dug into the environment day after day.

Again, it doesn't matter what position they hold; talk with them and record their views. You will undoubtedly gain real insight into your operation and what is working or not working. Make sure you ask for both observations and suggestions for improvement. Over the years I have heard some great ideas.

I caution you to understand that not everyone will be brimming with observations and ideas, but don't let that stop you. Not many people will have experienced this type of behavior from leadership. You are placed in the trust versus mistrust syndrome. Only by consistently engaging in this type of activity will you overcome the mistrust issue. I will just say this—it is worth waiting for!

Summary

The relational model complements and energizes the business plan. You can't have one without the other. In the end, common sense drives the model. Test common sense with associates any time there is conflict. Know that the right people will get the job done, and it is up to you to make sure they are in place. Be certain to do self-observation; if the idea of relational leadership is not possible because of your personality or demeanor, don't do it. Never, ever forget that your people drive your success. More to the point, remember that your people are more than your employees or team; they consist of your customers, vendors, shareholders, and even community.

Remember, as the leader, it is your responsibility to always set the example. Live, act, and preach the gospel of relationships. Drive the precepts through the organization and do not tolerate those who shun them. It doesn't take much to throw the group off focus. One inappropriate hire can do it. You are the sentinel at the gates; be attentive to the atmosphere you have created. Always be on guard for a change in the barometric reading.

Keep in mind that change takes time. The conversion from non-relational to relational is a big one. The investment will take great effort, but as some great philosopher once said, "There is no great reward without great effort!"

In researching for this book, I didn't find much in the way of models for relational leadership outside of academia. In talking with the many leaders I thought to be relational by nature and deed, I found that they had no script to follow. That was certainly true of me. It was a maturation process for all of us. We picked up pieces along the way by observation or intuition. However, we all started with people; and then an understanding of what people need enabled us to embellish the original ideas with more and more substance over time.

Your advantage is that the whole system is laid out for you in this book. You know what your next steps will be, and ultimately you will find ways to improve what is now in front of you. I have a personal trainer, Jermaine Richardson, whose mantra is, "Slow and steady wins the race." Getting off the mark is the most important thing you can do for yourself and your organization.

KEEP IN MIND:

- Common sense more than anything else will lead you to appropriate and successful leadership decisions.
- Hire the right people, and then treat them right.
- The leader always sets the example, so live, act, and preach the gospel of relationships. Drive the precepts through the organization, and do not tolerate those who shun them—be authentic.
- It is easier to create energy from chaos than it is to sustain that energy once stability is in place.
- *People* include not just staff but also your customers, shareholders, community, and vendors. All are central to the success of your team and organization.
- Relational leadership is a framework superimposed on a solid business model.
- The greater the plausibility of a leader's style, the greater the possibility that she will be followed.
- People crave affirmation of their value because it gives them a sense of worth—common sense!
- If you say something, either do it or retract it, but don't ignore it.

Chapter 6

Developing the Leader in You

> "When you know a thing, to recognize that you
> know it, and when you do not know a thing, to
> recognize that you do not know it—that is knowledge."
>
> —*Confucius*
> *The Analects Book II #17*
> *(Translated by Arthur Waley)*

- Apply Discipline
- Execute Winning Activities
- Avoid Shortcuts
- Manage Risk
- Develop the New You
- The Effect of Misuse of Power on Leadership
- The Many Faces of Leadership
- Summary

If you accept the premise that leaders are made, not born, then you will want to do everything you can to enhance your leadership qualities. You have control over the type of leader you become. What you know about leadership and what you do to make yourself a leader is within you.

My personal belief is that people have tendencies as part of their personality at birth that can help them become leaders. Having said that, I also believe that you can learn the craft of leadership over time, assuming you pay attention to the world around you. Either way, becoming a leader is hard work. It can be done if you want to do it and you commit to doing it. You must be purposeful in your approach.

You have probably heard the story of the chicken and pig; it's a fable that has been around for a long time. One version goes like this. The chicken and the pig were in the barnyard, and passing the farmers kitchen window, they noticed breakfast was on the table—ham and eggs. It looked like the family was enjoying the meal. The chicken noted to the pig with pride his involvement in the meal, while the pig thoughtfully replied, "For you, it was involvement; for pigs it is total commitment!"

I am not looking for the pig's level of commitment for you to extend your leadership capabilities, but you will need to be determined and disciplined to pull it off. So get fixed on that right now.

It was Napoleon Hill who said, "Whatever the mind can conceive and believe, the mind can achieve." Your mind is a powerful force within you. People who study such things say it is the most underdeveloped part of our being. There are five areas you want to concentrate on as you exercise your mind toward a relational leadership thought pattern.

- Apply discipline
- Execute winning activities
- Avoid shortcuts
- Manage risk
- Develop the new you

Understanding the implications of each area provides you with the foundation necessary to develop qualities of leadership that you are comfortable with. Just because you are relational doesn't mean that you are the same as another relational leader. Each person will apply his own style based on his strengths.

Apply Discipline

Discipline is like fuel for your automobile. As long as you have it in your tank, you can move forward. If you don't stop once in a while to refuel, you will eventually run out and stop dead in your tracks.

What about this discipline business? You need to be clear on this concept: Without discipline in your thoughts and actions, nothing happens—nothing. You are the sum total of your internal and external life—what is in you and what you see outside of you. Together, they become your personal mosaic. The key to bringing these parts together (the glue, if you will) is your capacity to apply discipline in your life. Discipline is the answer to so much of what makes you a better person because it keeps you on the road you have chosen.

> **TIP**
> An Axiom: The discipline to remain committed, to push away distraction, to keep your goal in view, is the doctrine of a winner.

To become a better person, you must create the will to get started, to stay on the course you began, to keep out distractions, and to do the right things repeatedly, even if they are uncomfortable. Winston Churchill kept an entire nation focused with his iron will and determination when he spoke these words in October, 1941: "Never give in. Never give in. Never, never, never, never—in nothing, great or small, large or petty—never give in."

Discipline keeps you from becoming lazy. It stops you from taking the easy way. It makes you strong. It fuels your determination. It reminds those around you that there is no quit in you, that you will finish and you will win. So decide right now. If you are going to improve your lot in life, if you are going to become relational, if you are going to make a difference, you must become disciplined. Easy to say, but not so easy to do. Yet there is no alternative to success.

I believe there are five principles that you must adhere to if you are going to acquire the discipline you need to succeed:

- *Focus* is about knowing what you want and why you want it. It is visualizing in your mind what the final destination looks like.

- *Commitment* is about understanding what the activity will do for you and why it is so important to you to achieve.

- *Readiness* is about accepting that now is the time to act. Your mind must be receptive to the idea that this activity is worthwhile.

- *Applause* is about recognizing yourself when you hit a milestone along the way to your goal and taking the time to pat yourself on the back.

- *Partnering* is about enlisting help. Team up with someone you trust to remind you if she sees you straying. There is no disgrace in this; it demonstrates character and determination.

Acquiring discipline is a lot like quitting smoking. You have to be ready. Try to quit smoking before you're ready, and you will be puffing again in short order. Because someone wants you to quit is usually not enough motivation. Your mind has to be engaged in the process before you make a decision to quit; that's what gets you ready. When you quit, your mind is in charge of the process—that's discipline. If you are not ready, it is improbable that you will be able to muster the discipline to sustain the effort.

Execute Winning Activities

The power of being positive has long been held as an affirmative strategy. Smiling is a proven results driver. Treating people with respect produces their best efforts. Setting high standards and believing that you can achieve them makes for positive outcomes. Expectations will often deliver the end product. Here are some examples of winning activities.

Visualization

Visualization is a concept that coaches use effectively with their players. Think about your coach exhorting you to do this: *See yourself crossing the goal line. Bring the image of the joy in your heart when you cross the goal line. Feel your teammates slapping you on the back, congratulating you when you cross the goal line. Keep these visions in your mind and repeat them often. You will cross the goal line.* That is the power of positive thinking at work—the power of visualization.

Visualization is a winning strategy, and like discipline, it involves the mind's active participation. I have used visualization all of my life. It works. Know what your goals are. Know where you want to be in the short term and long term. Create scenarios in your mind that show you achieving your objective and receiving the accolades that reward your victory.

Since 1994, I have worked with a partner, George Slook, in a small consulting business we started called MetaFocus. We were all about getting people to think differently about their situation. Visualization was an integral part of our process. It was often challenging for our clients, but the effort was always worthwhile.

When doing vision work with our clients, we engaged them in "right brain" activity. One favorite activity presented them with a set of facts. The second part of the exercise required them to draw a picture that represented the scenario. You could actually see the tension that this activity created in the audience, but it produced exceptional results. Right brain activity is hard work for some people, but it can be done if you don't set yourself up as an art critic!

Visualizing is a step process. Here are the steps you need to engage in to be effective:

1. Be clear on your end result.
2. Think about how you would feel achieving the result.
3. Identify the resources you need to get the job done.
4. Fix in your brain your physical environment as you achieve the result.
5. Identify who is around you at the time; who cares about what you have accomplished?
6. Know what is different because of your success.

Make notes if you must, but to the extent that is possible, do as many of these steps as you can in your mind. This is a means of connecting your brain fully to the activity. The following is an example of what you might be thinking:

I am a successful executive leading a productive team. The group respects me because I give them the freedom to think and act. I watch their back and provide the resources they need to get their job done. The consultant I hired is driving home the new continuous improvement system I put in place. I can see my team energized and working long hours to bring their projects to fruition. They come to work spirited, particularly Kelly, Meredith, and Kenny. Their attitude is spreading to others on the team. Caitlin and Daniel are more active and involved in staff meetings. Everyone is responding to the mini celebrations we hold when we reach an objective. Work seems to be fun and purposeful again because people are all pulling in the same direction. Carolyn, my boss, tells me frequently that she likes what she sees coming out of the group, both their attitude and work product. She seems very pleased with me. Productivity is up for four straight quarters. Carolyn is pulling the group together in the corporate board room with Dan, the new vice president, to reward us with bonuses for the excellent team work we are displaying. In her speech, she tells the group I have been working very hard to become a relational leader, which she supports, and it seems to be working for the team.

Every day, at least once a day, think these thoughts. Add details as you go along. All of this will affect your attitude and your actions. It will have a similar impact on the attitudes and actions of those around you in a very positive manner. This takes discipline and time, but the results will be worthwhile.

Remember that visualization begins in the mind. It is in the mind where your thoughts control your actions. The mind rules—engage it! Create your own winning strategies.

Giving Is an Essential Part of Getting

Understand that to get, you must also give. The famous motivator Zig Zigler lives by the philosophy that you can have everything in life you want if you will just help enough other people get what they want.

Decide too, in your mind, what you are willing to give. Will you give the requisite time and energy to the project? Will you sacrifice what it takes to make your objective? If you focus your mind on what you want, do the work required, and give what is necessary (and more) to achieve your objective, you will get where you want to be.

Giving extends beyond what you are willing to commit to doing within a project. It is a life mind set. Helping others to achieve their goals is giving. Picking people up when they are down is giving. Being available when needed is giving. Donating to charity, or better yet, volunteering for a cause, is giving.

All my life, I worked with people who gave and gave generously in many instances. They were great people to be around. They were nicer, happier, and better adjusted than the average person. Volunteers are healthier and live longer because the act of giving produces good feelings all over your body. The attitude of volunteers impacted me as well. Being around people like this and the environment that they fostered made my work satisfying. Their vibes became my vibes. All was good.

Doing What Failures Won't Do

There is a saying I heard people quote early in my career that had many different variants. I don't know who said it besides my branch manager at Sun Life of Canada, but the version I like best went like this: *Winners will do the things that failures refuse to do*. It impressed me to the point that I made it part of my personal belief system. Over the years I have uttered the same declaration to my associates.

What a powerful statement! Winners will do the things that failures refuse to do. If you can get your brain around this statement and its implications, you are well on your way to success. What do I mean?

Winners prepare; failures don't. Winners listen and observe; failures don't. Winners study, question, and research; failures don't. Winners give; failures take. Winners are positive, helpful, supportive, and receptive; failures aren't.

Winners have an attitude that success takes work, and they are willing to put in the time and energy, diligence and care to make it happen. Failures take the path of least resistance. The attitude of failures is one of entitlement and often connivance.

TIP
Winners do the things that failures refuse to do.

A winner who fails, gets back up and digs in again, confident that this new effort will get her where she sees herself. A failure seeks to place blame for her inability to achieve results, but that blame rarely is placed where it belongs—on herself. Winners are stalwart and bold; failures are uncommitted and weak.

Avoid Shortcuts

In short, shortcuts don't work. I have never met a single person whose climb to success was generated through a series of shortcuts. I want to tell you a story about a childhood friend who lived his life as a shortcut. It will illustrate my point better than anything I could say to you.

My friend had talent. He was smooth. He believed he didn't have to work hard because he had all the answers. He was likeable enough, but just below the surface there was a bit of the con artist in him. Actually, there was quite a bit of this character trait in him.

He had a job working in security for a major manufacturing company in town—back in the days when companies were very paternal. The covenant was, "Show up, work hard; you have a job for life and a pension to go with it." Well that kind of situation is not for everybody, and it certainly wasn't for my friend. Today, those company styles no longer exist.

He quit the job two weeks before he married. Personally, I didn't think moving on from this position was a bad idea; I did think the timing was peculiar. He just quit; he had no place to go, and hadn't even thought about what he would do next. What he believed was that he was better than what this secure position offered.

No doubt he was right about something better, but he had no idea what that might be. What he did know about himself was that he didn't go to college and didn't perform very well in high school academically, nor did he distinguish himself in any extracurricular activities. Aside from being glib, he had no real training or preparation for professional work. And now he was unemployed by his own volition. My friend lacked discipline in a big, big way. He also lacked the powers of observation and listening. He could visualize, but he wouldn't do the work.

His life after that became a pipe dream. Someone was always promising him an important job but never delivering. He skipped from one position to the next because there was always a new dream. But the dreams lacked substance, and the dreamer never put forth the effort to actually improve his personal capability. He was his own "dream blocker."

> **TIP**
> True success is born of hard work, determination, a good idea, an effective plan, and belief.

So now after a lifetime of chasing windmills like Don Quixote, my friend is no farther ahead than he was at the beginning, except he is quite a bit more cynical today. His world is his own creation. In this world, he succeeds and this makes him feel good. However, in the world the rest of us live in, he is, on his best days, no more than average. With him, there was always an excuse. It was never anything he did wrong that took him off course. I lost track of how many jobs were lost or how many promises were broken. What I do know for certain is that the formula for success can't be a shortcut.

Manage Risk

Jim Kelly is another member of the JA Delaware board and National Gold Leadership Award winner—one of 12 in the country that year. At his day job, he is the Chief Operating Officer of ING Direct, the hugely successful Internet bank. During an extended conversation about risk, we discussed how risk is fundamental to the American business system. I am sure you have heard the expression, "There is no great reward without great risk." It is a basic economic principle. Jim's view of the world, which is similar to my own, is that risk is important but must be managed.

Risk management is about calculated risks, not wild, thoughtless, from-the-gut risks. The type of risks Jim and I would advocate are ones that have been well thought out, offer a challenge (so the reward factor kicks in), and fall within tolerance parameters. Well, what does that mean? It means that you don't bet the house! You only put at risk what you can afford to lose.

Risk is exciting and enticing. It is an area of life that the "devil" enjoys. It is very hard to resist for many people. Talk to any gambler in Vegas or Atlantic City—risk has the capacity to overtake all your senses. When you get caught up in the excitement of winning, it is hard to quit, even if you know you should. Earlier I talked about discipline. Risk management is the area of leadership that screams out for discipline, perhaps more than any other.

Jim postulated the following scenario relating to risk management. What if someone came to you in 2006 and told you that house prices would fall 30% to 40% nationally. You would probably say, "It'll never happen. You're out of your mind! Nothing like that has happened since the Great Depression." At the time, you are intent on capturing a piece of the housing market expansion. So if you were starting a lending business around that time, you would not start it on the outside chance that a global recession could happen. In fact, you'd be so convinced that it could not happen, you would make a couple of bets that it wouldn't occur. You lower your underwriting standards and take on more customers. You're building up steam and thinking about more ways that you can cash in on this ever-expanding market because you know full well that housing prices can't drop 30% to 40% nationally.

The reality is that they can and in fact did. If you actually pursued this strategy, you lost big time. The recession would bankrupt you. Your actions were not calculated to protect against the downside risk of a housing market freefall. You put everything on the line—an "all in" better's strategy.

So what does this scenario mean? Should you never take a risk? Should you always play the middle and avoid the upside and downside? No, that is not the answer. Playing the middle may be just as dangerous as going for broke. So what is the message here? Well, for sure, you have to try things, you have to take risks, and you have to gamble a bit, but you never bet the house! If you are going out on the margin, you go out with money you can afford to lose, recognizing that if you win, the payoff will be big—very big.

Jim says, "I think that playing the margin with what you can afford to lose is something that a lot of people lost in this last bubble. Everything looked so good; it could never be bad. The financial wizards said inflationary control was solid. The models pointed to a rosy future, and they were all wrong. We end up with what we got!"

As a leader you will be called upon to take risk regularly. "Betting the house" is a desperation move, not a leadership move. Circumstances constantly change, but not always when you think they will. Be aggressive for sure, but do so with care. Many people depend upon your discretion.

Skip Schoenhals told me the story of what he encountered when he took over the reins at WSFS Bank. The bank was in very bad shape, the stock was trading at one dollar per share, and the primary reason was asset quality. Loans and investments were worth a whole lot less than what the bank paid for them. How did the bank get into this situation?

Well, obviously there were some poor decisions and some unintended or unanticipated economic events, but even more than that the bank was simply not prepared for any sort of economic downturn. Skip says, "You have got to be sure that you have structured the bank so that in the inevitable occurrence of a downturn, you haven't bet the farm. Unfortunately, previous leadership had bet the farm on a series of bad decisions." The decisions that caused the problems at WSFS were loans in the commercial real estate market. The market was over-built because it was driven by tax strategies. The bank's lending practices simply were not based on fundamental economic needs.

So what do we take from these two examples? It is not a good idea to bet either the house or the farm! Get to the basics of your business and make calculated, well thought out risks that you can cover in case of disaster.

Develop the New You

Developing anything new takes time. Changing how you personally operate to become a relational leader is a big project. So don't think a new person is going to miraculously emerge from the pool, as in the 1985 film *Cocoon*. Build the new you one step at a time; definitely take no shortcuts here. Sustainable change in behavior is a process. You will become what your listening and observing skills bring to you.

Attentiveness is a critical success factor for life. It is a pillar among the attributes of relational leadership. It is what will help you to become something different. It is a behavior that anyone can adopt. Keen observers will pick out actions and traits in others that they can add or avoid within their own repertoire. A question that arises, often by younger people is, How do I differentiate between good and bad behavior? Most of the time, it will be obvious. If your sense of fidelity and appreciation is solidly based, it will be even more evident. Certainly you can check the behavior against Bob Albin's Average Person Theory.

What would the average person say about whatever it is that you are observing? Does it make sense? How will most people react to what you are seeing or hearing? If you think about it and apply your thoughts to the world that you live in, more often than not, you'll get the right answer. Mind you, I am talking about behaviors that shape your character, not necessarily the issues that arise in the political mainstream.

When you use your powers of observation and listening to help you shape the kind of person you want to be, you actually take on the personas of many people. The objective is this: Meld the many into one—you. Your goal is to be selective. Think of yourself as being a very exclusive club with specific criteria for entry. Sift through what you hear and observe in others and take only the best for you, for the you that you want to be. Remember what Mom used to say, "If Howard and Marie jumped off a bridge, would you jump off the bridge too?" Become the person someone else will admire and want to emulate.

If you don't know the story of Don Quixote, he saw windmills and he thought they were a giant avenging enemy that he must destroy. After all, in his madness, he was a knight-errant, and it was his duty. Think of the windmill as the giant avenging enemy of a mind that is slipping away. Do not allow your mind to move in this direction. Stand up for the discipline to change, the discipline to succeed. And don't wait another day!

It is vital to invest the time and energy required in order to change. Some folks say if you repeatedly do something over and over for a period of 28 days, it will become a habit. Only four weeks—but while you are inside those four weeks, they could seem like an eternity. You must be ready to change, you must be committed to the hard work change demands, and you must be disciplined to see your personal quest to the end.

When the new you emerges, it will be a sunny day. You will feel the power you now hold over yourself. You will see potential for real gain where only fantasy existed before. Your team will hold you in esteem, your organization will move forward, and your life will become harmonious with your objectives. You will achieve a oneness with your spirit that will make you whole. It is definitely worth the effort!

The Effect of Misuse of Power on Leadership

A major focus of this book is to encourage leaders to use power positively. One of the most important principles of relationalism is that it precludes the misuse of power. It is focused on people and provides an atmosphere and motivation where people can flourish. It builds upon moral and ethical behavior.

Power and leadership are closely aligned; they are a natural outflow of each other. But how the leader handles power is another subject. Depending upon how much power a leader has, he can shape events around him either positively or negatively. When those who misuse power are exposed, their corruption chips away at the integrity of our system causing doubt and creating unrest and unease in the citizenry.

In 1887, Baron Acton of Great Britain sent a letter to Bishop Mandell Creighton. Acton was an historian and moralist who had a somewhat dim view of the world. He is widely quoted today for saying, "Power tends to corrupt; absolute power corrupts absolutely." He continued with, "Great men are almost always bad men." This part of his quote doesn't get much visibility. Well, I am not sure that I completely agree with his statement, but I get his point. If you take on the "my way or the highway" mentality, it is pretty easy to be a bad guy.

When someone is in control and is able to establish the parameters for his own actions, then the potential for bad is always there; unfortunately, it often happens. I have mentioned the countless times leaders have gone astray, even just considering the past 15 years or so. They come from every background and walk of life. In most instances, they have gone astray because they could, because the opportunity presented itself. Think about Enron, Wall Street, the hi-jinks of our politicians, and on and on.

The immorality and corruption that seems to prevail in society today will cripple the nation's capacity to grow and prosper. Leaders will no longer be revered, and the upheaval will be catastrophic. Many commentators postulate that America has risen to its highest level and is on its way toward international mediocrity. This trend, if in fact it is as bad as some say, can be reversed if we take hold of character and morality individually and collectively, now!

TIP

An Axiom: Adherence to relational principles ensures that power is not intentionally abused.

A relational leader can't misuse power because his moral and ethical compass is well fixed. He is governed by attributes that do not permit bad behavior. Greed is not part of his makeup. If you doubt this, examine the qualities of the element of fidelity again (refer to Figure 4.2 in Chapter 4). If you practice and commit to fairness, trust, and character, you cannot then be greedy, corrupt, unethical, and immoral.

The intent of this chapter is to encourage you to believe that you can become a relational leader, and you are desperately needed in this role. Relational leaders create spirit, good will, effectiveness, and respect. The country and the world need leaders willing to be relational in both their words and actions.

A Demonstration of the Misuse of Power

I want to tell you a story that illustrates the concept concerning absolute power. Probably more than anything else in my life, this story I lived through provided the backdrop and set the course for me to become a relational leader. The following tale is not about earth-shattering, wide-spread corruption like a Bernie Madoff "Ponzi" scheme. It is primarily about one man and the effect that the misuse of power had on him. I think we tend to forget that for something to be bad, it doesn't have to be on the scale of a tsunami. In many ways, to the extent that one is affected, all are affected.

Early in my career I worked for a man, Jack Talcott, who was like a second father to me, and I loved him dearly. Like most father-son relationships, we had our moments of tension. I thought I knew just about everything when, in fact, I didn't know much. I was at the front end of active observation. So I studied Jack constantly and paid attention to everything that he did.

As mentioned earlier, Junior Achievement in the early 1970s did little with hiring or training. It was all a random walk. So, if you had a deficiency, it was more likely to get worse rather than better.

Jack had a boss, the JA board chairman and a senior officer of the Gillette Company, who took delight, it seemed, in beating him up mentally. For purposes of the story, I'll call him Jim. Whatever faults Jack had, Jim would blow them up larger than life. He never talked about Jack's strengths; it was almost as if they didn't exist. Actually, Jim liked to do this with anybody he encountered, but he seemed to take extra special zeal with Jack.

There was a time that I was charged with creating and running a conference for students in the Massachusetts area. We hadn't attempted anything like this before, but we did know about kids and what they responded to in situations like this. As Jim was chairman during this time and a person who reveled in control, he wanted to know all the details of the conference. He came up with some ideas on his own that he felt the students should be exposed to.

We had a meeting at Gillette that was attended by Jim, two of his reports, Jack, me, and two other program managers, Bob and Elliot. Jim wanted to know what I thought of his ideas, and I told him respectfully but frankly that I didn't think the students would relate very well to the concepts and topics.

Jim was disenchanted with my response to say the least, and there was silence in the room for what seemed like an eternity. Finally, with an air of authority, Jim called me up to stand next to him at the front of the room. He demanded that I relate to him. I was pretty much lost for words or actions. I had a feeling that my next words would shape the rest of my life, and if not that, certainly the immediate future.

I was 23 years old and being challenged by the chairman of the board and a senior executive at one of Boston's major corporations who I knew was not such a nice guy. I didn't seem to be getting any support from my associates, nor did I think any would be forthcoming. I was hanging on a limb, which didn't seem very secure, and even I couldn't stand the silence much longer. So I took what I thought was the only defensible stance and told the truth. I said to Jim, "I have no idea how I could relate to you." I don't think that was the response he was looking for. His face reddened, and he spit out that he was leaving the room and would return in 20 minutes for an answer on the agenda.

I was berated by his direct reports, who at JA we affectionately referred to as Pebbles and Bam Bam (from the *Flintstones*). There is more to that story, but it seems best to leave it where it is. However, I did not give any ground, and right on schedule, Jim returned in 20 minutes wanting to know what the decision was that we reached. Bam Bam told him that I would not relent on my conviction. Without hesitation, Jim said that Gillette would have nothing to do with the conference, picked up his papers, and stormed out of the room.

I had already seen and heard all I needed to know about this man. As I retell this story here, I am reminded of the element of fidelity and how Jim allied to its attributes. He turned out to be an effective instructor for me. He taught me that station in life is relative. Not only did you have to earn your way to the top, but you had to continue to operate at a high level once you got there. Because I did not hold him in any sort of esteem and because my primary responsibility was to run a great conference, I had little difficulty holding my ground. (Well, that's not exactly true, but I did it anyway.)

The conference was a huge success and grew to become a regional conference in the ensuing years. Students from as far away as Ohio and Virginia attended. Clearly, I couldn't relate to Jim, but I was able to relate to the students who were my customers.

The interesting thing about Jim was that he never offered any support if you disagreed with him. You were expected to capitulate. Somehow, you were going to be able to do things better just because he didn't think what you were doing was very good.

With Jack, in particular, he never offered any help or training opportunities to overcome the deficiencies that Jim saw in him. He just battered him privately and publicly. There's that fidelity again. He had the power to do good, but didn't.

I was in a meeting with the two of them once where the remarks that Jim was making about Jack and his performance was making me uncomfortable—who knows what it was doing to Jack? It certainly had to be a monumental embarrassment to him personally. After all, I was only a couple of years in the work force and 25 years younger than Jack.

I could never figure out why Jim did these things. Because he could, was one thought that came to mind. It was unfair. It was brutal. It was debasing. In my mind, whatever Jack's deficits were, they were nothing compared to Jim's ruthlessness, thoughtlessness, and mean spirit.

As time moved on, Jim's attacks eroded Jack's confidence. Before long, my observations of Jack's activities changed. I saw a man who rarely left his office. He seemed to become increasingly timid around the board, particularly with Jim. Around the staff, he lost his temper a lot. Most importantly, we seemed to lose our direction as Jack became unsure of where to take us. He was a shell of the person I knew.

Reflections and Nuggets Taken from the Story

I learned some important lessons early on. I learned that you had to stand up for yourself and your reports. Sometimes that was very hard, and it took what we used to call "intestinal fortitude"; today we just call it guts. I also learned that you had to point your organization in a direction, right or wrong; there had to be a destination that everyone was heading toward. Finally, I learned that Jim put his pants on the same way I did, and he (or others in similar positions) was not omnipotent. There were other "take aways" as well but these three stuck with me my entire career.

Still reflecting on Jim's actions, I wondered could he possibly think that humiliating and grinding people into the ground as a successful leadership strategy? Was he getting this type of treatment at work, and this was his opportunity to dish some of the same out to others? Was his objective to get Jack to quit? This became a conundrum that I never was able to solve, but I wonder about it to this day.

Often, there are no answers to life's questions. In the end it, wasn't going to matter as Jim's term as chairman was coming to its finish. Thankfully the chairmanship of the board was a two-year deal. While he did indeed move on, he never left me. Even though I didn't have the why about Jim, I did learn something very early in my career, which was how not to treat people. I saw what his style of leadership did to people, and I was bound and determined that I would never be that way. Breaking people's will and spirit is a despicable act. It happens more often than we realize.

What I did was to turn my observation into a personal philosophy. It was grounded in the negative and that's a shame, but *so what?* The important point was to take away from the circumstances what was productive. Exercise the discipline to form a value system into a way of conducting your life. This was my first remembrance of what was to become my leadership style. I determined then and there that when I was in a position of authority, I would make my decisions and provide leadership on the basis of people and their needs.

The Many Faces of Leadership

So what does the face of leadership look like? It is certainly different from one person to the next and one perspective to the next. Some people claim they can see a leader just by looking at the person. Do leaders have a certain demeanor? Some say that they can just feel the aura of power and leadership when they stand next to a person. Well, they may not be far off. Observation is one of the qualities anyone who wants to be a leader or remain one must employ—look and listen. It takes commitment and discipline.

Former Vice President Dan Quayle was certainly a leader. He took what seemed like constant abuse from the press during his time in office. He was regularly ridiculed for things he said or did. The press influenced the country to think of him in a somewhat buffoonish manner. I had the opportunity to meet him several times, and I can tell you that this man exuded power and leadership. It just seemed to pour off of his body. When you stood next to him, you stood straighter! I must add, by this time in my career, I regularly associated with powerful people from all walks of life and was not intimidated by the powerful. He was a leader, taken down by a haughty press.

The press demonstrated conceit as they magnified his mistakes while never allowing that everyone slips up from time to time. In the case of the Vice President of the United States, the individual is constantly under the microscope. Everything he says or does is recorded, photographed, and reported.

> **TIP**
> An Axiom: Make up your own mind about people based on your interaction and observation of them.

Faces of Leadership Through Leaders' Eyes Thinking about leadership and how it plays out in you must be a constant in your life. You can always improve your style. As you have seen, attentiveness can be a major factor in who you become. Of course, developing the capacity to exert the discipline to make adjustments is a critical success factor. I have picked a sampling of anecdotes to share with you that demonstrate the face of leadership. Effective attentiveness can help you to find similar examples in your own life. These stories reflect many different faces but may not reflect the individual's most important face. Following is the list of attributes you will read about.

- Composure
- People
- Goodness
- Inclusion
- Integrity
- Rules

One of my most admired people is Mark Suwyn. He was incredible under fire. Mark would listen carefully and respond evenly. He was always trying to salvage whatever was possible from an interaction. Losing his temper was just not an option, because it is then that you are most likely to make a serious error. Observing Mark under duress, you didn't observe any visible distress: his demeanor was even-handed, his eyes focused, his voice modulation normal. He would seek clarification and often offer alternative means of dealing with the situation. Because of how he responded to stressful situations, he more often than not came out ahead in the interaction.

Everything he did was observable and workable for the observer. It was easy to see that he was assuring that the circumstances didn't disintegrate further, and if they did, it would not be because of him. While Mark was keeping his composure, often the opposing individual was losing his more and more. Before long you could easily see where confrontation was going to end. You could tell that he was always in control, and therefore he held the upper hand. Composure and control are faces of leadership with Mark.

Bob Albin feels the face of leadership is his face in the field with his people. The best way to keep everyone on message and to promote loyalty toward the cause is to be out in the field with associates on a regular basis—walking in their shoes with them, riding in their cars with them, going to dinners with them, or visiting their customers with them.

Bob talks about his trips in the field with his staff this way: "I got the chance to reinforce the message about the goals for the year, got a reality check of field versus Ivory Tower, and I built relationships with them. They could then always say, 'Remember when we did thus and so?' It was a shared relationship."

When the staff came into the home office for meetings, Bob knew who they were. He spent meaningful time with them, and for the staff, there was a certain comfort in that knowledge. He concluded with, "When you have those kinds of legs on the stool with staff, they have a tendency to support you and to do missionary work for you." All good! Bob's face of leadership involved being with his people on a regular basis and embracing them as an important part of the team.

When Jim Kelly thinks about the face of leadership, he sees someone who is trying to do good. He believes that you can choose to do good with your staff, customers, shareholders, and community, or you can choose to take advantage of them just to make more money. He says, "The amount of money you make, either as a person or a company, is not indicative of the quality of the business you run. It says something about the way you run your business, but it doesn't say anything about the way you treat your people or your customers."

Jim talks about how he wants to see himself and how he will be judged when his work life comes to an end. He believes that it is important to be seen as someone who did something beneficial for everyone he came in contact with—he believes that is the face of leadership.

To Ed McKenna, the face of leadership is inclusion. From personal experience early in his career, he discovered what it did for him when senior management asked him to participate in Chase's first attempts at developing credit scoring as a means of eliminating discrimination in lending. He was a member of the team but the only one who was passionate about the potential benefits for the consumer. He was allowed and encouraged to push this forward, which he did; one thing that impressed him the most was that he was not told to do it.

Ed included people when developing new systems or installing new processes. "Here's why we're doing it; here's what we expect to accomplish." What Ed realized was that, every time, at least one person would say, "How about this?" They would add something to the process, and by bits and pieces, they made the product better. At the very least, someone would raise a question that made him stop and think. Ed then had the opportunity to explain how it was going to work, so they could use it to do better. If the question pointed out a deficiency, they were on their way to a solution. Ed says, "People came away much more capable of doing their jobs and much more capable of making the way their job was done operate better."

Now, not everybody wants to share their thoughts. There are many reasons for this, but for Ed the number-one reason was trust. The only way you can overcome this sensitivity to trust is by consistently doing the same actions. You can't one day act in a fashion that is different from the next day. You can't treat one individual one way and others in a different way, which is the more common failing. People talk, and your actions get around. In time, you will build trust. For Ed, this is the face of leadership.

Mike Kozikowski is a different kind of politician. He stands for integrity and service. He is always available to his constituency and maintains a very high standard of ethical behavior, commitment to service, and efficiency of operation for his staff. He has gone to great lengths to improve how the office works and how people can access their documents. He has also created innovative DVDs to educate the public about the work of his agency. The people are the center of Mike's universe. Delivery of effective and efficient service with a human touch is the face of leadership for Mike.

For Russ Owen the face of leadership is integrity. To have people trust you is the only way they will follow you. So much energy is wasted in organizations with people protecting their backsides. "It far exceeds the productive output of the group," says Russ. "It can be difficult, but at all levels and in every decision you make, you as a leader must be a person of integrity."

Fairness and integrity are guiding forces for Russ. He believes that you should always tell people the truth because the interest earned on deceiving people just grows with time. If you don't have any secrets, then the kind of people who make their marks by manipulating information can't get their tracks on you because you have told everyone what is going on. "Those are the principles that I have carried with me throughout my life," concludes Russ.

When Chris Coons took over as county executive, he faced some severe challenges. His predecessor spread lots of rumors about what Chris was going to do upon taking office. None of them were good! Many people were fearful that they were about to lose their current position and perhaps even their entire careers.

Here's what Chris did. At his inaugural address he laid it out succinctly. He said, "To those of you who are willing and able and ready to change the way you work in this government and to be focused on serving the public, being accountable, and being respectful, I extend my hand to you. I am ready to work with you. I mean everybody. Those of you who are unwilling to change and are committed to an old way of doing things—there's the door."

He believed firmly that this posture was a matter of integrity, and from the very beginning he had to set the tone for his new administration. He kept his word, and to this day some five years later, he has avowed loyalists to the prior administration working with him at the highest levels of county government. His only interests are in how well you do your job, serve the public, be good stewards, and work together well. For Chris, that is the face of leadership.

Not all the faces of leadership are relational. The following is a story of a person I am friendly with who experienced non-relational leadership first hand in the waning days of his career. We had similar careers in the non-profit world and have known each other for a long time.

He served his organization with distinction for over 30 years and was coming upon retirement time. He was determined to retire with 35 years of service, but for some reason he miscalculated and turned in his papers with 34 years served. Because there were a couple of breaks in his service, he asked that his time be rechecked and recalculated if appropriate, but to no avail. It was done properly.

The report he received was accurate, including the dates of service along with the dates of his time away. When looking at the actual dates from his personnel records, he noticed a mistake in his starting date. He had actually worked part time during the two years prior to starting full time and that wasn't captured.

This is where the story gets interesting. When he reported the mistake, he was told by personnel that nothing could be done about it and that he should have questioned the discrepancy a long time ago. Personnel backed off this stance, but told him that he would have to prove that he worked there some 39 years prior; his word on the issue was not enough. The problem was that anyone who could have corroborated his time on the job back then had died or couldn't be located. Personnel would not back off of this requirement.

As it turned out, he was able to locate his tax return from 1971, and lo and behold, there was his W2 from the organization. Personnel was astonished by this but did accept it as proof. They now calculated his time on the job at 36.2 years.

But a problem still remained. Personnel had a rule, internal to the department, that they wouldn't recognize publicly service anniversary dates once they had passed. So they would provide the pin and certificate and the memento, but they wouldn't publish his picture in the awards program or allow him to speak to his colleagues from the podium (which was traditional for 35 years service).

Protests to higher authorities including the president of the organization fell on deaf ears—after all, a rule is a rule. It did not matter that his family would be in attendance at the ceremony, nor did it seem that much value was given to the three and one half plus decades of highly successful service he dedicated to the organization. The rules must be enforced as they are written! This statement would sum up the organization's face of leadership.

As I replayed this story in my mind, it was clear to me that people were not the central focus of this organization's belief systems. Knowing other people who worked for the company, I knew this wasn't always the case, and I wondered what this new attitude would do to its future success. Time will tell.

And then there is the tale of a gentleman who took advantage of Chris Coon's open door policy early in his tenure as county executive. He came to tell Chris about an incident which happened a year or two before. For this person his only job was with the county, and he had worked there diligently for 30 years. He was not highly placed in the county, but he served the people well in his capacity, worked hard, and was pleased to be a government employee.

Here is his story. As he was approaching his thirtieth year on the job, he knew he would receive a handsome clock as a token of his tenure. He was proud of his work record; he wasn't one of those stereotypical lazy types. He wondered with his wife what they would do for him on the actual anniversary day. He even prepared a little speech, though he was not accustomed to public addresses.

The day came; he was a little nervous but glad the day was here. He looked forward to the next eight hours with anticipation. Nothing happened in the morning or at lunch; not a word was said to him in recognition of his anniversary. When he returned from his break later that afternoon, much to his surprise there was the clock sitting on his chair. There was no note, no card, no flowers, no ceremony, no cause for the little speech he made up.

He went to his boss and asked hesitantly if the clock on his chair was the extent of the remembrance for his 30 years. Yes said the boss, and he was lucky to get the clock. That is what you get for 30 years on the job, nothing else is required, and he, the boss, would appreciate it if he got back to work!

The worker told Chris that he shared the story with him because he still hurt to this day by the way he was treated. He hoped that Chris could bring a new sense of respect to county government.

The lesson for a relational leader is clear—don't hide behind rules. Always favor people over rules. Use common sense. Respect the fuel that makes the engine work—your people. Both of the preceding stories could have ended differently and far more productively if common sense and respect were part of the fabric of the respective organizations, if their leadership was relational.

> **TIP**
> To create your face of leadership, you must first know how you want to be remembered after you've left the team.

It is you who must decide for yourself what kind of leader you will be. Your face of leadership will paint your company or team with the brush of your choosing. This is a consideration that you must spend a fair amount of time thinking about. It is almost like the management consultant asking you to write out what epitaph you want written on your tombstone. How do you want to be remembered after you have left your team behind? If you can get clear on that, then you can begin to build the foundations that will become your face of leadership.

Ingredients of Your Leadership Style

To be clear, as a leader you will pull from inside of yourself, the person you are. You will simultaneously pull traits from those around you whom you admire and mix them with your own personal style.

The fusion of your inner self with the exterior influence becomes your leadership recipe. What would be the ingredients? What makes you a leader? Is it the way you dress, comb your hair, or the manner of your speech? Does it have to do with your actions, personality, or reputation? Is it your style, connections, or athleticism? Is it your wit, track record, or demeanor? Just what is it that makes a leader a leader? Why would anyone follow you? These questions have been asked time and again throughout the ages. For some, the answers are elusive; for you they don't have to be.

We know today intuitively that people are not born leaders. They may have tendencies that would enable them to lead, but many people do if we develop what we've got. So in order for you to develop what you've got, you have to know what it is that you've got! You also need to know what other people have got. It is the combination of who you are and what you can pull from others whom you admire that will enable you to become a great leader.

The surest route toward developing a comfortable style of leadership is to observe others who are leaders—watch what they do and how they comport themselves. Analyze the individual. Much like a sports team studying an opponent, you need to break down the person's tendencies. What's on the surface? What's inside? What seems to be working for her? Why did I feel that this person was so admirable in the first place? Perhaps an even better question is, What seems to be working for her that I can incorporate into who I am?

148

In order for you to successfully employ this strategy, you need to have a good understanding of who you are. A self inventory is a good idea. What are the ingredients that make up you? Take a look at both sides. What are your good traits, and then, what are your not so good traits? You can make a list, and certainly your friends and associates will help you add to it, if you ask. You can take a personality assessment or a career assessment. Both are very common on the market today and not very expensive.

> **TIP**
>
> An Axiom: Leaders are mindful of who they are, what they are made of, what they stand for, what they will tolerate, and what they cannot tolerate.

Once you understand who you are, you can begin your search for people who can help you become who you want to be. For instance, let's say that you have a tendency to lose your temper easily. You might want to seek out people in your acquaintance who are able to keep their "cool" under any circumstance. Or you may just decide that any good leadership is worth examining, even if it doesn't fill a hole for you right now. This strategy is a good one, too. You can always improve upon the personality and character traits that you currently display. Why not do so with someone who proves to you that they are outstanding at what they do? Remember, we are all a sum total of our experiences.

Summary

It is important to understand that the mind controls much of what you are able to do when you are involved with change. You must be convinced and ready to change, and you have to let your mind in on it—open yourself up, free yourself! By doing this you put your mind in control, enabling you to apply the discipline it takes to adopt new behaviors.

Leaders are not born, although people may come predisposed or "hard wired" with leadership qualities. The development of these qualities depends entirely upon the will of the individual to embrace and nurture them. People who do not have such obvious qualities with genetic coding can still be effective, even great, leaders. It depends upon your will to become a leader.

In either instance, it depends further upon your motivation to listen and observe. To the extent that you can identify people whom you admire and can identify what makes them admirable, you are on your way. The idea is to fold in the best of who they are with who you are. You become an amalgamation of many people, which becomes the new you, a distinct individual. This process happens anyway, but when you are purposeful about it, the results are better and more predictable.

Discipline and visualization are both mind games that are vital to your success. Staying on course and creating a picture of you succeeding will make your goal of becoming relational much easier. Doing the hard work of taking on this process of change step by step gives you a firm foundation from which to move forward. Taking shortcuts weakens the foundation making your long-term success less reliable. Risk is a significant part of the American economic system but not the "bet the house" type of risk taking. You only want to risk that which you can afford to lose.

Power is a funny thing. The more you have of it, the more you control events and people, the less control you seem to have over your own ambition. This causes you to do things that at another time and place you wouldn't. A firmly rooted character will block these tendencies to take advantage of your power position. Being relational precludes the misuse of power simply because its elements won't allow it. This should be reason enough to embrace relationalism as a philosophy that counteracts immorality and ethics-less behavior.

There are many faces of leadership. You will show the face that is appropriate for the time and situation. You saw examples of some of the faces, such as composure, people, goodness, inclusion, integrity, and even a nonrelational face, rules. It is important to realize that you will acquire these faces over time, not overnight. They will develop as you sharpen your skills.

In the end, you know that discipline is the key to incorporating the principles of relational leadership into your life. It is what keeps you on task. Attentiveness is what attracts the experience of people you admire so that you can emulate their makeup and actions. Attentiveness also helps you to understand the negative character traits and events that you should avoid as a leader. Applying the principles of focus, commitment, readiness, applause, and partnering will enable you to develop discipline.

Remember and commit to the philosophy of Napoleon Hill: "Whatever the mind can conceive and believe, the mind can achieve." It is a powerful tool, maybe the most powerful tool you have in your entire arsenal.

KEEP IN MIND:

■ The discipline to remain committed, to push away distraction, to keep your goal in view is the doctrine of a winner.

■ Your mind has to be engaged in the process before you make a decision to take action; that's what gets you ready. When you take action, your mind is in charge of the process; that's discipline. If you are not ready, it is improbable that you will be able to muster the discipline to sustain the effort.

■ Winners do the things that failures refuse to do.

■ Visualization is a winning strategy, and like discipline, it involves the mind's active participation.

■ A winner who fails gets back up and digs in again, confident that this new effort will get her where she sees herself. A failure seeks to place blame for her inability to achieve results, but that blame rarely is placed where it belongs—on herself.

■ What I do know for certain is that the formula for success can't be a shortcut.

■ When you use your powers of observation and listening to help you shape the kind of person you want to be, you actually take on the personas of many people. The objective: meld the many into one—you.

■ A relational leader can't misuse power because his moral and ethical compass is well fixed. He is governed by attributes that do not permit bad behavior.

Chapter 7

Tips for Building the New You

"Be a person of character versus
a person of convenience."
—*F. J. McIntosh*

- Discovering Yourself
- Summary

hapter 6 discussed strategies for developing the leader in you. In order to be an effective relational leader, it may be necessary for you to change how you do certain activities. There is nothing about becoming relational that is detrimental to your being. The shift, to the extent that you must shift, will simply make you a better person. As your relational skills become more pronounced, you'll transform into a better leader. Building your strengths, visualization, risk management, and attentiveness are among the many strategies that, if effectively implemented, will make your leadership qualities shine.

With that in mind, this chapter will help you be purposeful in designing the new you and enacting strategies to bring the shift about. I am a firm believer in hands-on learning. Personal involvement in a project will engage you at multiple levels. The outcome will have more value to you, and the end product will likely be a better one. Actively engaging in the process of change will help you to assist others as they strive to change and make you an authentic leader. The tips contained here will give you the keys you need to alter yourself to the necessary degree. You will learn to engage in the process of change as well as appreciate just how much more this engagement enables you to retain the information in order to use it practically and effectively.

TIP

There is a powerful Chinese proverb that goes like this: Telling me, I forget; showing me, I remember; involving me, I understand.

Discovering Yourself

First and foremost, you must understand yourself. What are your character traits? What strengths do you possess? This knowledge will help you make decisions about what you need to focus on to improve your relational style. The focus should be on your strengths. Building on your strengths is the most effective way to improve your capabilities.

If you have participated in any sort of personality assessment in the past, dig out the results. If you haven't and would like to, there are two very good books put out by the Gallup organization that I highly recommend. *Now Discover Your Strengths* and *StrengthsFinder 2.0*. They also have an excellent online assessment called StrengthsFinder, which is free if you buy one of the books (though the extended report costs money). If neither of these work for you, the following steps will help you acquire the sketch of yourself you need.

1a. Go online and complete a personality assessment of your choosing.

OR

1b. Create a comprehensive spread sheet of personality traits. (You can get examples of traits from an Internet search.)

2. Ask friends and family to check off traits that are descriptive of you; also inform them they can add traits that are not listed on the form if they think that is appropriate.

3. Do this same exercise yourself.

4. Compare the results by highlighting traits that are mentioned multiple times, as they will become the top traits in a new list you will make.

5. Decide for yourself if this profile is descriptive of you. If it is, create a new list. Separate what you perceive as your strengths and weaknesses in the list. Put the most prominent of either category at the top and work in descending order of relevance until you get to the point where you deem you have a trait, but it is not a very strong one. Draw a line across the page. You have now created a list of your most prominent strengths and weaknesses.

Just a word or two about this exercise before moving on: There is really no need to be scientific here. It's about you, and you probably know quite a bit about yourself, even before doing the exercise. What you are trying to do is get an objective viewpoint of the kind of person you are and the character and personality traits you possess. This knowledge will help you make decisions about what you will focus on to improve your style. A word of caution, though. Don't make it a big project or let it overwhelm you. It's pretty easy, particularly with the Internet. The key is getting good feedback from friends and family.

TIP

Give your friends and family the character list you created from the Internet search (leaving room for additional traits to be added by them, if they choose) and a self-addressed stamped envelope. This way they can remain anonymous, and you will get better feedback. Be sure to give them a deadline for returning the survey. It should be within a very brief timeframe to maximize returns. The checklist should only take them a few minutes to review and evaluate.

Building on Strengths versus Improving Weaknesses

In the preceding exercise, you separated the strengths from the weaknesses because you are going to concentrate on building your strengths. You listed your weaknesses because it is nice to know what they are, and if you can do something about them, you should. Marcus Buckingham and Donald Clifton, authors of *Now, Discover Your Strengths* (The Free Press, 2001), strongly suggest that strength building is the most productive method of improving your performance.

In my experience, Buckingham and Clifton are right on target. Too much time is wasted on trying to correct people's weaknesses. At best, try to neutralize your weaknesses. Spend time on making your strengths stronger. This is much easier to do and frankly much more profitable in terms of results. You will be well ahead of the game.

TIP

You have a much better chance of building up your strengths than you do of improving your weaknesses. Your strengths already come naturally to you, and therefore, will increase as you practice them.

Twenty years ago, no one was thinking about building strengths. Performance reviews concentrated on an individual's weaknesses. You were sent away to training to help make your weaknesses disappear. It was your weaknesses that your manager discussed with you, and rarely your strengths. Enlightened leaders of today realize that it is your strengths that will drive your performance, and their success is about their ability to match your strengths with the jobs the company needs done.

I had a person working for me back in my Denver days named Howard. His father was the CEO of the major utility in town, and his brother was a senior vice president. Howard was one of my program managers at Junior Achievement. Business might have been in the family's blood, but it wasn't in Howard's. He tried and tried to shore up his weaknesses because that was what I told him to do. (This was before I had my epiphany on strength building!) There was never a lack of effort on Howard's part; he just didn't get it. He made the same mistakes over and over again. He did not understand how to plan his day to achieve maximum results from his efforts, goals were a nebulous concept, and timelines challenged him.

Finally, we had to let Howard go. He was relieved because, even working as hard as he did, he wasn't able to put it together. The stress he suffered was overwhelming him. In fact, he and I both believed his efforts were causing even more problems as he tried to improve. The good news was that he went on to become a dental hygienist and was very happy and productive at this work. He brought his strengths with him that included friendliness, a concern for people, and being very accommodating. The business world did not play to his strengths. Concentrating on improving his weaknesses did not improve his performance significantly. Instead, it actually frustrated him more. Had I worked on his strengths and if I had had a job that aligned with those strengths, it could well have been a different outcome.

> **TIP**
> Define yourself; don't let anyone else define you.

Skip Schoenhals, who commandeered the revitalization of WSFS Bank, believes deeply in building on strengths. He gives the example that he is smart enough to be a pilot, but you would not want him in the pilot's seat flying a 747 to Los Angeles if you were a passenger. He is not "hard wired" in the way a pilot is hard wired. He is a big picture guy, not a detail guy.

Early in Skip's career he had the job of comptroller in a bank. It was clear that he could do part of the job, but he was missing important pieces along the way. Senior management thought they could "fix" him with more training, so off to "comptroller school" he went. Well, he is smart, so he was able to improve by a modicum. However, he did not improve to the standard that was needed. In his words, "I probably improved from a 3 to a 4 when I needed to be at an 8." It was very stressful and trying for him, as it usually is for anyone placed in that situation.

I don't want to leave you thinking that you never do anything with weaknesses. Skip improved at comptroller school but not enough to make a significant difference in performance. As a CEO, where his strengths lay, he far exceeds the average. Weaknesses can be improved, just not as quickly or productively as your strengths. In my view, you simply want to put yourself in a position where your weaknesses don't get in the way. You want to neutralize them as best as you can.

Your energy must be placed on strength building. The reason why strengths can be built upon more easily is because you already possess them and are successful using them in your day-to-day existence. If your strengths are strong enough, they will overshadow your weaknesses.

Applying Your Self-Knowledge to an Improvement Strategy

Now that you have a clear picture of yourself, you are going to put it to work building a better you. Now is the time to be purposeful about the knowledge you have of yourself and others. The object of the following exercise is to identify traits of someone you admire that you want to have others see in you. You are going to convert your observations into something concrete that can help drive the change within yourself.

Begin by selecting someone you respect and know well from observing him over time. This would be a person who is successful at whatever it is he does and that you hold in high regard. Conjure up in your mind's eye a picture of this person. Make notes about him on a piece of paper. What are his best traits? What does he do well? How does he do it?

Now create a simple chart like the one shown in Figure 7.1. (Additional copies can be downloaded from www.fjmcintosh.com.) Write the person's name at the top. List a trait of the individual you admire in the first column. Check if that is a trait that you possess, rating it on a scale of 1 to 5, with 5 being the highest. Now do the same for how important you think this trait is to your success as a leader, rating it on the same scale. Continue until you have listed all of their admirable traits that you can think of.

Look over your results. You may notice that you share some strengths relatively equally. You may also find that the subject's strengths are not your strengths. By looking at the importance you assigned to the strength, you will get an idea how much effort you should put into replicating it for yourself. Finally, jot down some strategies you could use to incorporate this trait into your own personality. This becomes your roadmap to improving your status as a relational leader. The best leaders will consciously study the habits of people they admire to improve themselves.

Let's look at an example of a person I once worked for in Denver, Dale Baxter. He was a really good boss and became a really good friend. When I agreed to work for him, friends told me that this would be a big mistake; he was impossible to get along with, and I would be constantly struggling and frustrated. Had I misjudged Dale because of my interview with him? I wasn't getting these vibes.

My friends also said he was very argumentative (what do you want from a National Debate champion?) and he was very controlling (not unreasonable from a "world class" wrestler). They said he wouldn't let you do anything interesting. The truth was he didn't argue, he challenged; he didn't control, he tested. If you had your facts and could put forth a case that demonstrated something good would occur from your actions, and you established some

Style Improvement Strategy Chart

Name			Date
Trait	**I Possess This Trait** 1(low) to 5(high)	**Importance of This Trait to Me** 1(low) to 5(high)	**Possible Strategies**

Figure 7.1 *Use this blank copy of the Style Improvement Strategy Chart to start an exercise.*

sort of positive track record, the green light was always on. I'm thinking my colleagues didn't know Dale very well.

So, if I were filling this form out with Dale in mind at that time in my life, what would it look like? For purposes of this discussion, I filled in a couple of lines to give you an idea of how this works (see Figure 7.2).

As shown in this example, I would have concentrated on observing and improving the traits of being detailed and analytical. You can see that I have some strategies that will help me improve in these areas and incorporate them into my regular routine.

Style Improvement Strategy Chart

Name Dale Baxter			Date
Trait	**I Possess This Trait** 1(low) to 5(high)	**Importance of This Trait to Me** 1(low) to 5(high)	**Possible Strategies**
Detailed	2	5	Research important projects: facts, what if's, projected outcomes, ask Dale lots of questions.
Trustworthy	5	5	No action needed.
Analytical	2	4	I'm instinctive and want to stay that way—will improve by observation of others.
Fun loving	5	5	No action needed.
Intelligent	4	4	Always try to be smarter—use observation and listening skills.

Figure 7.2 *The chart gives an example of how the traits of an admired person are rated and the strategies that you can build on surrounding the trait to improve yourself.*

Being trustworthy and intelligent are already pretty much in line between my skill level and his. They are also fairly important traits. Therefore, I do not concentrate on these traits, but I would keep track of possible areas of improvement that Dale may show me from time to time. I would check my own strategies from time to time to ensure that I was getting what I needed from my observation or listening activities. I would check with myself and others to see if they thought I was doing better with details and analysis. I would try to be very specific about where I saw improvement, what it was, and how I could do even better. I might want to tweak my strategies if I felt I wasn't improving at the rate I believed I was capable of.

I would also bring Dale in to partner with me if I thought I needed his direct person-to-person assistance. If you decide to involve the individual personally (you don't have to; it's up to you), you can do this at any time in the process. You simply explain what you are up to, why, and how he might be involved.

There is one caution: When you let the individual in, it is unwise to restrict his input. If you are opening the door, then you should be ready to receive what he has to say, without being defensive. As I am sure you are aware, this is easier to say than to actually do.

Summary

Observation is an activity that we all do but not always effectively. Observation is listening with your eyes. Unfortunately, not everyone is a good listener, but as human beings, we seem to talk more about listening than seeing. While listening is a vital trait of a leader, observing is too.

As you begin transforming yourself into a relational leader, you want to concentrate on strength-building. This is where you are most likely to succeed. As you build your strengths, your weaknesses will become less important.

Finally, develop strategies that will help you capitalize on what you already have and additional strategies that can incorporate your mentor's strengths into your personality. Pay no attention to the mentor's deficits, unless you line them up with opposing strengths. Spend your energy on where you are already strong or where you believe that you have the capacity to become strong.

Now you have a tool that you can use to build your inventory of leadership strengths. Pay particular attention to your strengths that are relational by nature. As you build your inventory, you will be continually upgrading the most important traits you possess; the most important ones will always be the relational traits that enhance your interpersonal skill set.

In time, you will do all of this in your head. It will become instinctive to you. You will see someone doing something and know immediately where it fits into your plan. Then you will develop a strategy to adopt it over time. Like most activities, the more you implement the plan, the better you will get at it. Practice on multiple subjects. Observe activity, and then filter what you observe. How does this particular activity impact relational leadership? Critically appreciate what is going on in the scene; is this a positive or negative? Can I take something away from what I am observing? What is it? Can I do something that will help the person I am observing?

If the behavior you are observing is negative, don't discard this type of input. It can be as instructional to learn from poor leadership as it can be from good leadership. Many people will tell you this. In fact, Skip Schoenhals has said that virtually everything he learned about being relational and running a business came from observing behavior that was negative, at least in his eyes. He knew what he wouldn't do.

You may recall my example of the start-up bank back in Chapter 1. Much, if not all, of what I observed there was negative. The CEO regularly strayed from virtually all of the principles of relational leadership. Any attempt at building a relational atmosphere was clearly a pretense.

One example of this entailed what appeared to be a very relational activity. Just like Nathan Hill, whom I described as having a "walking around" strategy, the start-up bank CEO liked to roam around the office from time to time to demonstrate that he was available and he cared about his staff. So, like Nathan, he would often stop by everyone's cubicle or office upon his arrival for work and chat for a moment. However, unlike Nathan, it was clear to the people that he was typically distracted while conducting this ritual. In fact, by his actions, he was shouting out, *I'm not available and I don't really care.* What could have been effective relationally became simply an interruption that had little value.

Instead of attempting to engage in small talk, which the CEO demonstrated by his body language that he really didn't want to do, he could simply have gone from person to person and said with a nice big smile, "Good Morning, and have a great day," or something to that effect. The effect would have at least been positive. But however you approach this process of observation and interaction, your objective is to build your relational skill set. The leader in you demands it. Take the time and make the commitment to do it right.

TIP

Sincerity is vital to your interactions. People read you easily. Your insincerity is transparent and becomes quite detrimental to your overall objectives. Do only what you mean to do, make it purposeful (not what looks good), and never promise that which you have no intention of delivering.

KEEP IN MIND:

- Beware of non-relational behavior that is dressed up as relational behavior, and be cautious of the individual responsible.
- Building on strengths is easier and far more effective than trying to improve upon weaknesses.
- When you personally involve yourself in any activity, you are likely to see a better and more permanent result.
- Demonstrating sincerity and empathy for people are cornerstones for developing a spirit of trust in an organization.
- It is almost impossible to fix somebody. Divorce courts are filled with failed attempts.
- Don't let anyone define who you are; take the time to figure out the real you, and then allow yourself to become that person.

Chapter 8

Creating a Great Place to Work

"We will either find a way, or make one."
—*Hannibal*

- The Building Blocks of Trust
- Make Stress a Positive Force
- Summary

Sue Linderman, a former Junior Achievement student member, board member (chair), and National Leadership Award winner created a great place to work when she recast the performance measurement metrics of the regional sales group she managed. The measurement would now be based on collective performance of the entire team. She wanted to create an environment where the sales people supported each other for the overall good of the business as opposed to looking out for themselves alone. People were skeptical in the beginning. They didn't like the idea of working together on a sales call. But it worked and people were much happier on their jobs thereafter. Sue said about the program, "There were 20 sales districts in the country. We went from 17th to number one in only two years' time. It happened because they were helping one another and pooling their strengths. This turned out to be one of my greatest accomplishments from a bottom-line perspective." Sue's career included assignments in Information Systems as director and business director for the X-Ray business at DuPont, and later as president of Sterling Diagnostic Imaging.

Investing in your people is one sure way to create a great place to work. I really liked what Russ Owen said about his people because it really puts the importance of people into perspective. It bears repeating. "Ninety percent of our intellectual property takes the elevator home at night. We have to take care of our people to maintain our competitive edge."

He describes his style as "leading from the heart." By this he means being collaborative, trusting, having integrity, doing the right thing, being supportive and challenging, and finally being compassionate. As he went into managerial and leadership positions, he realized that he needed to shift his style from "an accomplisher of things to an understander of things." Russ quotes Dan Fogelburg, the singer/songwriter, when Russ thinks about relationships with staff as "a sculptor of souls." Russ says, "As a leader, you try to develop people to succeed, and your job satisfaction shifts from things you built to people you built."

According to The Great Place to Work Institute, Inc., trust is the foundation and defining characteristic of a great workplace based on its research over the past 20 years. You will get no argument from me except to say, in my view, that it goes beyond trust.

The relational leader makes trust important, along with the other attributes of the relational model. It is the combination of all of the elements that cements the concept of trust. When they stand together, they are all stronger, as is the leader and the organization. The organization emerges as a great place to work because of the focus on its core—its people.

So ultimately there are two pieces to building a great workplace: (1) a relational style of leadership and (2) an environment energized by positive tension. You are fortunate indeed if you can say about your employer, "This is a great place to work." However, no one policy, individual, or benefit will make this statement become a reality. It is the combination of many related ideas, activities, and people that make it so. This chapter will explore many aspects and specifics about creating a great workplace, where people feel valued as individuals and where stress becomes a productive and positive tension.

The Building Blocks of Trust

You cannot have a great place to work unless trust is inherent in the entire organization. You generate a trusting environment when you pay attention to the things people value. It is not about what you value or even what you think your people value. It is always about what the people themselves value. The following principles are the *building blocks of trust* and will get you started. They are not meant to be all-encompassing, but each is a concept that people care about.

- Be consistent.
- Be fair.
- Align words and actions.
- Admit mistakes and correct them.
- Encourage ideas and give the owner authority to implement them, if possible.
- Celebrate people's accomplishments, both large and small.
- Hire people who demonstrate relational tendencies.
- Connect to your people in ways that demonstrate you care.
- Have fun (don't be stuffy).
- Treat people as you want to be treated.

People are valued when their environment "speaks" to them with respect, challenges them with work equal to or greater than their competence, and expects them to succeed by providing resources that enable them to achieve their objectives. I would always tell new employees that I accept no responsibility for their success, that it was up to them personally to succeed. I was responsible for providing an atmosphere in which they could succeed, and I held myself accountable to that end.

> **TIP**
> Advertise the building blocks of trust within your organization so that every-
> one knows what you are trying to accomplish as a leader.

So that you better understand the building blocks, I will discuss each one individually. It would be wise to build a company implementation plan that
expresses the values laid out in the blocks and provides measurable objectives
for delivering against the values and producing an atmosphere of trust.

Consistency

Consistency is vital to any relationship. It is very upsetting when you do not
know what to expect from leadership. You will adjust to just about anything
if you know what to expect, even if you don't like it.

Take baseball, for instance. Baseball has a well-defined strike zone, and it is
the umpire's job to judge a pitch to be either a ball or a strike based on this
defined zone. Batters are trained to swing at pitches thrown in this area.
Because all this judgment is not an exact science, umpires call pitches strikes
that technically should be balls, and batters swing at pitches that are not
strikes. What matters most to a batter is that the umpire consistently calls the
pitches the same way throughout the game. He can adjust. What a batter
can't tolerate is an umpire who has a "moving" strike zone, that is to say, he
is not consistent with his calls.

The people who work with you must know what to expect from you at all
times. It is very important. You establish who you are by regularly doing the
same things over and over. You must understand that your staff makes decisions about their own behavior based on their perception of your behavior.
If they view you as an individual who will bend rules to your favor, they will
take license to bend rules to their favor, and so on.

One of Nathan Hill's goals for his organization at Discover Card was consistency. He wanted Discover to be a great place to work. He put a plan in
place and worked the plan month after month, never veering from his objective. He believed the company should be a place of consistency so that it
could also be a place of trust. I trust you, you trust the leadership team, and
together everybody achieves more.

His philosophy went like this: I will be honest with you always. I will provide
you with the necessary training, tools, and feedback you need to do your job
well. But most importantly I will provide you with recognition for the things
you do well. You will be challenged to give a bit more; then we are going to

celebrate it, and then we are going to ask you again to do a bit more. Anyone who worked at Discover Card during Nathan's tenure knows that this was the way he operated—they could "bank" on it.

Consistency is reassuring. It provides stability. It builds credibility. It is reliable. It is a building block of trust. Trust is a critical success factor in a great place to work.

Fairness

Fairness is another building block of trust. It means that you treat people respectfully and equitably, regardless of their position in the organization. It means that hiring and promotions are considered without bias. One group is not favored over another group for benefits. Pay is based on the economic contributions you make to the business's success. Gender, ethnicity, race, or myriad other statuses are not considered in policy decisions or business planning. Essentially, each person, as much as possible, is treated as a human being deserving her own sense of dignity.

For example, at WL Gore and Associates, expertise is honored over station (where you stand in the company's employee structure). Bill and Vieve Gore, the company's founders believed that individuals would naturally rise to leadership roles in areas where they had a specific expertise. Everyone in the company was respected and treated with dignity.

Chris Coons, prior to being elected county executive, worked at WL Gore and Associates. He talked with me about the company's methods of operation. Gore is known for its workplace practices, and particularly for its lack of a hierarchical structure. Essentially, anyone can speak to anyone in the company about a business process, a new idea, or any pertinent activity concerning Gore and its success, even if the person's last name is Gore! At Gore, this level of communication is accepted, but it's not so true at most other companies. The barriers presented in communication can be quite detrimental to success.

Mark Suywn approaches this communication challenge differently and systematically. He talks about how he addressed this challenge at New Page with a program he called "Speaking Truth to Power." It is a format that all employees were taught to use when having difficult conversations with senior managers (the Power). Difficult conversations are defined as any time you have to speak to someone at any level where you are uncomfortable. Because everyone knows how to conduct a conversation using Speaking Truth to Power, it is a lot safer, particularly for the subordinate. Everybody behaves better, because all agreed to use the format. It designs the conversation so that it (a) identifies the underlining emotional issues, (b) teaches participants how to express their concerns without emotion, (c) offers both sides the ability to respond, and (d) provides an "off-ramp" that asks, "What do you want me to do?" Speaking Truth to Power flushes out the hidden agenda that can sometimes develop when issues are left to fester. People learn to respectfully bring up issues and ideas, and they learn to force their managers to be better managers.

In Mark's words, "The key is to give people the courage, skills, and training to handle the confrontations on difficult issues. The process reduces stress, and it helps create a positive environment. I want every part of the organization to be a dramatically better place to work. When you're emotionally engaged, you will work harder to make things work better than if you are just following orders."

> **TIP**
> Having the ability to speak across functional lines and employment levels to address issues is a positive force in achieving objectives.

This type of program reinforces fairness because it levels the playing field for all participants. It encourages people in the company to speak up when there are areas of conflict. It gives every employee the capacity to make suggestions. It changes the dynamics between and among employee groups. It builds trust.

Align Words and Actions

When your words and actions fuse as one, you are seen as authentic. However, when you are disconnected between what you say and what you do, you're a fraud. You are viewed as autocratic and from the old school of "Do what I say, not what I do!" Not very good, if you mean to be a relational leader.

Back in the early 1990s, we were in a major economic turndown. Money at Junior Achievement was extremely tight. I was confronted with a situation that tested my alignment between saying one thing and doing another.

At this time the organization was not very "tech savvy," but I could certainly appreciate the value of a computer and the part it would play in our future. One person on the staff tended toward the geek-like personality, or at the least, he was computer literate. In those days for most of us, it was hard to tell the difference. The organization and I relied on him quite a bit.

One day he arrived at my office with a Cheshire grin on his face. He announced proudly that he had acquired the new Microsoft software that we really wanted to buy but couldn't afford. There was a moment of elation tempered on my part by the grin on his face. When something is too good to be true, it most often is not true!

I asked how he came about getting the software, and he indicated that he got it through a friend. Being a bit of a spoilsport, I asked if the friend also gave him the licenses to go along with the software. He became crestfallen, and that was all I needed as an answer.

I told him, "We don't do that here, and you know it. Please return the software immediately." I added that he should never accept such an offer again, suspecting all the while that he had probably initiated the request.

The consequences of this very brief discussion could have been ruinous. If I hadn't responded as I did, it would have given him and the rest of the staff license to be dishonest. It is a very slippery slope from there.

> **TIP**
>
> An Axiom: Know yourself and what you stand for, as well as what you will not tolerate. Know this before you are placed in a situation that requires you to act decisively and quickly.

For the most part, if you are well grounded in your beliefs, you will be okay. However, as a leader you don't get very many breaks. There is an expectation that you will always act as you talk and sometimes you may slip. Most people will give you a "bye" on this but not everyone, probably because you haven't yet reached the highest level of trust.

Keep in mind that you are in ground-breaking territory when you establish a relationally lead organization. Most people haven't experienced anything like it yet in the workplace. So for them, it is still a test, and you're the one being tested. You don't want people saying, "See, I told you so. He's no different from…." You must be very careful about what you say. Commit right now to never—and I mean never—saying anything that you are not prepared to back up with action.

Admit Mistakes and Fix Them

It is only the ego that stops you from retracting a decision, which upon reflection, you deem to be wrong. Get the ego out of your head. Categorically, ego-driven certitudes and relational leadership are mutually exclusive.

Everyone makes mistakes; it's part of being human. To pretend otherwise diminishes us in the face of our peers and subordinates. Leaders sometimes get caught up in always being right. They think that is an expectation of leadership. The contrary is true. I believe that leaders are elevated in the eyes of peers and subordinates when they can admit they have made a mistake and are willing to correct it. The idea is to get it right so that the organization can move on effectively.

When you accept the concept that anyone can make a mistake—even you— it frees you to act. The freedom to act allows you to make a decision and to make it more quickly. The direction is set, and your organization is moving. Organizations need action to be effective and to achieve results. No doubt you are in a leadership role because your decisions are usually right. Ultimately, the only mistake that will be held against you is the one that you refuse to admit and don't attempt to fix.

TIP

An Axiom: Arrogance is not a quality that is admired by many. In a leader, it goes hand in hand with omnipotence, which is generally not applied to humans. Admitting mistakes makes the leader more of a real person in the eyes of the people he leads, which is generally viewed as good.

Following is an example of a mistake I made and what I did about it. But first a word about decisions—when you make a decision, it is based on the best available data you have in front of you, and for most leaders, what their instincts tell them. More often than not, mistakes come about because your data was insufficient or faulty or circumstances change and you don't. So at the beginning, the decision can look okay, but over time it loses its potency because of new factors that come to light. Now, here is my personal example.

The early 1990s were as bad to Junior Achievement as the late 2000s are to everyone (just about)! JA could not meet its normal budgetary requirements. One of the concepts working its way around business at the time was *self-managed teams*. (I spoke about this briefly in Chapter 4 in a different context.) The theory was that by reducing layers of management and putting authority directly with those on the front line, you could get better results for less cash outlay. In fairness to the self-managed team enthusiasts (assuming there are some left), it was more complicated than what I just described. At its very essence, though, this was it and for purposes of this discussion, I will leave it at that.

I tried to do all the right things, including talking to the self-managed team gurus and attending workshops on the subject. I brought in a consultant to facilitate the system turnover, and we even took to the "ropes course" all in the name of *team*.

> **NOTE**
> The *ropes course* was an activity that brought the whole team together to participate in some physical outdoor activities, like wall climbing, trust walks, and mazes. Some of the activities (like the maze) were centered around a group, where the team members needed to help each other to complete the exercise; others were individual activities, where the role of the team was to encourage a single participant.

The idea of self-managed teams was that everybody shared in the decision-making, including compensation. Work functions blended according to ability. There was little in the way of individual accomplishment. It was all about the team, and as you have undoubtedly heard said, there is no "me" in team, unless you rearrange the letters, which of course doesn't make it team anymore.... Okay, I'll move on.

To make a long and painful story short, it wasn't working very well for our team. They did want to be part of the decision process but only on a selected basis. For instance, there was no interest in being involved in areas such as determining salary increases. With regard to the big company decisions, the team still wanted me to make those calls.

It was also interesting that the same people who complained about their colleagues' performance in the pre-self-managed days found these same people to be average performers when it came to salary review in the new system. As a matter of fact, it seemed that everyone was average. Staff could not really bring themselves to this level of evaluation. When it came to salary decisions, everyone was egalitarian. Please understand, that did not mean that in their hearts they really felt this way. They just were very uncomfortable expressing it "publicly."

As it turned out, what they truly wanted was the right of input, which is a very different concept. In actuality, they already had that, and they continued to maintain it after I put self-managed teams "to bed for a long winter's nap!" With the training they received in the team concept, their input became much sharper and more on point. So this was a good result from the effort—perhaps the only one.

When you make a mistake, admit it, fix it, and move on! No one protested when we dropped the project after about 18 months of effort.

Encourage Ideas

How do you think the group feels when you ask for ideas, get them, and then nothing happens with those ideas? How do you think a person feels whose idea is accepted but then she's cut out of the loop?

The answer to the first question is pretty easy. Most often, people will feel like you really don't want any ideas, as you have already cornered the market on them. People are unlikely to quit over this circumstance, but you will never get their full efforts while they are with you.

The answer to the second question is a bit more complex. Much of the answer revolves around the capacity of the person who came up with the idea. It doesn't take a rocket scientist to come up with an idea, but it might well take a rocket scientist to implement the idea. If it is within the individual's skill set to implement the idea, give her the opportunity to do so. You will be amazed at the new level of interest people will have in thinking about better ways to accomplish tasks.

TIP

It's not just about encouraging ideas; it's about giving the person who came up with the idea the authority to oversee the project to completion. When people are involved in the idea generation of the company, they take on ownership that otherwise did not exist and are willing to work harder to achieve results.

The big leap of faith for a leader is accepting the ideas of others. After all, most leaders got to be leaders because they had ideas that were good, and they knew how to implement them successfully. This is where you have to be serious about shifting your viewpoint on ideas. Even you had ideas that were a bit iffy along the way. Skip Schoenhals refers to rejecting other people's ideas as *dream blocking*. Don't be a dream blocker; be a dream maker.

You probably remember the story I told from Mark Suwyn and his Maine New Page plant. One of his mill workers came up with an idea that cut down-time on a process to zero hours, saving the company millions of dollars. This person had been working there for 32 years. Mark says, "You have to ask yourself, why now, after all these years did he come up with the idea for this final tweak of the process? He is emotionally invested. He understands if the mill runs better, he will have a job longer. He might have had this idea before, but he had no way to express what he knew. We created an environment where he was either comfortable or compelled to think of ways to help the business."

One of my staff, Dave Nichols, came to me with an idea for improving one of our signature events, The Character Rally. This program was the brainchild of General Chuck Krulak and myself. Chuck was the former Commandant of the United States Marine Corp and a member of the JA board. Character flowed through his bloodstream. We were both pretty vested in the construct of the program and not very interested in changing much of it.

Dave put together a competent argument for the change, and after much discussion and soul searching, I gave him the green light. He took charge of the program and was fully responsible for its outcome. I did this not because I actually wanted to make the change; I did it because it was important that he and other staff see that change was okay, that they could be part of it, and that I would support it, even if it messed with one of my very own "babies."

You build trust when you create an environment where people feel that their thoughts are valued and that they will be recognized for their thinking. Relational leaders understand that the idea maker is vested in the concept he thought of. The leader will give the individual the opportunity to take on the implementation of the project wherever possible.

Celebrate Accomplishments

Celebrating accomplishments does more than just recognize the individual(s) involved—celebration sends a clear message to all people in the organization about what is valued. It is often said that what is measured gets accomplished. It is just as true with what is celebrated. What we honor is sought after.

A key component to any non-profit organization is its board of directors. As the CEO, it was vital to me to recruit the right board members (no less important than hiring the right person), keep them happy and engaged, and to keep them focused on achieving the organization's objectives. To this end, I had an effective device that I began in Junior Achievement of Denver where I served as a senior vice president before going to Delaware. I called it "Driving for JA." Here's how it worked. At the end of each board meeting, I awarded JA logoed golf balls (of reasonably high quality) to members who had accomplished something of worth between meetings. I created a legend around the ball that suggested it would repel water and sand. You can imagine this was sought after by the many "hackers" on the board. To receive a golf ball, the something they did had to be above and beyond what was expected of them in the regular board assignment. If you were present, I would also site the reason for the recognition.

This recognition, which celebrated their accomplishments, caught on fast and became an important part of the meeting. It clearly demonstrated what I valued from board members. The fact that it was at the end of the meeting and you had to be present to receive a ball, and that was the only time I read the accomplishment aloud encouraged members to stay until adjournment. Everyone received credit in the monthly leaders' board, regardless of attendance at the meeting. A running total of the number of golf balls awarded was kept throughout the year, and at the annual meeting, the individual who was awarded the most golf balls received an impressive plaque with a driver mounted to it to honor the accomplishment.

The folklore surrounding Driving for JA grew (intentionally) over time. We had fun with it. It didn't matter how serious the discussion at a meeting was, the members always left the room on a high note. Members knew what I cared about because every meeting it was in front of them. You have no idea what people will do for a $2.50 golf ball that repels water and/or sand! There is little doubt that board members remembered this activity with fondness more than anything else I did. It didn't matter if they golfed or not. The non-golfers would often display their collection in a bowl in their office. This was a win-win activity for all.

There are many ways to celebrate accomplishments. In this example I connected a volunteer's activity with a need of the organization and recognized the individual for the contribution in front of their peers. It strengthened the relationship between myself (and JA) and the board member. While people do not necessarily do things to receive recognition, they do like to be recognized. They want to know that you are paying attention. When you recognize people's contributions, you are building trust because it sends a message that what a person does matters.

Hire the Right People

It is not possible to have a great workplace unless you have people who are right for the business. Every hire is important because people need to work together to achieve whatever the objectives of the company might be. Any time you have a weak link, the overall team suffers. Leaders who demonstrate that they understand the importance of people to the business by the kind of people they hire also build trust. The people already in place can trust that their efforts will be fruitful.

Hiring the right people has several dimensions. Certainly it means finding people whose strengths (which include technical capacity, training, and work ethic) match the jobs you have to offer. But it also means to hire people whose personalities are relational. A hire that only has one or the other of these profiles will be challenged in a relational environment.

Think of these dimensions like the relationship of the business plan to the relational leadership model. The business plan is the engine; the relational model is the fuel. An engine without fuel, no matter how great the engine, goes nowhere.

In order to hire the right people, you must be in tune with all aspects your business, including its objectives and the people who currently work for you. When you are clear about the business and its people, you will be able to determine what kinds of people you must recruit to enhance the potential of the organization.

Skip Schoenhals' business philosophy revolves around hiring the right people. He says, "Know your goals, know your values, make sure you know your priorities, and get the best people you can get. Give them clear direction, and then get out of their way!"

He elaborated with this scenario. If he got his best friends (all smart and successful people) together for the purpose of flying a plane to the west coast, it would be a problem. It really wouldn't matter how accomplished they were; they were not going to get to the coast because they lacked the requisite skills to do so. You have to blend the skills of the people with what you are trying to accomplish.

"The best strategic plan in the world . . . that is poorly implemented is much worse than a mediocre plan that is very well implemented," points out Schoenhals. The implementation comes from the people, and the people must be multi-dimensional—technically appropriate and relationally tempered.

Finally, don't be fooled. You cannot fix people. If they are not relational, you are not going to be able to make them relational. We tend to be wired in a certain way; we grow accustomed to this way, and we don't want to change it. You may achieve a temporary change in behavior, but fundamental, long-term change is quite unlikely and certainly not worth the effort. Pay attention to both dimensions (technical capacity and relational personalities) in your hiring practices, and you won't have to worry about it. You create a great place to work when the people who work there have both the technical and relational skills necessary to contribute to the success of the business.

> **TIP**
>
> An Axiom: You can't fix people.

Connect with People

Relational leaders are people centered, and thus tied to their employees. When someone focuses on another person and show they care, trust is built. Where there is trust, people are more comfortable in their surroundings. All of these are ingredients for a great place to work.

Connecting with your people in a way that demonstrates that you care is a consideration that is often ignored in leadership. It is not the big things that make an organization that cares. It's all the little things. It is how the company is viewed in the community. It's how your vendors and customers, and increasingly your shareholders, talk about you.

I have driven home the concept of attentiveness time and again in the book. It's important for your development in becoming a relational leader. Keep in mind, though, that you are not the only one looking and listening. All of your stakeholders are doing the same. It is one of the principal means by which they have to evaluate you.

> **TIP**
>
> An Axiom: Connecting with your people is a state of mind. It is doing what is right for your people whether you're seen or not, whether they know you have done something or not; it's what you do.

It is important to understand the ways you can reach out to your staff or the way your actions can impact them (positive or negative). People are affected by all sorts of outside stimuli. Something you say or do or a policy you create can greatly impact how you connect with your people. The following are examples of how small courtesies can deliver big results in the caring department.

Recently, I was at a funeral, and I saw Skip Schoenhals and his newly minted president and CEO, Mark Turner, paying their respects. The individual who passed away was a long-time associate of the bank but not a senior manager. That's respect, and I know the family appreciated the caring demonstrated by Skip and Mark.

If you were getting married, Charlie Cawley and MBNA let you borrow the antique car of your choice from the bank's collection to use as your wedding carriage.

From time to time, when I knew the parents of a staff member, I would send them a handwritten note on their child's birthday. The message was simple. Their child was doing a great job at Junior Achievement. I thanked them for instilling in their child the values and work ethic that was contributing greatly to the success he or she was enjoying.

Whenever I was in the presence of a parent (which was frequent because of all of the events we operated and the relative age of our staff), I made a point to say something positive about their child. What parent isn't thrilled to hear something nice about their kids?

Actually, it got to the point where my predominant means of communication was by handwritten note, particularly if I was thanking someone for a special deed or congratulating a person for a special accomplishment. By doing so you are telling the person that he is important enough to you that you will focus on him alone with your personal message. You are elevating the individual in significance, and he will feel it.

Alan Burkhard shows he cares by understanding the needs of his workforce (mostly young college students); he invests significant time teaching them how to maximize their potential. Alan lays out the relationship between his employees and leadership from the outset of their employment. Because he is now in the restaurant business (among others), he employees lots of young people, many still in college. He is a teacher and believes leadership must teach. He wants his employees to feel no limitations, fewer rules, less policy and procedure, fewer steps, fewer lines in the sand, and fewer walls. He teaches them how to maximize their own productivity. Those who stay with him, flourish. They know he cares.

Sometimes your connections to people are affected by someone else, before you even enter the scene. For example, a worker commented at one of Chris Coon's early meetings that what he most cared about in whatever Chris did to lead the county was to restore the pride he once had in working for the government. He just wanted to be able to hold his head high once again among his neighbors.

People want to have pride in their company, like the government worker in the previous example. For many, the company they work for is an extension of themselves. Even the stature of the company has an impact on the connection with its people. During hard times, it is more important than ever to be cognizant of the company's situation and the impact that it is having on the employees.

I recall as DuPont was struggling to reinvent itself, it began to pull back on its visibility within the community. There were layoffs now when before there weren't. The company was losing ground as a world industrial leader. There was a lot of reorganization, and whole divisions were being sold. It affected how people felt about working there, and their pride was diminishing. Leadership just didn't care anymore in the view of many. Here was a company that for 200 years had enjoyed an impeccable reputation and was known worldwide for its concern for its workers. It doesn't take much to tarnish your reputation.

Sometimes your presence alone can demonstrate a caring connection to your people. Nathan Hill held a monthly staff meeting for all of the associates of Discover Card, some 2,000 in several locations. At the meeting, there were company announcements and an update on the company's progress, acknowledgment of milestone events like birthdays, anniversaries and recognition of volunteer activities and other such items. The meetings tended to be celebrations of contributions and life events of the employees.

Nathan made it a priority to attend all of these meetings. The staff loved it and felt appreciated for who they were, both in their business and personal life. Virtually every meeting had a moment when Nathan would burst out in song to help celebrate whatever was being honored at the moment. Not many could do this but Nathan could—he possesses a great voice. His constant refrain to staff was, "I want Discover Card to be a great place to work, and I will do whatever I have to do to make this so!" He did, and it was.

Jim Kelly summed up his feelings on caring by indicating that it was more global than many people thought. He feels strongly that it should touch the entire stakeholder base. He said, "I think to be pure, you have to be on the path of relational leadership. Your relations with everybody have to be above board. You can't mistreat one constituency and expect the others aren't going to see that. Your culture will be hollow, and people will be talking about you behind your back."

As in the preceding example, if you want to connect with your people and demonstrate that you care, you have to do it across the board. You can't treat one group one way and another differently (negatively, that is) and expect people to fully trust your ultimate intentions with them.

To wit many years ago we bought a Toll Brothers home. We are still in it, and we appreciate the company's attention to detail and their commitment to their customers. However, I never liked the way they treated their vendors. Management was very hard on them, and they squeezed the vendor's profit margins tightly. I often wondered if this method of operation was going to impact how my home was built. While it did not turn out to be an issue for us, I believe it had to be for others. It made such a negative impression, it still hangs over me these many years later.

So however you do it, understand that you are always being watched. If you care, it will show. If it shows, it will be valued. If it is valued, your people will produce. They will produce a great work product or lionize your organization with great stories.

Treating your people with respect demonstrates that you care. Making sure that it is part of your organizational culture is leadership's responsibility. As Mister Rogers and Captain Kangaroo taught us as children, always say please and thank you. It is a winning strategy!

You can see there are many ways you and your actions can impact your connections to people. Your positive connections build trust in you and your company. A leader who is consistently and successively connected to people will be a leader in a great place to work.

Have Fun

People rarely complain about having fun, and if they can do it at work, it is a great place to work indeed. When leadership promotes fun, it is telling the employees that they are trusted.

One of your roles as a leader is to manage the tension within your organization. Tension and stress are good to a point, as nothing really happens until there is some. However stress can be debilitating and destructive within a team. You need to keep your eye on the barometer in your organization and do something to change the pressure before it gets out of hand.

Once I had the opportunity to meet Herb Kelleher, the CEO (at the time) of Southwest Airlines. Herb is a very funny guy, and I was telling him so in our conversation. I also told him that I believed his spirit transferred to his staff universally. It was a pleasure for me to fly Southwest, absolutely my favorite airline.

He told me that Southwest is focused on making the experience of each customer outstanding no matter where the customer encounters an employee, be it in the cockpit, on the phone, at baggage claim, or the ticket window. Part of the customer experience he talks about is the attitude of the employees. Have you ever been on a Southwest flight when an attendant burst out in song when the plane landed? How about the customer service representative who pleasantly stays with you until your issue is solved to your satisfaction? These are not normal actions from employees except if you work in an environment that cares about you.

People who act this way are not the ones who dread going to work every day. They look forward to it because, in part, it is a fun place to work.

The Golden Rule

How can you go wrong with the Golden Rule? It makes sense. It has always made sense, and it always will make sense. The issue materializes when you get out of synch with your common sense. I think what happens is, you get caught up in the turmoil of your day-to-day existence, and you forget the impact that certain actions can have on others.

So for me, the best check on behavior is to regularly look internally. How am I measuring up to the person I think I am? Are my decisions consistent with how I would like to be treated in a similar situation? If not, why not? The test is to be able to look in the mirror and see the truth. You might say, *speaking truth to yourself!*

You also must look at what you have established as your operating procedures. What do you say is acceptable for the group? Are your actions measuring up to that standard? If not, why not?

If you find yourself out of character with the person you know you are, or you see that you are violating your own established policies and principles, then you must act immediately. If you make a mistake, it's okay; if you do not correct your mistake, then it's not okay. When you are at odds with the Golden Rule, you have a big problem facing you that needs to be addressed immediately. As in most things, let common sense rule, and more often than not, everything will work out.

People who employ common sense as part of their day-to-day living tend to be admired and trusted. In business, they tend to create great places to work because they instinctively embrace the building blocks of trust and carry them out effectively. They are relational and place their trust in the people around them. Bob Brightfelt is one such person.

Bob is an individual who possesses huge quantities of common sense. I knew this from the first day I met him. This character trait is very transparent. His people knew that he could be trusted to always use his common sense and for that reason (not to mention his impeccable record of sound business decisions), he was viewed universally as a person of character. It was never more apparent than at his retirement party. I have rarely seen such love pouring from hearts of people who worked under his tutelage.

To wrap up, it is the combination of these ten principles that will make your organization a great place to work. All are important and should be addressed as part of your way of doing business. They are the building blocks of trust.

Make Stress a Positive Force

The leader will tend to create all the stress in an organization or, less likely, cause there to be no stress. How you handle stress personally and organizationally will determine a lot about the success of your team. By the way, an overly stressed organization is rarely viewed as a great place to work! An under-stressed organization is thought of as a morgue—typically not good!

There is a natural stress in most organizations, whether it be a company, a work group, or a committee. Stress occurs because there is an expectation that something will happen, and this is good. Once that expectation is in play, then sooner or later there will be a conflict. Conflict equals amplified stress. This is usually not good.

As a leader, you want just enough stress. Too much and there are problems; too little and there are problems of a different nature. Neither are good. You must always check yourself to ensure that you are not the cause of the *too little* or *too much* syndromes. Your behavior will have a tremendous impact on your employees' or team's demeanor. Therefore, it is incumbent upon you to set the right tone and monitor the state of your personal being to minimize the occasions where stress spikes.

> **TIP**
> An Axiom: The goal of every leader should be to promote positive tension within his or her organization.

To maintain positive levels of stress in your environment, you must maintain control of yourself. What's that old expression? "Never let them see you sweat!" It could be that the walls around you are caving in, but you have to look as if you're just rearranging the office. Panic doesn't work. You must position yourself as clear-headed, mission-focused, and vision-driven. You are a problem solver, not a problem maker.

Whatever you do as a leader is monitored by those who follow you, including other leaders within your organization. Therefore, you are giving license to all based upon your actions. This section will discuss some tips that will help you manage the stress levels in your organization, enabling you to get the zip you need from your people without the anxiety of overblown tension, and thus creating a great place to work.

- Keep your emotions in check.
- Monitor your language.
- Maintain your sense of humor.
- Stay consistent in your behavior.
- Communicate the needs of the organization clearly.
- Set and check intermediate objectives.

Each of these items is fully within your control as a leader. You choose how you react to situations.

Keep Your Emotions in Check

Remember, you are the one who transfers levels of stress to your people. If you are all over the place with your emotions, you will certainly start a chain reaction among your staff. No doubt, though, if you are feeling this way, something is going on, and it has your attention. This is a time when you need a lot more determination than emotion.

Leaders with temperaments that tend to be emotive cause reactions among those they come in contact with. The reactions include a belief that the leader is not using her best reasoning powers. When a leader losses control, it is often upsetting to the people around her, and they can question her judgment. This situation leads to an erosion of trust. Because of that, you must minimize the occurrence of emotive behavior.

TIP

An Axiom: People who lose control regularly are viewed as unstable. This is not a quality that is often ascribed to a leader.

Think about all the mobster movies you have seen. The mob boss is most often portrayed as unemotional. He speaks with a soft voice making you strain to hear what he is saying. He is very deliberate, and you always get the feeling he means what he says! He's in control. The person he is talking to is always somewhat jittery and is often the emotional one, largely because he believes his life just took a bad turn.

If you appear to be in control, people are much more likely to follow you. The prophets of doom don't have a lot of followers. Stay in control and release your emotions away from your staff.

Monitor Your Language

Foul language has limited value. It gets attention, but when it is used regularly, it becomes deleterious. When what you say gets to this state, you are in trouble. A leader is expected to rise above the fray. Be prepared, because when you show yourself to be part of the weeds, people are willing to pluck you out of the ground. In effect, your language will delegate you to a place that you may not even deserve. At the very least, you will not be admired and your leadership will be in jeopardy.

TIP

An Axiom: By and large, any good cussing uttered by you (unless it is really creative and non-vulgar) is usually a bad reflection on you.

Depending upon how foul you get, there is a shock value that might have limited impact, but it is short-lived. You proved you were mad, but so what? Lots of idiots get mad. Plus, the shock value will ultimately lead to disrespect in most cases. It makes your staff uncomfortable and could be grounds for a harassment charge. People are more sophisticated than that today, and they expect more from their leaders.

Maintain a Sense of Humor

Effective and appropriate use of humor can diffuse a situation and put people in a mind-set that the job can be done, even if it will be challenging. By using your sense of humor, you are demonstrating that whatever the circumstances are, they are not insurmountable; more importantly, they are not the end of the world as you know it.

If you can find some humor in the situation, it can't be as horrible as people might think. Changing how the situation is viewed enables the leader to get people thinking about how to improve the state of affairs. That is the psyche that can change outcomes.

By diffusing the problem with humor you are then in a position to reset the challenge in a way that seems doable. After all, if you can laugh about it, how bad can it be? You are able to refocus the group's energy in a positive manner by setting the stage with your wit.

Now you can use stress to your advantage because you are environmentally controlling how people are thinking about it. How powerful is that? They are able to use their individual skill sets to fullest advantage and stress is now a positive factor.

Remain Consistent

People respond best to situations where there is some predictability. It gives them a level of reassurance. They know what to expect in general, and more importantly, they know what is expected of them. This is the value of consistency, and it is a positive force for your organization. You have expectations and ways of accomplishing objectives that your employees are familiar with. They know how to respond.

If you are viewed as inconsistent, you will cause harmful stress within your organization because everything about what employees know is questionable. You create a mindset with employees that tells them what you say is true today is likely to change tomorrow or the next day. It is hard for them to decide what to do because the employee knows that conditions, rules, and tasks change regularly. This situation causes havoc and is very stressful.

People appreciate folks who have an air of confidence about them. Consistency seems to follow a leader who demonstrates an attitude of confidence. People will follow a leader whose persona suggests that he knows what he is doing. Ultimately, when you regularly act in the same fashion, you build trust because you are seen as reliable. By doing this, your people believe you will get them where they need to be. They are prepared to follow. If people will follow you, your leadership has taken hold in the group, and the stress levels are kept in check because of the confidence the group has in you.

TIP

A relational leader portrays himself as clear-headed, mission-focused, and vision-driven particularly in times of stress.

There is a caution I want to leave you with here. Often inconsistency comes about because the leader doubts his course of action. It's really okay to have doubts, but you must have faith in your ability to manage the situation and work with the resources that are available to you. Share your doubts with a trusted friend or colleague who can help you stay on course and maintain your consistency. You don't have to be alone in your pursuit of organizational objectives. If you don't have someone whose "shoulder you can cry on," you need to find one. Sooner or later, you will need a shoulder!

Communicate Clearly

In my experience, one of the significant roadblocks in an organization is the lack of clarity in what is communicated to staff. When clarity is missing, people will often take the wrong path on a project or task. This will ultimately wind up in some sort of negative performance discussion. If clarity becomes an ongoing issue, there will certainly be a dramatic rise in negative stress. Many organizations experience a significant rise in employee turnover as a direct result of lack of clarity.

Skip Schoenhals said, "Know your goals, know your values, make sure you know your priorities, and get the best people you can. Give them clear directions, and then get out of the way." Ambiguity is disastrous to an organization.

TIP

An Axiom: Lack of clarity in delegation is a principal complaint of people across all organizations. It causes delay and failure to perform. Always check for clarity of instruction.

Keep it simple and stay on your course. Spend the time necessary to align your people in the jobs for which they are best suited. Make sure the jobs are aligned with the task at hand. Communicate the objectives of the business plan. Be certain that everyone knows what is expected and then, as Skip says, get out of the way.

As a leader, your primary business objective is to focus on the organization's vision and be sure that the organization is similarly focused. Remove the roadblocks so that your people can get the job done. But most important, make sure the people know what the job is and what they are personally and collectively responsible for delivering. Each and every one of your associates must understand their roles.

Set and Check Intermediate Objectives

An excellent strategy you can employ as a leader to manage stress is found in the planning process. By setting and checking intermediate objectives for your staff, you can help them stay on course and achieve the desired result. As the leader, you should have a handle on what it takes to get a job done— what needs to be done and by when.

There is another old saying that goes something like this: What is measured gets done! Don't you love old sayings? You know they get to be old because they have that ring of truth to them!

Anyone who has achieved any degree of success will tell you where they spend their time—in areas that matter. Obviously not all activities are equal, so it becomes leadership's responsibility to sort through the activities and order them in terms of their importance. This practice sets the expectations of the workers.

TIP
Be sure you measure all the critical success factors that make your organization effective.

Depending upon the maturity level of your team, your checkpoints will be closer or farther away. In any case, always make sure that the checkpoints leave you enough time to switch gears without crisis. In order to do this, you have to know the end date, know what is being measured, know that the measurement will give you the information you need to evaluate your position, and know that the time of the measurement leaves you the flexibility to alter your strategies if necessary.

Once these parameters are established, get out of the way. Let your people do their work. If they need you, make sure they know it is allright to come to you; otherwise, get out of the way.

Look at the situation this way: If you have the right people, the right plans, and the right measurements, and you have removed the roadblocks then implementation should be smooth. You undermine confidence and present yourself as an annoyance when you look for updates before they are scheduled. Remember, people will tend to perform as you expect them to. When you help your staff achieve their objectives, you are creating a great place to work.

Summary

Creating a great place to work is synonymous with becoming a relational leader and installing the Relational Leadership Model into your business or association. The first part of creating a great place to work is relationalism. It is a place where people are at the core of the organization and trust and character form its backbone. It is a place where people believe they get a fair shake in their day-to-day work lives. They have fun, they are listened to, and they are noticed for who they are and what they do. They see purpose in the mission of the organization, and they are proud to be a member of the team.

It is incumbent upon you as a leader to be very deliberate about creating the environment that supports a great workplace. This means you communicate the values of relationalism, you train your leadership team to understand and deliver the concepts consistently, you encourage your people to give feedback on how to improve the business, and most of all, you walk the talk every day.

The second piece to creating a great place to work involves promoting an atmosphere of positive tension. It is true that without some degree of tension, nothing happens. When tension becomes unchecked stress, you begin to see the pressure build and decisions weaken. Unchecked stress takes on a life of its own and seemingly becomes unstoppable. It causes false assumptions and leads to failure, oftentimes unnecessary failure. For many, it becomes a self-fulfilling prophecy.

Being the leader means you control the environment so that stress becomes productive, not destructive. Your people understand that positive tension is good, and it will result in reaching or exceeding performance objectives, which is good for all. You demonstrate leadership by how you act, your language, your sense of humor, and by consistently living up to the principles you espouse. You have empathy for everyone on your team, and you treat people fairly.

Doing the right thing is a constant refrain among all the people I spoke with in preparing this book. When you do the right thing, it sets up everything else. It makes your people proud of where they work and lights their internal flames around a personal work ethic. By most any standard in the Delaware community, WSFS is considered a great place to work. Schoenhals indicated that he built trust, which was vital to the turnaround by transparency; leadership did what they said they were going to do, and they admitted their mistakes. He summed it up by saying the following: "[WSFS is a place] where doing the right thing is the norm and not just a slogan. We match the talents of the individual to the needs of the job (this is done quite carefully) and provide good supervision. We do a survey every year and follow up aggressively at the work group level, creating a culture where people are encouraged to do what they do best."

Bob Brightfelt provided an environment where it was clear to the team that he cared about them, not just at work but in their personal lives. He made it his business to know things, to celebrate in good time, and to be by someone's side in times of sorrow. Time and again, I heard from associates at Dade

Behring that the company was "a great place to work!" When this is the case, stress takes on an entirely different character. It is no longer destructive—it is invigorating. People engage themselves at higher levels of their own accord. They intuitively understand that their workplace promotes an atmosphere of constructive and monitored tension rather than anxiety-based stress. They like this place, and they want it to succeed. It's a great place to work.

Creating a great place to work is difficult but infinitely worth the effort. The reality is that you work hard at whatever you do. You choose to be a relational leader because it makes sense to you and because it will make money for you. Happy people produce results, and ultimately, that's what you are looking for—results.

KEEP IN MIND:

- There are two pieces to building a great workplace: (1) a relational style of leadership and (2) an environment energized by positive tension.
- Engage the building blocks of trust, and you are on your way to building an organization that values people and that people value.
- Never *ever* promise anything that you are not prepared to back up with action.
- Everyone is not equal, but everyone should be treated equally.
- Always give public credit to the individual who developed an idea, and whenever possible, give him the opportunity to bring the idea to reality.
- Be approachable.
- Don't be a dream blocker—be a dream maker.
- You can't fix people. Understand the strengths they have and the strengths you need, and then match them to the jobs you have.
- Clarity of expression and expectations is essential to getting a job done correctly.
- Manage the stress in your environment so that positive tension is the norm.

Chapter 9

The Value of Relationalism Outside the Workplace

> "Do not let what you cannot do
> interfere with what you can do."
> —*John Wooden*

- Working with an Outside Organization
- Community Leadership Opportunities
- Summary

To this point I have talked about relational leadership largely in terms of the individual leader within the workplace or workgroup. I have touched upon utilizing relational skills outside the workplace and suggested that it is appropriate and helpful for anyone trying to develop or hone the skills of leadership. In fact, there are business and personal reasons for the relational leader to practice the craft outside of the workplace.

Business leadership is changing, out of necessity, as the world increasingly adopts market-driven economies. The same old advantages America has enjoyed are not working quite so well anymore. Technology is available everywhere. The cost of goods produced in emerging economies is significantly lower, and the quality of those goods is higher. Companies are losing market share to foreign competitors that didn't even exist in the not-so-distant past. There is a worldwide zest for "free" markets. People and their commitment to the organizations they work for will be one of the keys to our country's success in the decades ahead. This is why relational leadership makes so much sense as global competition intensifies.

So what does this mean for today's leader? She must understand the value of relationalism in the workplace and commit to perfecting her approach to the style. Concomitantly, she must also understand that government resources are being challenged like never before. As a result, services for citizens are being reduced even though the needs are unchanged and in many instances increasing. This provides both an opportunity and a mandate for relational leaders in particular to demonstrate their commitment to leading in the broadest possible manner. Employees want to see their senior management acting relationally in their internal relationships and supporting the community with their personal and corporate resources.

Progressive business leaders will spread themselves beyond the workplace, but not everyone wants to do this. Involvement in the community is like the debates throughout our country's history (until 1940) regarding isolationism. Generally, we did our best to mind our own business. But with the outbreak of World War II, it became clear that we could no longer sit on the sidelines, and America became a world leader.

Business itself must also get off the sidelines, if for no other reason than to attract and retain committed, energetic, enthusiastic, and knowledgeable workers. This is an important factor of rising to the top in the competitive global economy. In Chapter 4, I pointed out Mark Suwyn's study that determined in his words, "If you found a group of people who were invested, not money-wise but emotionally invested, in the outcome of the business and how it was operating, that business tended to be successful. The people environment that you created and how people responded to that was the only correlation that we could make about successful businesses."

Increasingly, I see that enlightened business leaders are becoming involved in activities outside the workplace. The expertise you possess adds value to community groups, public discussions, and political agendas. Often the objectives of these outside groups impact your business needs. Therefore, it is wise for you to be a part of the community and support its well-being, not just as an individual, but as an individual who represents your company. People will then see you in a broader light. When they see you demonstrating your leadership capabilities, they will begin to trust and appreciate you more. They will seek your advice and council. They will see you as a skilled human being and not some profit-making ogre hiding behind the corporate flag. You become one of them, and better yet, you become a person who is contributing to improving the community. Because of this, you will gain their sympathies in time of need, their support as consumers, and their dedication as employees (if they wind up working in your organization). There is an old saying that is very apropos here: "Those who give, get."

I urge you to get involved outside the workplace. Pick organizations or causes that you believe in. Even better, pick groups that you believe in that might be helpful to your business somewhere down the line. However, there is one caution: Don't go into volunteer work with your agenda "on your sleeve." Volunteer knowing you possess the capacity to help the organization through your leadership skills. You will be surprised how quickly people will begin asking you what you do and what your business issues are.

The role of the leader is constantly evolving. The complexity of the world we live in demands an expanded viewpoint of leadership. Practically speaking, volunteering extends your ability to practice your leadership skills in a different environment, one where you have less control and knowledge, and thus it demands extra effort on your part to accomplish your objectives. It is important that you continuously practice the craft of leadership, and what better place to do it than in a non-threatening environment? With regard to your outside relationships, you will find the relational model as presented will work effectively. Remember, the best and most gifted performers arduously and continually practice to improve their skills—you are no different.

There are many leadership opportunities outside of work for you to get involved with as a volunteer, which include the following:

- Committee established by a non-profit, such as United Way or Junior Achievement
- Task force commissioned by a government agency
- Commission formed by a school district
- Work group created by a political party
- Special interest organization built upon a perceived community need

There is a leadership gap in this country that gets a little bit wider each day. I believe that you as a relational leader have an obligation to serve your community where you can to improve the quality of life for your fellow citizens and to develop your personal capabilities so you can lead more effectively. In this chapter, I will explore the leadership challenges and rewards these kinds of opportunities present for a business person outside the workplace.

Working with an Outside Organization

One example of how this might work is my own experience with volunteering in the schools in Delaware. My employer was Junior Achievement, a finance and economic education organization that serves students from kindergarten through high school. Thirty years ago, JA was making a major shift in how it did business, which involved a much closer working relationship with educators. Our programs, increasingly, were placed in the schools during the school day. While JA was a highly respected organization, it was not well known among educators and had no real reputation for being an educational group.

At the same time, when I moved to Delaware, my children were just approaching school age. Therefore, I was very interested in the schools and how I could support them so that my children could have the best educational opportunities possible. It made perfect sense for me to become involved in public education as a volunteer. I had both a business and a personal interest.

So, I joined the PTA, became a school-based president, and later state president. I was appointed to school reform committees at the local and state levels. I chaired referendum campaigns for my school district, assisted other districts, and I did much more.

It wasn't long before people noticed my contributions. They came to me wanting to know more about Junior Achievement. They began to draw their own conclusions about how JA could be helpful to the schools. Before too much time passed, we went from another good community group for kids to an essential partner with the schools.

After serving a term as a local unit president, I was asked to serve on the state board. I brought many new ideas and resources to the board and, increasingly, it was clear that the people valued what I had to offer. I never tried to promote myself or Junior Achievement—I was focused on helping the PTA become a better organization. I knew if I did that, I would benefit by increasing my skill set, and JA would benefit through better relations with the schools.

One day, there was an article in the paper that was not particularly complimentary to the PTA. I thought it was way off base and factually incorrect, so I wrote a letter to the editor stating my views and clarifying facts. As it turned out, I was the only person who did so, and my fellow board members were very impressed that I took this initiative, even though I was still new to the organization. Before long, I was asked to be president-elect of the state PTA, and two years later was elected president of the state organization.

What came from this involvement? Well first of all, it opened more opportunities for leadership. For example, I was appointed co-chair of the Governor's Mentoring Commission and a member of the Leadership Committee of the State's Education Reform movement. There were many other appointments to committees. As my name grew in stature, opportunities for Junior Achievement grew at an even faster rate. JA went from a "best kept secret" to a highly recognized and respected organization. And I never directly promoted JA. Of course, I answered questions, and when people thought we might be able to help them as a collaborative organization, I pursued the opportunity.

The bottom line is that my volunteer involvement worked at every level. PTA grew (as I was stepping down as president, the PTA was very near its greatest membership numbers), JA grew (Delaware was one of the top JA franchises in the country), I felt really good about the activities I was involved in, and I matured as a leader. It was a win-win for everybody.

Community Leadership Opportunities

Volunteerism, or giving back to the community as it is commonly referred to, can be an effective way to make a name for yourself and your company. It puts you in front of people whom you normally may not associate with, creating new contacts and allowing you to demonstrate your leadership skills. It makes your community a better place to live. By and large, your relational skill set can be transferred directly to the volunteer opportunities that you pursue. Better yet, you will grow your skills as you practice them.

However, be cautioned about the challenges that you will face, particularly as you begin this process. You are entering unfamiliar territory. You are not likely to know many of the people involved; you will not know the organization well (certainly not at the level of your own business); and you will not know much about the history, structure, or culture of the group. Also, it is very likely that the people you meet will be a very diverse group, often with viewpoints decidedly different from your own. And there will be "power brokers," people who for whatever reason hold influence with the group. You will need to identify and understand their relative value to you.

None of these people in the group report to you. They don't owe you anything. You are not supplying the funding stream for the organization. On the surface there is no reason for them to accept you into their midst; in fact, you may be viewed as a threat to them because you are an outsider. At this point you might be asking, "Remind me again why I should get involved in a situation like this?" The challenge is great, but as the fundamental economic principle states—*there is no great reward without great risk.*

Just imagine how you can hone your leadership skills in situations like this! There is no better way because how you make your living is not threatened by the results. You can be a bit more daring and take a risk that you might avoid on the job. You can test out theories that you are thinking about. You can make the volunteer experience a laboratory for your personal development.

When you bring your relational leadership skills to the group, you will find that they allow a point of entry. Displaying fidelity, appreciation, and value will ensure that your new associates take notice of you in the best possible manner. Patience is very important in the early stages (well, in most stages). You need to give your fellow volunteers enough time to get to know you and appreciate what you are able to bring to the group that will help it become more successful.

Summary

In this chapter I explored utilizing the relational model outside the workplace. I built a case for volunteering in the community and provided business reasons for doing so. The differences between work and personal relationships are not significant by themselves, but how you address the components of the model is certainly different. The dynamics of the volunteer opportunity or the workplace will often call for alternative tactics.

You can expect to develop personally through volunteerism by learning more about your community, becoming more astute at relationalism, and growing in stature among other community leaders. You are likely to grow your business by increased profits and by attracting better employees.

KEEP IN MIND:
- Volunteering in the community is a winning business strategy that will boost your reputation and profits, create new contacts, and attract better employees.
- Volunteering is a winning personal strategy, as it greatly enhances your leadership skills.
- There is no great reward without great risk.

Chapter 10

Applying the Relational Model at Home

"A hundred years from now it will not matter what my bank account was, the sort of house I lived in, or the kind of car I drove. . .but the world may be different because I was important in the life of a child."
—*Forest E. Witcraft*

- The Relational Leader at Home
- Relational Similarities Between Work and Home
- Summary

While the community is a perfect place to practice your leadership skills, there is another area that is much more personal and meaningful to you that requires your expertise—your personal relationships. I am talking about your connection to a friend, significant other, spouse, or child. These associations need your leadership as well but can be quite a bit more sensitive than those at work or in the community.

Private relationships, particularly ones that encompass children, are vital to society's well-being today. The quality of interpersonal relations impacts how individuals act both inside and outside the relationship. Do not fool yourself into believing that dysfunctional families are economically stratified. The children who are products of a dysfunctional family are everywhere and are becoming a burden on the support systems in our country, including schools, judiciary, medicine, and the workplace.

Because effective relational leadership can have a positive impact on dysfunctional families and because your leadership approach will be different in the personal arena, I am going to concentrate in this chapter on using your leadership skills within a family. If you don't have children, it is still a very good idea to put your skill set to use with any relationship you may have. This chapter will help you with that as well.

The Relational Leader at Home

There are many good reasons to bring your relational style home to your spouse, your friends, or your family. The most obvious is the central piece of the model—people—and how you successfully interact with them. Having fun and celebrating adds to the quality of life. Creating purpose and sharing in the pursuit of a purposeful life is significant to the parties involved. Being attentive takes discipline and must be practiced regularly. Practicing the craft of leadership is an essential exercise that should be attended to on a regular basis.

Has someone in your home said any of the following to you? "This is not the office!" "We're not paid to listen to you!" "I am not your employee!" These are usually references to combining your work persona with the daily patterns of your home life. Generally, this would be your spouse or a friend speaking! If you are hearing these expressions, you might want to take stock of your style at home. This potential conflict is very fixable for a relationally trained leader. Of course, if you don't make some adjustments, you may be in real trouble regarding your approach to the "internal work force," so to speak, which is not very good "speak" at all.

The elements of the relational style work perfectly in the home environment, but there are two big differences between work life and home life. At home you and your partner (if you have one) are equals, and the issues you face tend to be far more personal (thus, often emotional) than the work environment presents to you. However, if you and your partner are willing to negotiate and discuss, you can come to a consensus on the best approach to most situations.

For instance, Sue Linderman talks about logical consequences as a means of guiding her eight step-children. This made sense to her because she used the same methods at work. "Logical consequences work with kids just like they do with adults. Because children are known to say with frequency, 'That's not fair,' it is important that your logical consequence be fair. If you stay out later than your curfew, then you don't get to go out again. That's fair and logical. It you stay out later than your curfew, and then you can't have candy for a month—well that's just stupid."

So fairness is being aware that there are other points of view, and some may even hold more weight than your own based on the rightness of the argument. Fairness dictates that the minority has the right to express its opinion. In the case of family, the children are not always wrong. It is up to the parent to encourage discourse and to differentiate between what is right and wrong or reasonable and unreasonable as it pertains to family matters. By doing so, you will train your children to make logical and reasoned arguments as well as give them a life skill that will always be admired.

If you review the element of fidelity (of which fairness is an attribute), you understand that this is where the family derives its "moral compass." Here is where you define what is right and wrong in the household. You set up what is debatable and what is sacrosanct. You may debate curfew times, but the rule about not drinking and driving is sacrosanct. As you move through your family's timeline, these notions will change, and your attitudes may shift simply because you now know the personalities that you are dealing with.

A relational leader builds trust. In a family, the elements of trust can be touchy. Parents will do things that they claim are in the best interest of the child. Often the things they choose to do will not evoke a trusting environment. For instance, sometimes parents will read their children's personal mail. Now there's a trust builder! I have known parents who listen in on their children's telephone conversations. Open and consistent communication is a better method.

Trust is the essential foundation of any relationship. When it is lost or discounted, it is very hard to regain. Lincoln believed that caring and compassion inspired trust. Caring and compassion are basics in most family environments. It is not hard to start out with an atmosphere of trust; the challenge is to maintain it over time.

At work you can discharge a person who is not trustworthy. However, it is not practical to fire one of your family members. The key is to model the behavior you expect; if you do, you are likely to see that behavior expressed back to you.

Finally, consider the various ways that you can interact as a family. It doesn't require a lot of money to engage in adventures as a group. We found it was cost-effective to join one or more of the local museums that would be interesting for the children. As a result, we had the opportunity to enjoy and learn without spending a lot of money. We all loved going to the National Aquarium in Baltimore or the Philadelphia Zoo or the Hagley Museum in Wilmington. Best of all, we could afford to do it, and the children got to explore their world. It brought us closer together, and some of our best memories stem from those days.

TIP

Remember that there is unifying power in shared experiences, and it has great impact on relationships.

Review the chart shown in Figure 10.1. Let this be your guide in working your skill set with your family. Soul, spirit, and will—along with fidelity, appreciation, and value—are the fundamental underpinnings of relational leadership, and they are successful strategies in work or home.

As you review the entire model and think about the many opportunities you have to integrate its principles in your daily home life, I think you will appreciate what relationalism can do for you as a parent or partner. This is one time when you should not check your business hat at the door when you arrive home!

My Observations

In preparing to write this book, I collected and organized lots of information from my past and conducted several dozen interviews with people whom I believed were relational leaders (including myself). I compared characteristics of this group to find similarities. Along the way, I began to notice trends. In fact, they shared many common traits like the high degree of comfort they had with themselves. The degree of personal freedom they enjoyed was very high. The contentedness and happiness that enveloped them was very high.

The Essence of Relationalism

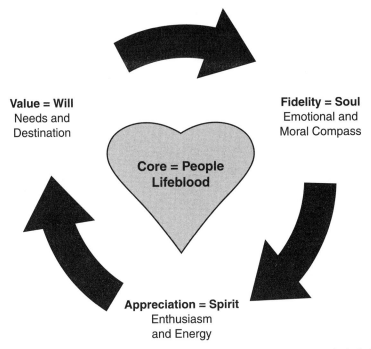

Figure 10.1 *Moral compass, enthusiasm, energy, needs, and direction are particularly forceful when applied to the family.*

Their personal health was high. While interesting and positive, I was not really surprised by these observations.

> **TIP**
> Commonalities among relational leaders interviewed for this book include personal freedom, happiness, contentedness, health, personal fulfillment, and accomplishment.

One day, I was thinking about my own situation and the fact that my wife, Carolyn, and I have been married for 37 years. I then started thinking about the interview group, and I recognized that many had lifelong mates for at least as long as Carolyn and I and in many cases longer. Did this mean something? I don't know the answer to that question. I don't think I have enough data points to draw any reliable conclusions. For the most part, these people are not connected with each other except through an association with me and Junior Achievement. But I do find it interesting that after more research, virtually every person in the group has enjoyed companionship with a life-long mate. Could this mean that by being relational as a manner of conducting yourself leads to stability in your home life?

Relational leaders tend to act a certain way consistently. They are fair, moral, ethical, and attentive. They create an atmosphere of trust, appreciation, fun, and purpose. Most importantly they have a deep respect for people. Individuals who possess and practice these attributes not only are going to be pretty good leaders, but they are also quite likely to be pretty good mates. This makes sense to me.

This revelation led me to think about the families of these people. Again, almost without exception the children in these families are well adjusted, professional, and contributing members of society. They are teachers, lawyers, bankers, health professionals, entrepreneurs, and more. Some have just started their careers and are on solid paths to fulfilling their goals. Others are established in their careers as successful leaders. There are some who are still in school doing serious academic work with a bright future ahead of them.

TIP

Relational leaders who employ their skill set at home seemingly have deeper, more harmonious relationships, longer marriages, and more well-adjusted, productive, and happy children.

This observation opened my eyes even more to the power of relationalism. The children's success can't be an accident or chance. All of us are products of our environment. These children were nurtured in an environment that respected them and valued their abilities while motivating them to think and contribute. Randomness is not the answer as the parents were purposeful in their actions. They were purposeful about being relational. If there was no other reason for you to adopt a style like relationalism, these observations regarding relationships, spouses, and children should be enough to move you in this direction.

TIP

An executive once said upon retirement, "My only regret was that I didn't spend more time with my family." Remember, when the day is gone, it can't be retrieved.

It is important to remember that a relational leader will be more productive simply because of how she leads. Her people will work harder and smarter, and she will find herself with more time—time that can be invested in family or other aspects of her life she wants to pursue. While leaders try to separate the business life and home life, it is a major challenge to do so. Do your best to make the two complement each other in a positive manner.

Reflections of Relational Leaders

I selected Sue Linderman, Nathan Hill, and Russ Owen to represent the reflections of home life from my leadership group. What they have to say is representative of other viewpoints. When parents conduct themselves similarly to these individuals, it is not hard to see why they fulfill each other and how they inspire their children to be responsible citizens.

Sue Linderman is stepmother to eight children. She says, "My work style made it easier for me to be a parent; I didn't have to adopt a new style at home. You have to engage the entire family in the process; it's all about 'We are in this together' and 'How are we going to make this work?'" Sue believes the difference between work and home is that emotion is involved. While there can be emotion at work too, the relationships are different. "There is much more involved with emotion at home because it is personal. If someone in my business doesn't like me, that's okay, but in the family, it is essential that you nurture each relationship," says Sue. As parents or bosses, you have to be cognizant of the forces that surround you in the world and the impact these conditions have on your decisions. There is so much access to information and different ways of doing things that authoritarian control doesn't work for Sue, either on the job or at home. With so many choices available, it becomes increasingly harder to control how people will act, thus challenging any form of authoritarianism.

Nathan Hill talks about his family meetings, where all were encouraged to give feedback about how their world was working: "John would say how he felt about things and was always brutally honest. Tonya, the older of the two children, was a bit more reserved but was also able to get her points across. This became like an opinion survey at work. It produced the opportunity for counseling, encouraging, motivating, and recognizing them for accomplishment. It was up to Laura [Nathan's spouse] and me to motivate each other, find common ground on things, and sometimes agree to disagree. This was about honesty and trust—all basic. The philosophy of 'do unto others' was an important part of what we instilled in our children. Anything that is worth doing is worth doing well; you need to give it your best. It's the same thing at work. The guiding principles you follow at work, you do at home."

Russ Owen says, "A lot of what I know about management I learned from my children. You try to guide them and be their inspiration, but you walk the fine line of encouragement and discipline. You don't want to break their spirit. You want them to take risks and be successful. Laurie and I tried to strike a balance. You learn to give them choices, rather than ultimatums, even if one of the choices is a bad one. Let them make mistakes and pick them up and encourage them to go on. Give them life skills. I even made them drive a stick-shift. They don't teach that anymore, but everyone should know how to do that! Nurture them so they can achieve their full potential. Give them space and let them enjoy an amount of independence. There is really no difference between office and home. It's about leading from the heart."

TIP

An Axiom: Relational behavior brings out the best in people in work situations; it can and will do the same in the home environment.

Sue, Nathan, and Russ are describing scenarios with their children that honor them as real people who are deserving of respect. Their opinions count. They have the right to make decisions on their own, but there is a safety net in case they get in over their heads. They can speak their minds. They can be themselves. They are exposed to the world around them in a way that enables them to be prepared for what is to come. All of these are representative of skills that the relational leader brings home.

Relational Similarities Between Work and Home

Russ Owen talked with me about "leading from the heart" in the workplace. He says it is part of integrity and trust. It's challenging people to do things they are not sure they can do but with the knowledge that you will be there to support them in every possible way. You are nurturing and understanding.

When he talks about his family, specifically his two boys, he comments wryly, "in this case you actually do know more than they do," and you use this knowledge to nurture your children. You lead from the heart at home just as you do in the workplace.

In the case of the workplace, you are interested in your associates being productive, driving the business plan, and committing to the vision. If you can get that, regardless of the sector you work in, you as a leader are pretty happy.

You have a product that you want to be successful, be it a policy for the public good, an item you manufacture, a service you provide, or a cause you care about. As a leader, it is your job to make that happen.

Regarding your family, you care about growing the love of your partner and preparing your children to take their rightful place in life, with a solid foundation about right and wrong and with the skills to contribute to the betterment of society. But parenting doesn't come with a handbook, so there is a lot of trial and error involved with bringing up children. You do the best you can to take that tiny baby to a functioning adult. You draw upon your experiences and try to make the best decisions possible.

The truth is that there are many support systems that can help you be a better parent, if you seek them out. Parenting is akin to a recipe with many ingredients, like nurturing, encouraging, disciplining, and a good deal more. You don't always know what the measurements might be. You could surmise instinctively that several cups of trust, fairness, character, fun, celebration, attentiveness, and purposefulness will make for a "well-baked" child who will be able to handle the rigors of adulthood.

TIP

An Axiom: A relational parent/partner demonstrates the elements of fidelity, appreciation, and value when interacting with their partner or children.

Undoubtedly, you are already doing much of what I have talked about in this chapter. The challenge is to make your home relationships as cohesive as possible. When you commit to putting the whole design of relational leadership together in your home environment, you will live in a place where civility, happiness, success, and love abound and are evident for all to see.

Most important, keep in mind that leadership is not confined to the workplace. When it is, it is insular. Great leaders take a broad view of the world in which they live. Because they do, they bring a grander prospective to the work situation that enables them to lead better. And don't be mistaken—your home life impacts your business life and vice versa, no matter how hard you try to separate the two. If you can achieve harmony between the two, you are better off.

Summary

Applying relationalism to your personal life is very doable and, if done, very productive. You are able to see that it works well in a business setting because it makes sense. Putting people first, establishing boundaries while giving freedom, creating trusting environments, and celebrating contributions all make for very enthusiastic and energetic employees. Putting your family first will produce similar results. Everyone wants to matter. Your family can certainly see the effort you put into making your work situation the best it can be. They want to feel you will do the same for them. If you do, they will respond, just like at work!

There is a lot at stake in creating a relational household. This includes your personal well-being, your attitude about yourself, and your degree of happiness and personal freedom. While there is not enough data to support this revelation conclusively, it appears there is a connection between relationalism, the harmony of your personal relationships, and the stability and adjustment of your children.

The goals of the workplace, while different, are comparable to goals that you have for your family. At work you are seeking to achieve goals, promote a safe and productive environment, encourage your associates to become a cohesive team, and execute the business plan. At home you want your love for family to grow and prosper; you want your family to be safe, healthy, and successful; you want members of the family to support each other; you want your children to appreciate the differences between right and wrong, to be educated, and to get off to a good start in life. When you break down what you want from work and from home, the objectives may be stated differently, but they are essentially the same.

There are two major differences between home and work that affect the relational model: The home has two equal leaders (unless it is a single-parent household), and the issues you face are more personal and potentially emotive. It is important to remember that communication and clarity regarding expectations on a regular basis is an essential piece of relationalism at home. Relational leaders will find a way to deliver this message effectively to their children.

In fidelity, you find the moral compass for your family. It defines what is debatable or inviolate. It sets standards of fairness that are likely to be upgraded as circumstances in the family unit change. It recognizes that the leaders are expected to be the role models for all the precepts that make up the family code. The leaders are responsible for communicating and reinforcing the code to the children on a regular basis. They also provide a means of allowing feedback from time to time about the standards and, when appropriate, allow the standards to be challenged.

Appreciation is clearly a critical part of the family plan. While recognition in the outside world might be random, inside the family, it is expected. Providing a fun-filled environment for the family is a means of bonding as a group, emphasizing the values of the unit, and reinforcing aspects of the children's education.

In the end, relational leadership is a business thing, a personal thing, and a family thing. The more you practice it, the better leader you will become.

KEEP IN MIND:

- The relational model at home involves both the partners as co-leaders.
- Your relational leadership skills are readily transferable to the home and will be just as positive there as they are at work.
- The greatest regret of many business and educational leaders after retirement is that they didn't spend enough time with their family.
- Talk with your family about what is important to you and allow them space to talk with you about what is important to them.
- Model the behavior that you expect to see.
- The power of shared experiences is incredibly strong.
- Don't try to fix everything—most of the time all someone wants to hear is the sound of your listening.
- Relational leaders seem to have life-long mates and children who are well adjusted and happy.
- The results you look for in work are similar to the results you look for at home; you just call them by different names.

Chapter 11

The Long and Winding Road

> LOVE is the virtue of the HEART
> SINCERITY the virtue of the MIND
> COURAGE the virtue of the SPIRIT
> DECISION the virtue of the WILL
> —*Frank Lloyd Wright*
> *The Organic Commandment, 1940*

- The Idea Comes to Life
- The Next Day: Billy and the Leadership Group
- The Board Meeting and Billy's Presentation
- Frank Meets with Billy and the Team
- A Private Coaching Session with Billy
- Nine Months Later
- Final Thoughts

I'm not sure if it is a good idea to end a business-related book on Chapter 11. I know Otis Elevator Company doesn't have a 13th floor, but I am not superstitious, so merrily on I go! I have chosen to end this book with a story. It is the story of the creation and implementation of a relationally led business, which includes seeing the relational leader outside the workplace interacting with his community and his family. It will give you the opportunity to see the entire model in full practice. While the business and the characters are not real, the model description and implementation is.

The Idea Comes to Life

Billy was leaving his office heading out to the parking lot. What a bizarre day it had been, but he was full of excitement about the future. The sky was still bright, and the temperature still held the warmth of the mid-afternoon sun. Billy took that as a good sign.

Earlier in the day, a surprise announcement was made to the senior leadership group by the board chairman. Peter and Jack were tending their resignations as CEO and COO, effective immediately. Rob, the chairman, indicated that the board was disappointed by the company's performance of late and what seemed to be a lack of *esprit de corps*. The board simply could not wait any longer. Rob finished up by saying that it was the board's desire to fill their open slots internally, and the focus would be on hiring the CEO first.

Rob said that anyone on the senior leadership team was eligible to "throw their hat in the ring," as he put it. Anyone interested should devise an outline of a plan to move the company forward and be prepared to present it at a special meeting he was calling next Friday. He would be at the meeting, and he would have fellow board members Tracy and Jim with him. Time was of the essence he proclaimed.

The buzz around the office after that was incredible. Not much work got done. People wandered down to Pete and Jack's workspaces, where they were cleaning up and preparing to leave, to wish them well. For most of the leadership team, it was a perfunctory exercise as Pete and Jack were real controllers. They weren't very interested in an idea unless it was their own or a version of their thinking coming from one of the "team." They just didn't get the importance of the people thing, and it seems it was beginning to show in the numbers.

Billy loved classic rock music, and he usually played it loud on the way home as sort of a de-stressor. Today, though, he left the radio off, thinking about what happened and what it meant for him. Pete and Jack were decidedly non-relational, and he figured the board finally realized that this style was not moving the company forward effectively.

There had been many solid people, strong performers, who had left the company lately or taken an early retirement, even though the job market was less than robust. We were losing lots of our best people Billy was thinking, and though he didn't know for sure, he believed it was because of how they were being treated. He had been thinking of doing the same thing. There is only so much a person can take. These folks were full of ideas, but they never seemed to go anywhere. Their opinions weren't valued, and no one at the top seemed to listen to them

Billy had just finished reading a book called *The Relational Leader*, and he was very excited about the model on leadership that it espoused. As he thought about the people leaving the company and the stagnant productivity of late, he thought there could be some answers in this model.

The board was clearly ready for something new. Pete and Jack didn't just decide they wanted to do something different today! They were pushed out. Billy decided that he was the guy for the job. He was never comfortable with Pete or Jack's style, but like the others on the leadership team, he adapted to their will. The company was solid, and it had an excellent and timely product, good distribution channels, and a loyal customer base. Yet it could not be ignored that numbers were falling off, and the company seemed to have lost its energy and will to succeed—all of this was in spite of the fact that it was still profitable. Not many could see the early signs of demise, save perhaps the board.

Billy concluded that in order to reverse the downward trends, the answer was in a new and dynamic style of leadership. He was going to bring a proposal to the board based on the relational style he read about. He would convince them that this is what the company needed and that he was the person to make it happen. He believed that people were the driver of any business; the company had good people whose individual capabilities were left unchallenged. Maybe this was the answer.

Later That Night

Dinner was full of conversation. Billy caught up on all the news about the grandchildren from his wife, Linda, and he told her all the details he knew about the big day at the office. They talked about the implications for them if he were selected for the CEO's job. All was good, and off he went to his study to create his plan for the board.

Because the organization was not very people-focused, he thought the advice given in the book about starting slowly was a good idea. People would be leery of a radical shift. While he valued people himself, he didn't have any real training in this stuff. It seemed to be pretty much common sense, particularly if you saw people as a primary asset.

He made a list of the issues that a relational style of leadership might initially encounter from the employees. Billy pared the list down to four manageable areas. He made notes next to each item, and the list looked like this:

- *Trust*: Wasn't I part of the regime that was being replaced?
- *Fairness*: Never perceived that there was any, so why now?
- *Belief*: This is too good to be true!
- *Motivation*: Are they just looking for ways to get rid of me?

As he was thinking about these potential road blocks, it struck him that he should get more input from the other members of the leadership team. Sitting there in his study working up a plan on his own was really no different than what Pete and Jack did. They never much valued other people's opinions. Talking to his associates would demonstrate that he was committed to a new style of leadership.

The Next Day: Billy and the Leadership Group

The office was still abuzz with yesterday's dramatic resignations. The time was ripe to talk about how to move forward. Maybe coming to consensus on a plan was behind the board's idea of keeping the CEO position in-house. Billy would ask the leadership group to meet with him. He would open with the consensus idea, discuss the current atmosphere, then talk about the concept of relational leadership, and finally, if all was going well, he would seek input on the roadblocks he identified.

With some trepidation, he pulled Doug, Bonnae, Alan, Joyce, and Linda together for a meeting in the conference room. In some respects, what he had to say was not new. They had all talked about the leadership problems in the company individually, however, never collectively. It was always clear that leadership would not tolerate people talking badly about their actions or decisions. Frankly, it was a bit dangerous to be too open on how the organization was being led. Several people were let go because of it, and others were shunted to less desirable jobs.

The conversation was going well. Billy knew that this team often looked to him for advice, but he still made sure that he was low-key about his own ambitions. He didn't know for sure how any of the others might be thinking about their own future. Billy was ready to lead, and he was at the top of his game in this meeting. He was sensitive but direct, thoughtful and solicitous, which facilitated a smooth flow to the discussion.

It was interesting that without Pete and Jack around, the conversation was much more open. No one in the room seemed to like the treatment of people in general within the company. You couldn't trust anyone—thinking about the dismissals and reassignments. People were often treated unfairly. If you supported leadership and played up to them, you seemed to get ahead. If you stood up for something that leadership didn't want, you were treated like a pariah.

Billy sensed that it would be okay to take the next step. He put forth his proposition in this way: "If there was a way to change the environment and get people focused on delivering the business plan, not fussing about how they were treated, would they be interested?" He also asked if they liked what he had to say, and would they support him if he became the leader? Talk about ALL IN!! All were interested in how things could be done differently. Regarding Billy himself as leader, responses ranged from general affirmation to enthusiasm, but no one was negative.

Billy began by telling them he had read *The Relational Leader* and was really impressed with what it had to say and how it matched so well with how the company needed to change. He described the focus on people and talked about the interrelationship between the three elements of fidelity, appreciation, and value. He certainly had the attention of everyone in the room. As he talked about trust and fairness, heads nodded and knowing looks came to their faces. When he talked about fun, Bonnae spoke out saying, "There's not much of that around here."

The concept of making people the core of the business and being attentive to them was clearly striking a chord with the leadership group. Doug said, "If we could do this, it would turn everything around; no one could stop us. Better than that, we would stop all the defections."

Joyce, always impatient to move on once her mind was made up, said, "I've heard enough. What's the next step?" Billy almost started to talk about his issues list and his timetable, but he remembered that Alan and Linda had yet to say anything, and he was reluctant to move ahead without their input. So he asked how they were feeling about what he had presented so far.

Neither one had quite the enthusiasm of their peers, but they indicated they were willing to move to the next step. Alan was thinking to himself that perhaps the CEO job would be something he would like and be good at, and Linda was a bit uncomfortable because she had a reasonable relationship with Pete and Jack, although only on a social level.

Billy discussed the roadblocks he foresaw on implementation. He talked about the admonition from the book regarding moving too fast in a non-relational organization. He said, "If we try to do this all at once, I think we will overwhelm the associates. We have to build trust first. That will mean dealing with the fairness, belief, and motivation issues. We will have to be consistent enough and do it long enough that our associates will believe we mean what we say."

Everyone understood this point. They dug in and began to address the issues. What would be different that would change how people responded to the new manner of operating? It was clear that the element of fidelity, which dealt directly with trust, fairness, and character, was the key to gaining wide-scale acceptance of leadership's plan. Once they were able to make progress on that piece, Billy would be able, with the team's help, to put the whole plan in place.

Alan, warming up to the discussion, decided to join the conversation and indicated that he saw no reason why they couldn't start being attentive while they were concentrating on fidelity, and Linda said something similar about celebrations. They both seemed to be showing more enthusiasm and energy for the idea.

Later in the afternoon, everyone emerged from the long but fruitful meeting feeling they had accomplished much for the company that day. Doug had a final reassuring comment: "This was the most productive day I have had since I hired on here. We just reinvented our company, at least in the way we treat our people, including our customers and vendors. I feel really good about our work. Billy, I don't know where we would be without you."

Billy thanked Doug for the comment and then wrapped the meeting up by saying, "I will put a plan together based on the work we did today and circulate it via e-mail. Mark it up as you see fit, and I will make the revisions and send it back for final approval. My intent will be to develop a straight-forward and crisp presentation for the board. We only have until Friday when the board is meeting with us, so let's be prepared to be stay on top of this."

On the way out Joyce remarked to Bonnae, "Billy certainly is sounding like a CEO." Bonnae responded, "Not only that, but he is acting like one, too. I really liked the way he is keeping us in the loop and continuing to seek our counsel. That's a breath of fresh air around here!"

The Board Meeting and Billy's Presentation

The day had come. Billy and the leadership team worked very hard to arrive at a consensus on the points of the presentation. Doug, speaking for the group, surprised Billy by saying they would join Billy at the meeting as *his* team and support him for CEO. All of them had known Billy for a long time; they knew he completely understood the business from the ground up, and most important, they trusted him fully. They knew him to be a fair and ethical man, and he certainly demonstrated those character traits throughout the process of developing the plan for the board.

After calling the meeting to order, Rob asked if there were any proposals for company reorganization. This time Joyce took the lead, surprising Billy. Rob, Tracy, and Jim held Joyce in high esteem, both for her work and her personality. She quickly recapped the events since the resignations. She indicated that there was a proposal that the entire group came to consensus on and that it was Billy who led the process. If the board liked and supported the proposal, the leadership group supported Billy wholeheartedly for CEO. He was their candidate without reservation.

Billy now stepped up to make his presentation. He started with an assessment of the current state of the company and made the following points:

- The company's product line, distribution channels, and customer base was solid.
- The business plan was well thought out and capable of delivering the profit projections.
- There was a general malaise among associates who didn't feel valued.
- There were some complaints emerging from vendors about fairness.
- There were comments from customers that no one seemed happy at the company.
- The best plan, poorly executed, would fail.

Billy's comments were right on point from the board's perspective. They believed all the ingredients were there for a highly successful company except the people, which was why they moved on Pete and Jack. It was clear that the employees were not "happy campers," and even the customers were noticing it. It was wrong to treat vendors unfairly, and in the end it would hurt the company. Billy hadn't mentioned the shareholders or the community. If the company stayed on its current track, the stock would surely drop. With the lack of spirit among associates, there had been a marked drop-off in community "give back" programs.

All of the company's constituents must be served if the company were to reach its objectives. In Rob's mind, the associates were number one on the list. Surely, if their attitude didn't change, Billy's comment about the best plan, poorly executed, would fail was spot on and dead right. Not surprisingly, the same thoughts were going through Tracy and Jim's heads. But what are board members for? To think and act correctly!!

Billy then introduced the concept of relational leadership. He showed a slide that demonstrated the model and how the components interacted with each other (see Figure 11.1).

Billy walked the board through the model. He concentrated on people as the focus of the model and pointed out that *people* were thought of in the broadest sense, meaning associates, vendors, customers, shareholders, and community. He indicated that value is shown for people by the manner in which the three elements were introduced. All were important and all needed to be implemented, but nothing could happen until the company got a handle on fidelity.

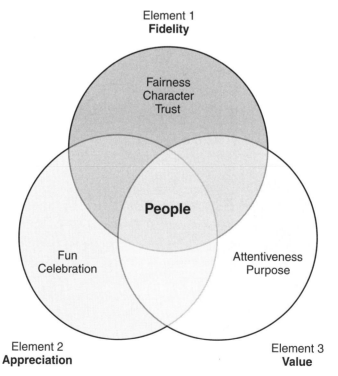

Relationship Diagram

Figure 11.1 *Relationship of the core to the elements in the relational leadership model.*

Fidelity was where the company established trust, fairness, and character. All three were ebbing low, and until they established a consistent treatment of fidelity in the company, the associates simply wouldn't believe that real change was here. They had been taught over these past few years to accept management's command structure. Their attitude was not going to change overnight. Because of this, early emphasis would be on fidelity with a little side introduction of some of the other attributes. Each member of the leadership team was prepared to support this through their individual departments. Billy also recommended contracting the author of *The Relational Leader* to come in as a coach and consultant.

The board members were very impressed with what they had heard so far. They understood the concept of the relational model working in tandem with the business plan. Billy showed them a slide that made the connection quite visible (see Figure 11.2).

Relationship of Business Plan to Relational Model

Figure 11.2 *Relationship between business plan and relational model. The model supplies the energy to drive the plan.*

The board was pleased with the plan. It was well thought out and certainly emphasized the problems the company was facing. They were particularly impressed with the willingness of the leadership team to agree to work together under Billy, who plainly was the leader of their group. Finally, bringing in an expert on the subject was a great idea—it would be the first demonstration that the company meant business about change.

To wrap up his presentation, Billy gave some examples of the kind of things the company could do to build on fidelity with the caveat that he wanted to meet with Frank, the author and expert on relational leadership, to really nail it down. He thought the following might be good places to put a stake in the ground:

- To build trust, he and the leadership group would meet in small groups with everyone at headquarters, and then meet by video conferencing, again in small groups, for their satellite offices.

- Regarding fairness, they would establish a policy that gave rights to all associates to question a performance review with impunity.

- Regarding character, they would engage the workforce to develop a document concerning what was acceptable or not acceptable in the business from an ethical viewpoint.

Having made these points, he ended his presentation and asked his team if anyone had something to add. No one did, so he asked the board if they had any clarifying questions or comments.

Tracy was first to jump in by congratulating the whole team on the work they had put into thinking about the issues of the company and preparing for this meeting. She thought they were right on target and could see good karma coming their way. Tracy always brought the human touch to the business equation.

Jim revealed that he had just finished reading *The Relational Leader* book. From one chapter to the next, he kept feeling that this relational leadership concept was exactly what the company needed. He was very enthusiastic about its potential. However, he did caution that he thought it was going to be a lot of work and wasn't going to happen overnight.

Rob had the final say, and true to his personality, he got right to the point. He said, "Hire this Frank expert of yours and get going. There is no time to waste."

The Meeting Postscript

Immediately after the board left, Billy and the team met to digest what happened and decide on a path forward. They all agreed that the outcome exceeded their expectations. There was a lot of excitement, high-fiving, and relief from passing their first test as relational leaders.

Billy noted that the real work was about to begin. He would contact Frank to see how he could help and when he could be available to hold an introductory meeting. Joyce agreed to set up a timeline and schedule for all the meetings that would be coming up. Bonnae thought they should get copies of the book for all the associates and board. She would work on that piece. Alan, Doug, and Linda would rough out guidelines for the three fidelity initiatives they proposed. Each would take one to work on. Everyone agreed to meet the following week to give an update.

Frank Meets with Billy and the Team

Billy was very enthusiastic about the company's path forward. His initial contact with Frank went well, and when Frank arrived, he and Billy had a private meeting to get to know each other better and to review Billy's expectations. They were in tune regarding the concept of relational leadership and shared an excitement about its potential in solving the company's problems. Even better, they were both avid Red Sox fans and enjoyed a good cigar. Billy was certain that Frank would be a person he would like working with. "This really is coming together," thought Billy.

At the meeting with the full team, Frank reviewed the entire scenario. He congratulated all on their excellent work to date. He acknowledged the thoroughness of their analysis of the company and approach, specifically the following:

- People were not highly valued in the company.
- Enthusiasm and energy were low throughout and extended to vendors and customers.
- Trust and fairness were issues with associates and vendors.
- Productivity was slipping.
- Fun and celebration didn't seem to exist, at least on any consistent basis.
- Trust had to be rebuilt with the people before anything else could happen.
- Fidelity was where the turnaround should start, and the initiatives recommended to the board were a good starting point.
- Initiatives in appreciation and value could be melded into the plan fairly soon.

Using the recap as a jumping off point, Frank then turned the meeting over to Billy. Billy reviewed the steps at the beginning of Chapter 3 about getting started on creating a relational organization. The team had already done steps 1 through 4 and would now concentrate on step 5—creating a plan to introduce the model to the company.

It was clear Billy understood that relational leadership was about people—the core. He was absolutely right to focus on fidelity and, more specifically, trust. Trust is a critical success factor particularly in an organization that is moving in polar directions. That type of movement makes people uneasy.

Billy explained the thoughts that were likely to go through people's minds when they were introduced to relational leadership: "Even though I do not like how I am being treated now, what makes this new system any better? Could this be a ruse for leadership to solidify their new positions? Why should I believe that leadership is now acting in my best interest? Where were you before and why didn't you do it then?"

Frank related that it would probably be better not to address these issues directly. They were the past, and new leadership was going to be the future. What they needed to do was put together a convincing plan that demonstrated they were serious about the future and serious about the welfare of the people. They needed to make that their driving force and back it up with actions. Their objective needed to be to make the company a great place to work. That was their focus, and they intended to do whatever it took to make that happen. They needed a clarion call to arms for the support of the people to assist them in creating a new way of doing business!

Designing the Associate Meetings

Billy's idea of the leadership team meeting with the associates in small groups was an excellent one and vital to establishing a ground floor of trust. He recommended that the meetings include vendors and customers as well. He also suggested that, because there were only two satellite organizations, the leadership team should split into groups of three and personally visit one site per team. Conducting the meetings in person would send a strong message to the associates, vendors, and customers.

What they needed to do was change the thinking of the people. They needed to move them along a series of thoughts like the following:

- Maybe this could be a great place to work.
- This is starting to feel like a great place to work.
- I want to help make this a great place to work.
- This is a great place to work.

Frank discussed the content of the meetings with Billy and the team. The focus should be on the future. They needed to acknowledge that there were issues but not dwell on them. They needed to make it clear that the object of this exercise was to build a new company, that is, pay attention to its people so that the business plan can move forward.

With those thoughts in mind, the team decided to develop some questions that they could bring up at these meetings. The leaders had a lot of energy for this process, and a lively discussion ensued. Doug suggested, "What should the business look like as new systems are implemented?" Bonnae added, "What role does the vendor and customer play in achieving the objectives of the company?" Joyce, who liked getting at the heart of the matter proposed, "What would make this a great place to work?" Joyce's question prompted Linda to add, "What is the one biggest problem you personally have here at the company?" Alan's idea was, "What do you like best about what we do here now?" Billy thought it would be good to identify the top area associates felt needed to be addressed through change, so he added, "If you could change one thing that would help the company as a whole, what would it be?"

Frank pointed out that this meeting was where leadership should get its data dump on fairness and ethical behavior. The associates, vendors, and customers would be right in front of them, and they might not have such an opportunity again. It would also be a good idea to mix the vendors and customers in with the associates for these group meetings. It would be as important for the associates to hear what is on the minds of vendors and customers as it would be for leadership to hear what they have to say.

Billy thought this would be a good time for a break, and besides, he needed a cup of coffee. As often happens at breaks, side conversations began around the refreshments table. Alan and Bonnae started talking about listening and observing. They decided that the upcoming meetings presented an excellent opportunity to utilize attentiveness skills. Everyone could make separate notes on what they observed, such as body language, eye contact, tone of voice, energy level, and so on. This would be an important assessment tool when the leadership team came back together as a group to analyze the results.

Doug and Joyce talked about what would happen after the meetings were completed. They needed to compile the data as quickly as possible, synthesize it, and understand its implications. Doug felt strongly about the need to assess the mood of the people as well as the frame of mind of the company's key publics. Joyce agreed and added her own thoughts: "What will the team do with the feedback, and how will it be presented?" Both were concerned about correctly capturing the intent of the people because it would determine how quickly the organization could move forward.

When the present meeting was called back to order, it was clear that the team was focused on the subject at hand while munching on their donuts and coffee. The team was eager to share their thoughts, and Frank captured them on paper to facilitate the discussion. Billy was pleased with the excellent points being made and felt he should start to wind things down. He made his last points, and offered the floor to Frank to make any concluding remarks.

Frank felt it was important to point out that while they focused their discussion on fidelity, it was possible to implement parts of the other two elements—appreciation and purpose. "But don't go overboard," he warned, "because you will take energy away from your focus on fidelity, and of course, there is still a business to be run." Frank added that during the meetings the team should look for people who could help move the process forward. The leaders should observe and listen so that they could identify those people, and then plan to include them as leaders in the next phase. While doing this, they could also look for causes to celebrate accomplishments and find a way to announce the deeds to the organization. Something as simple as a phone call or an e-mail message from Billy would be significant. Frank concluded with hearty congratulations for the great progress the team had made. The team left the meeting feeling very good about themselves and the progress that was being made on behalf of the company. There was a sense of excitement and determination about them as they returned to their departments.

A Private Coaching Session with Billy

Frank prepared for a private meeting with Billy. He felt it was critical to reinforce that Billy was on the right track but that he still had a lot in front of him. Frank reflected on some of the important beliefs and observations he had concerning Billy. He was pretty confident about Billy's ability to handle this new style of leadership. The more Billy practiced it, the better he would get. He was intuitive and smart. The leadership team liked and respected him. They put aside their own egos to raise his up. He was off to an excellent start. He had the support of the board and his leadership team, and he had a well thought out plan to address the people of the company. He also had some strategies ready to go. This was going to be a lot of work in a very short period of time. It would be both exhilarating and exhausting. What Billy needed to understand was that it was only the beginning. The hard work had yet to come. Frank decided to begin the session by soliciting thoughts from Billy.

Billy was pretty upbeat for the coaching session. The activity from the past couple of weeks was certainly building his self-confidence. Responding to Frank's questions regarding his thoughts, Billy said that he felt he had caught on quickly, but that he knew it was only at the beginning. He knew there would be many tests along the way. He might even have to let some people go in that some people would not accept the relational style, while others just wouldn't believe that leadership was serious about this change. He also mentioned that he might need to talk with Frank again when this time came because it would be very hard for him to fire someone. Billy astutely observed that it was going to be a bigger challenge to maintain and grow a relational system within a mature company than it would be to start one from infancy.

Billy also told Frank he recognized that patience and discipline would play major roles in the success of this venture. He needed to accept that mistakes would be made; when they were, he would have to own up to them and then dig back in again. The hard part for Billy would be remembering that people are typically not used to relationalism, particularly when it is implemented on a broad scale using a model as a framework. There were going to be bumps in the road, but Billy felt that he and the team would be prepared.

Billy wanted to know more about staying on top of associates' attitudes as time went on. He understood that the leadership team really needed to stay attentive, but what else needed to be done? Frank discussed taking temperature readings in the form of surveys to stay on top of changing needs and views. Frank also indicated that the leadership team had to drive down the relational concept to the next level of leaders, and then down again from there. Frank pointed out that the relational style must become the way of life throughout the entire company.

Billy understood this right away and said he would draw upon the many different examples given in *The Relational Leader*, and, of course, he and the team would develop their own style over time. He knew that the people who accepted this style of leadership would respond to it with gusto! But it would take time because there was little precedent for it in their workplace. The trust (or perhaps it was a *mistrust*) factor wouldn't go away easily. This was going to be a big factor for the team.

Frank interjected at this point and told Billy about the car plants in Delaware. They were known throughout the industry as manufacturing sites where both labor and management trusted each other, and both acted in the best interest of the company. The GM and Chrysler plants flourished because of enlightened local leadership. Management established a relationship with labor that was unique. Each trusted each other and treated each other with respect. They acted *relational.*

Frank told Billy that time and again, from the mid-1980s until the great recession of 2008, there were rumors that the plants would be shut down for one reason or another. However, that did not happen (until the total collapse of the two companies involved) because of the relationship that had been established between management and labor. The quality of work and the dedication to excellence was hard to replicate in other locations. In fact, a new manufacturer was signing on to buy the GM plant largely because of the workforce that existed there. Frank said that Billy could reasonably expect similar performance from his workforce once the relational style took hold.

Billy's eyes lit up. He felt that this was what was in store for his company—associates dedicated to making it a great place to work. Associates who appreciated that they were recognized and valued for what they did every day and who gave their full efforts to make the business successful.

Billy wanted to set up a company-wide training on relational leadership. Everyone needed to have a good understanding of how it worked and what part they played in making it work. He wanted everyone to appreciate what work life could be like if it were approached in a relational manner. He was going to buy a copy of the book for each employee, an idea Frank could hardly argue with!

Leading in the Community and at Home

Before heading home, Frank wanted to press Billy on the relational leader as a community volunteer. He knew Billy was in tune with this idea, but it was important that they discussed it, at least briefly. Frank brought up the subject, and Billy was quick to respond.

Billy understood the value of working in the community. He and his team could certainly use the practice such opportunity would give to their relational leadership style. But it was more than that for Billy, as he saw his company emerging as a great place to work. If it was to be such an organization, then partnering with the community was essential. He knew that his team and the company's associates would develop a sense of pride as the company increased its prestige around town. Billy had even heard that some companies gave their employees paid time off to volunteer in community projects, and he said he wanted to implement a similar type of plan. He was ready to commit to this level of involvement—it was the right thing to do.

Billy looked at his watch and noticed the coaching session had gone well beyond its allotted time. They were behind schedule, and he knew Frank had a plane to catch. Billy suggested that he and Frank walk out together because he had one more item to bring up briefly.

As they walked toward the front lobby, Billy said he was struck by the idea that this would be a great way to operate within the family. He read about it in Frank's book, and it seemed to be successful on the home front. He could use a bit of that karma! Frank could see Billy's mind turning already. Supper with Linda was going to be interesting tonight!

Frank stopped and told Billy he had one final piece of advice to share with him. Frank acknowledged that there was every good reason to implement the relational style with the family because it could have some remarkable results there as well. Frank suggested that Billy follow the ideas expressed in Chapter 10, but he should be careful not to take on too much at once. He could start practicing some things at home, like attentiveness, and build from there. Frank indicated that attentiveness would be the best attribute to begin with, and if Billy had any questions, they could discuss them on the phone. Frank told Billy that regardless of the topic, if he needed anything to be sure to contact him.

Nine Months Later

Billy and the team felt a follow-up consulting session would be very important to keeping the organization on track. Frank's scheduled return to the
company nine months later turned out to be a joyous occasion. This visit was
a celebration more than anything. The company had indeed turned itself
around. Billy realized that Doug's words from that initial meeting rang true:
"We just reinvented our company, at least in the way we treat our people,
including our customers and vendors."

Rob announced that the third quarter numbers were very good, and it was
the second quarter in a row where this had happened. Joyce gave an update
on the code of ethics now employed on a company-wide basis. Bonnae
reported the results of the company survey just completed—every area
showed positive feedback. Alan discussed the non-profit organization that the
company had voted to support. The people were very happy and proud to
be serving the welfare of the community. Doug reported that customer relations were never better. He regularly received enthusiastic and appreciative
calls from customers who were amazed at the change in the attitudes of the
associates. Linda reported on recent negotiations with a group of vendors,
who were looking for ways to help the company move ahead.

Billy had the final say before the party began. He reported the results of the
survey from the Company Barometer Questionnaire indicated that 83% of
the people had said **this company was a great place to work!**

Final Thoughts

The relational style of leadership has the capacity to change the way we deal
with people on a wide-scale basis. Belief in the capacity of people is not new.
Douglas McGregor in his 1960 work, *The Human Side of Enterprise*, touts
Theory Y as the best means for motivating people to do great work.
Essentially, he said if you believe in people and support them, they will do
good work. He based much of his thinking on Abraham Maslow's Hierarchy
of Needs theory. Relationalism is an outgrowth of these two gentlemen's
thinking.

We can no longer afford the corruption, immorality, and greed that is rampant in our society today. The great recession of 2008 was caused largely by
these factors. It came close to tearing the entire world's economic structure
apart. Our business leaders, politicians, sports stars, and entertainers fall woe-
fully short as role models. Day after day, we see headlines about one or
another involved in cheating, drugs, crime, and all sorts of bad things. These
were people we once looked up to. It is increasingly harder to do so today.

The people you have met in this book are not among the liars, cheats, thieves, corrupt, immoral, or unethical. They are the real thing. Each is an ordinary human being who did extraordinary things. My privilege in life was to be associated with them and other people like them. I chose the ones I chose to highlight because each and every one had an impact on me, for which I will be forever grateful.

Certainly they made mistakes during their careers (and some of the younger ones are getting ready to make mistakes), but they never made one from fear. They did whatever they did because they felt it was the right thing to do. They know who they are, they are confident in who they are, they make decisions based on who they are, and more often than not, they are right. When they are wrong, they have the courage to admit it and change direction. Usually, they are not wrong twice.

They may not have the fame of Lee Iacocca or Jack Welch, but they are every bit as good. A hero is not about headlines. A hero does the right things based on his or her beliefs and does them consistently and wins consistently. There is no institution that could teach anyone what these people have demonstrated and taught by example throughout their careers.

There are only so many people you can highlight in a book and be effective. I offer my apologies to the many others who have influenced my life and the lives of so many others by their incredible energy, insight, and accomplishment who were not mentioned on these pages. That does not diminish what they did, who they are, or how I feel about them; it's just how it turned out.

If you are a true relational leader, be it at work, home, at the PTA, or a citizen's committee, you can make a difference. A true relational leader has character, is fair, can be trusted, knows how to have fun and celebrate, and has the capacity to observe and listen. The relational leader knows the direction he is headed and why. Most of all, he is not corrupt, immoral, or greedy!

If you would like to comment on the book or engage my services, you can contact me on the web at www.fjmcintosh.com. I encourage and look forward to your comments.

Appendix

The Company Barometer Questionnaire

This simple but effective questionnaire is designed to give you a sense of how your workforce feels about their environment. It is based on the attributes of relational leadership. Analysis of the results will give you a good understanding of the level of relationalism that exists in your company or business unit. Before beginning any changes in how you lead, I advise that you establish a baseline. Once you know how your employees rate the company according to these attributes, you can begin to put a plan in place that addresses the needs identified.

How the questionnaire is administered is vital to the validity of the results. I recommend that you use a third-party to collect and analyze the data. By doing so, you will give the employees a sense of safety in answering the questions honestly. This is critical because you will be making important decisions based on the results.

Instructions

Determine how you will distribute the questionnaire. For instance, you can send it via mail to employees' homes, have your managers hand it out, or include it with a paycheck. If your managers are going to hand it out, you must prepare them. Let them know the details surrounding the survey and what to say to their employees. If you are going to include it with payroll or send it via the mail, an accompanying letter of explanation is required.

Give them two weeks time to return the survey, and include an envelope addressed to the company that is collecting and analyzing the data. At the end of the first week, remind employees to return the survey by whatever means you use to communicate with your entire workforce. Thank all those who have already returned the survey. Announce the percentage of returns that the survey administration company has already received. Emphasize the importance of the feedback.

Determine how you will share the results and what the path forward will be. However you choose to provide the feedback from the survey and what your ongoing plans may be, it is vital that you do *something*. By starting the process, you have created expectations among your employees. It would be a mistake not to follow through.

If you wish, F J McIntosh Enterprises is available to assist you through this process. You can visit the web site at www.fjmcintosh.com for further information.

THE COMPANY BAROMETER QUESTIONNAIRE

Please circle the answer that most clearly represents your point of view on the statement. Comments are encouraged. Be as specific as possible, and feel free to use the back side of the paper to continue your answer if needed.

People in this organization are valued and respected for who they are and what they know.

    Always   Usually   Sometimes   Rarely

Comments: _____

_____

_____

_____

There is a sense of fairness in our workplace.

    Always   Usually   Sometimes   Rarely

Comments: _____

_____

_____

_____

Character and ethical behavior are evident in our company.

    Always   Usually   Sometimes   Rarely

Comments: _____

_____

_____

_____

I sense a trusting environment in this organization.

    Always   Usually   Sometimes   Rarely

Comments: _____

_____

_____

_____

We celebrate our big and small victories.

Always   Usually   Sometimes   Rarely

Comments: _____

_____

_____

_____

This is a fun place to work.

Always   Usually   Sometimes   Rarely

Comments: _____

_____

_____

_____

People in this organization are attentive; they observe and they listen.

Always   Usually   Sometimes   Rarely

Comments: _____

_____

_____

_____

I have a sense of purpose when I come to work in the morning.

Always   Usually   Sometimes   Rarely

Comments: _____

_____

_____

_____

Index